Health and Social Justice

Health and Social Justice

Jennifer Prah Ruger

OXFORD
UNIVERSITY PRESS

OXFORD

UNIVERSITY PRESS

Great Clarendon Street, Oxford OX2 6DP

Oxford University Press is a department of the University of Oxford.
It furthers the University's objective of excellence in research, scholarship,
and education by publishing worldwide in

Oxford New York

Auckland Cape Town Dar es Salaam Hong Kong Karachi
Kuala Lumpur Madrid Melbourne Mexico City Nairobi
New Delhi Shanghai Taipei Toronto

With offices in

Argentina Austria Brazil Chile Czech Republic France Greece
Guatemala Hungary Italy Japan Poland Portugal Singapore
South Korea Switzerland Thailand Turkey Ukraine Vietnam

Oxford is a registered trade mark of Oxford University Press
in the UK and in certain other countries

Published in the United States
by Oxford University Press Inc., New York

British Library Cataloguing in Publication Data
Data available

Library of Congress Cataloging in Publication Data
Library of Congress Control Number: 2009938558

Typeset by SPI Publisher Services, Pondicherry, India
Printed in Great Britain
on acid-free paper by the
MPG Books Group, Bodmin and King's Lynn

ISBN 978-0-19-955997-8

1 3 5 7 9 10 8 6 4 2

To Helen, Henry, and Margaret

Foreword

By Amartya Sen

I am delighted to have the opportunity of introducing Jennifer Prah Ruger's far-reaching book on health in general, and health policy in particular. It is a major contribution to a momentous—but very diffi-cult—subject. When I first met Ruger, she was a lively graduate student taking courses and excelling in each course she took. Her research ideas gradually gelled, and she went on to combine her remarkable talents with systematic preparation for making a definitive contribution on health policy in line with her deep commitment to the removal of injustice in the world. The book draws on her doctoral dissertation, and it is wonderful to see how Ruger has elegantly woven together different threads of argu-ments in her approach to health in the sickly world in which we live.

'The world is not an inn, but a hospital', said Sir Thomas Browne, the distinguished author of *Religio Medici*, more than three and a half centuries ago, in 1643. Things have progressed over time, and life expectancies have radically increased since Browne's days. And yet the prevalence of treat-able but untreated ailments across the globe is still shockingly large. Contrary to what Thomas Browne might have expected from a hospital, the afflicted population in the world often get very little medical atten-tion, not just in the poorer countries, but also in the richest nation on earth, namely the United States, thanks to the limitations of medical coverage and the absence of an adequately inclusive system of health insurance.

A person's inability—or lack of capability—to obtain medical remedy for treatable ailments is a hugely disturbing deprivation. If there is anything in the idea of our 'being together' in society, then society cannot but take such basic deprivations extremely seriously. A deep sense of injustice is hard to avoid in a field like this, but it is quite challenging to work out the precise demands of justice that can survive critical scrutiny and can be seen to be both conceptually well grounded and practically sensible. That is the exacting task that Ruger takes on powerfully in this closely argued book.

A preliminary question must, however, be addressed first. There are surely many inequalities and deprivations in the world. So why concentrate particularly on health? Part of the answer must lie in the fact that health is central to our being alive and happy (not dead, nor in constant pain and suffering). That must surely be a plausible beginning to answering the question of why health is important. But it cannot possibly be all that there is to say in addressing the question. There are further issues that link the opportunities of having good health to some of the basic freedoms of human life.

The perspective of freedom and capability has a long reach—longer than the alternative perspectives that focus only on utilities, or exclusively on liberties or resources for the derivation of social imperatives. Of course, health is *inter alia* a source of pleasure (and helps the avoidance of pain), and there are many issues of liberty and of fairness in the distribution of resources (or primary goods) that relate closely to good health. These specific concerns must receive attention, but going beyond them we also have to take note of the important fact that being healthy can add to our capability to do things. Indeed, health is, in general, freedom enhancing, by expanding our actual capability to do what we may have reason to do. If, for example, being healthy helps us to make cultural contributions, or scientific advances, or plays a role in political mobilization or in fighting for people's rights in any area of worthwhile human engagement, then the reasons for valuing health cannot lie only in the immediate linkage of health with well-being and other such single-focus concerns. Indeed, being in good health oneself may allow people to take better care of others, for example their own children or those of others, or of their neighbours, or simply of other people in the world—far or near. These freedoms to make a difference must be seen as one of the significant rewards of good health, going well beyond the pleasures that good health directly brings. Removing deprivations of health and addressing issues of health injustice is, thus, central to expanding significant human capabilities and freedoms that we have reason to value.

By locating her motivating concerns in this area, in what she calls the 'health capability paradigm', Ruger is able to present an understanding of health problems that has typically been neglected in the literature on the subject (important as that literature is in throwing light on many other problems). The light that Ruger's chosen perspective throws on old and new health issues is further extended through her far-reaching investigation and use of causal and evaluative connections, drawing on economics, politics, and ethics. A major distinction, which turns out to be central to Ruger's approach, is that between what can be called 'good health policy' and 'good policy for health.' The pursuit of health justice has to go well beyond getting the institutions of health care right, since people's health depends on a variety of societal influences, of which health care is only one. There is, thus, need for bringing the discriminating scrutiny of justice and injustice to all policies, and not just to medical attention and availability of specific health care. This broadening does not reduce, in any way, the importance of bringing about much needed reforms in health care (that battle is being fought right now in the United States, with attempts by the Obama Administration to bring universal medical insurance to the American population, against oddly powerful resistance). But it also draws attention to the need to go beyond these immediate issues to other concerns of central importance to good health (including, for example, the nature of patent laws, support for basic incomes, and informed understanding of the demands of nutrition or of the hazards of obesity or smoking or alcoholism).

Another area in which this book makes a noteworthy contribution is Ruger's pragmatic analysis of public reasoning, and her focus on the importance of arriving at agreements, even when the agreements draw on a congruence of different kinds of reasoning. Cass Sunstein's concept of 'incompletely theorized agreements' is put to effective use here, and while debates can be entertained on the status of agreements that are not only incompletely theorized but also imperfectly understood, there is every reason to think that Ruger's use of the idea brings an innovative approach to public discussion on health and health care.

Ruger enhances the reach of her powerful perspective by enlightening investigations of human flourishing and of the variety of influences that make substantial differences to the freedoms that human beings can actually have, and their ability to make well-informed and well-reasoned use of these freedoms. One of the central philosophical ideas on which Ruger has much to say is that of responsibility, and this applies both to individuals and to public institutions (through what Ruger calls 'shared health governance'). The robustness of her framework allows Ruger to shed significant light on a basic question that has important bearing on a number of fields, of which the pursuit of justice in health is only one.

By producing a book of such richness concerning a major area of human agency and policy, Jennifer Prah Ruger has substantially advanced the reach of public reasoning, not just about health care, but about social justice in general. I am happy to have the privilege of presenting this important book to the discerning public. There is much to celebrate here, and a strong message of hope even in the 'hospital'—to use Thomas Browne's depressing description of the world—in which we live.

San Felice Circeo, Italy
20 August 2009

Preface

Envision a world where every man, woman, and child has health insurance, providing coverage for high-quality health care services.

Envision a world where no one faces bankruptcy or poverty resulting from catastrophic illness or injury, where no one chooses to ignore a medical condition because he or she can't afford to see a doctor, where no impoverished person dies unnecessarily due to lack of care.

Envision a world in which patients and doctors make decisions about individual health care, not insurance companies or actuaries or government officials, a future in which these decisions rest on medical necessity and medical appropriateness, not profits or spending limits, where physicians are not reduced to rationing necessary health care.

Envision a world in which the health care system supports comprehensive prevention services, from nutrition education to smoking cessation programmes to immunizations and much more, thus averting the onset of disease and preventing both untold human suffering and economic drain on the health care system and the economy overall.

Envision a world in which the disabled receive the help they need to rise to their potential, a future in which victims of 'orphan diseases' receive care because decisions about research and drug development no longer rest on narrow profit motives alone.

This vision embodies an Aristotelian view of human flourishing, a view of society in which all people have the ability to realize central health capabilities—that is, to avoid premature death and escapable morbidity. This vision is the animating principle behind the *health capability paradigm*, a unique new approach in which not just health care (or even health alone) but health *and* the capability for health itself are moral imperatives. There are no guarantees of good health, but society can, if it will, design and build effective institutions and social systems, structures, and practices, supporting all its members as they seek to achieve these central health capabilities.

This is the vision. Can we make it reality? Many would say no, that it is too expensive, too contrary to political realities, too comprehensive and thus too daunting in its practical implications.

But can we fail to make it reality? Can the United States afford to continue the long slide into dysfunctional health care? Can we afford to stand idly by as the country's health outcomes standing in the world slips lower and lower, falling behind a growing number of other nations? Can we continue to ignore the system's failures, even as they push inexorably upward through the socioeconomic scale to reach well into the middle class?

Across the globe, can we continue to ignore human suffering?

I believe we can make this vision a reality, both in the United States and in nations around the world, and the health capability paradigm embodies comprehensive strategies for doing so.

The high costs of health care mean that fostering health capability for all will require a new commitment among the healthier and wealthier to help the less fortunate. Thus, the health capability paradigm may require a redistribution of income over different groups to pay for health care.

However, no great social change can take place if it is unsupported by the citizenry's values and beliefs. Moreover, this paradigm seeks to map out the steps of getting to a point in which individuals—through their health functioning and health agency—voluntarily embrace changes in the social structure, and in their own behaviour, to achieve this vision. Thus, income redistribution must be voluntary, and willingly embraced as the necessary cost of a valued enterprise. This kind of commitment rises out of shared public moral norms supporting our best aspirations. When societies recognize the need for significant change, they work by a variety of means to shape new norms and to affect their internalization. Grass-roots initiatives, strong leadership and public education are all part of this norm-building process. Through this process the social structure transforms from coercive incentives to libertarian paternalism to wilfully embraced social action. All types of programmes are needed at various stages of change. The goal for a theory of health and social justice is legitimacy in the moral, political, and policy implementation realms.

Norm-building must also address the misinformation embodied in erroneous and destructive norms. In sub-Saharan Africa, many men believe that raping a virgin will cure them of AIDS. This myth has spread AIDS ever farther and led to a child rape epidemic. In the United States, adolescents widely believe that their peers drink more heavily than they actually do, encouraging more alcohol abuse among teenagers. False norms often have deadly consequences.

A *norms-based approach to health promotion* is thus critically important. Internationally, the United Nations declared a right to health in 1948. Sixty years later, nations around the globe, including the United States with all its wealth, have failed to make it reality. Presenting a compelling case for health justice and shaping positive norms are key features of the health capability paradigm.

Patients and doctors are the central players in health care. Researchers, insurers, governments, actuaries, hospital professionals, individual citizens, and many others have legitimate though less central roles. The health capability paradigm envisions *shared health governance*, in which individuals, providers, and institutions work together to create a social system and environment enabling all to be healthy. Shared health governance encompasses consensus-building around substantive principles and distribution procedures, accurate measures of effectiveness, changes in attitudes and norms, and open deliberations to resolve problems. These deliberations among physicians, public health experts, citizens, and others will seek an in-depth understanding of problems and potential remedies. Health capability failures are not easily addressed through a single institution or group, multiple pathways are at play. The process embodies roles and responsibilities for all parties—individuals, providers, and institutions. It expects that each player will find his or her rightful voice and make appropriate contributions to policy decisions at the macro level and treatment decisions at the individual level. Because it focuses on methods and outcomes, it integrates both proceduralist and consequentialist approaches to justice.

Shared health governance rests on a *joint scientific and deliberative process* to produce and sustain a functioning health care system, an elaborated understanding of target levels of health functioning, and the benefits package needed to support them. The moral significance of health disparities is linked to *medical necessity and medical appropriateness*, both of which will be bedrock criteria.

In the health capability paradigm, deliberations take place at the national level, where policy is shaped and laws are written to implement it. They also take place at regional levels, in states or provinces, counties and communities. At these governmental levels, they embody a stepwise process that reviews scientific evidence about the consequences of policies on health and only then considers economic issues. They involve the legislative process, coalition building, citizen participation, and commitment.

Deliberations also occur at the individual level, as doctors and patients consider options for care and make reasoned, evidence-based decisions. Furthermore, the deliberative process must update its recommendations continually to account for changes in medical knowledge, technology, and costs when determining the worth of specific interventions.

How can societies reach agreement on seemingly intractable questions? Social choice theory offers a concept called *incompletely theorized agreement* that permits coming to workable consensus around some elements of an issue without necessarily agreeing on every element. Incompletely theorized agreements will be an essential building block in the health capability paradigm and will offer a means of public reasoning to reach consensus on health capabilities, on the scope and content of a right to health, and for proposed legislation for its realization.

In shaping these dimensions of health capability and a right to health, this theory seeks a global consensus about important health capabilities, applicable in most or all settings. A globally shared norm of health enables constructive comparisons and evaluations of health capabilities. While there might be no comprehensive unique conception of health, the health capability paradigm asserts that it is possible to identify certain primary, defining features of health and human life to which we assign priority for assessing political arrangements. There are, after all, things which reasonable people everywhere agree about—the evils of slavery, the death of infants and children, the critical importance of alleviating hunger, and providing potable drinking water. This is the 'view from everywhere.' Thus, the health capability paradigm promotes objectively assessed health, using standard mortality and morbidity measures.

Gaps in the health system—instances where the system is failing to foster health capabilities—will be measured in terms of *shortfall equality*, the extent to which individuals and communities fall short of average or target health levels. If data were to show extraordinary mortality from complications of diabetes in a minority community, for instance, the system would direct resources there to address that shortfall. This view, while eschewing a call for complete equality, is a hybrid of sufficiency and priority principles, since both are relevant for better understanding claims of justice pertaining to health. Sufficiency applies to our health capability goals whereas priority applies to triage in achieving these goals.

In some instances, of course, shortfall is not society's failing, but the individual's. Thus, *health agency* is a key component of the health capability paradigm. If societies ensure health capabilities, individuals must use their health agency, their freedom, to achieve the functions of health these capabilities permit. Indeed, ensuring health capabilities requires promoting health agency and equipping individuals and communities with the tools they need to pursue and achieve health outcomes they value and have reason to value. The diabetic, for instance, needs education about nutrition, exercise, glucose monitoring, medication and potential complications. He or she must adhere to testing and medication schedules and exhibit will power with respect to diet. In turn he or she must use these tools to achieve health functioning. Communities need education in constructive, positive health norms and collective organizing skills to ensure, for instance, safe water supplies. In either case, the responsibilities of the system to support health agency have their counterpart in the responsibilities of individuals, singly, and in groups, to exercise that health agency. Health agency thus brings together the moral importance and practical significance of both *responsibility* and *choice* for health in a theory of social justice.

Even in a wealthy country, resources are scarce and competition for them is fierce, both at the highest level—the total revenues available for government—and in the health domain itself. Fostering health capabilities for all will require *wasteless and corruption-free efficiency*. Moreover, justice does not require unlimited increases in expenditures to remedy shortfall inequalities. Wasted resources undermine important health capability goals. Expenditures in one category have opportunity costs in others. Funds spent to extend the lives of the elderly for a few days or weeks are unavailable to treat others with a high likelihood of recovery. Through shared health governance, the health system must strive to meet the standards of medical necessity and medical appropriateness, avoiding care that is medically futile. It must include effective safeguards against fraud and abuse, and the public health system must spend money efficiently. The health capability paradigm has a robust grasp of the opportunity cost issue and envisions applying the joint scientific and deliberative process to determine the wisest way to focus investments. A combined clinical and economic solution—that is, one that combines careful financial stewardship with competent medical judgement—is required. Under the health capability paradigm, economic solutions should follow and complement clinical programmes, not vice versa.

Because resource allocation in the health capability paradigm rests on medical necessity and medical appropriateness, not the ability to pay, progressively financed *universal health insurance* is fundamental, essential for human flourishing. Community-rated universal coverage distributes risk across the widest possible pool and protects individuals from disproportionate costs and penalties for their medical history. It will put an end to exclusions for pre-existing conditions, arbitrary denials of care, and a host of other practices that have prevented people from achieving their health capabilities. While universal coverage does have a seemingly daunting price tag, it will also reduce expenditures in a variety of ways. It will reduce illness and the need for more expensive medical care because it will cover and promote preventative services. It will pool risks over the widest possible population and thus reduce costs: and it will also reduce medical expenses to the extent that patients will no longer defer care until they are seriously, expensively, and perhaps even hopelessly ill.

Insurance not only pays for needed medical services; it also reduces vulnerabilities and insecurity, which diminish human flourishing. It protects people from losing jobs and savings, from the debt and financial ruin that can otherwise result from illness or injury. This *protective security* supports both overall health and capabilities beyond health—the capability to work, to manage a household and family, to engage in civic affairs, to live a flourishing life. As such, under the health capability paradigm, it is a moral imperative, a fundamental requirement of justice. The health capability paradigm focuses on individuals' exposure to risk and their ability to manage it adequately, rather than their preferences regarding it. By applying insights from mainstream economic theory, by reasoning through the insurance puzzle and the related issues of risk pooling, community rating, and progressive financing, the health capability paradigm incorporates this new and indispensable element.

Achieving universal coverage will in all likelihood require social systems characterized by partnership between the public and private sectors. The health capability paradigm values the private sector's productivity and efficiency; it recognizes as well the market's failures in promoting health capabilities. The market alone, for instance, is not equipped to prevent or contain epidemics, which require public health immunization and treatment programmes. Nor will the market alone correct the kind of information asymmetry that prevents patients from making fully-informed decisions about their own care. The health capability paradigm argues for a blended approach in which the free market and the government reinforce each other to improve health capabilities.

This book brings this vision and these strategies together to offer an imaginative new way forward. Other current frameworks have left us mired in inaction. This paralysis is a function of broad gaps these frameworks leave in the theoretical foundations underpinning health and health care. The current frameworks, for instance, do not provide the philosophical justification for the *direct* special moral importance of *health* and *health agency* as distinguished from *health care* and for the right to health. Indirect rationalizations of health, for example, in terms of equal opportunity or other egalitarian resource accounts do not offer justification for health as constitutive of human flourishing or well-being as accounts of the good life do. Nor do they provide a theoretical basis for prioritizing needs and allocating resources, particularly for individuals in addition to institutions. A truly joint scientific and deliberative model to guide collective choice is lacking and although comparisons among populations and population sub-groups are insightful for policy purposes, under this view individuals are of central moral concern. Other views give insufficient emphasis to shared governance and incomplete theorizing as opposed to quantitative or aggregative methods for shaping health policy and public health.

In short, an academic interdisciplinary enterprise encompassing health ethics, policy, and law is at a standstill. It is time for a new model, one that weaves together disparate constructs and original insights to create a foundational new paradigm for health. The need for this new paradigm will be increasingly clear as we review the existing frameworks. This book is an uniquely appropriate theoretical foundation for health policy and public health[1] because it envelopes moral intuitions that value both consequentialist and proceduralist principles.

This may seem like an idealistic vision for a non-ideal[2] theory of justice and in many respects it converges with various branches of perfectionism[3]. Yet, after more than fifteen years of work on these issues, this book aims to probe and offer insights into several fundamental questions, both idealistic and realistic, starting with the premise that the good life involves the development of human flourishing. How and why should social choices be made, and policies be implemented, at the national and sub-national levels to address health and health care disparities under conditions of resource scarcity? What values and principles should guide these decisions? What evidence should be brought to bear in the process and how should this evidence be utilized? Who is responsible for addressing different aspects and levels of this problem, and how should the successes and failures of institutions and actors, including individuals themselves, be measured and evaluated? How do different approaches to this problem fit with different theoretical schools of thought? How should health inequalities be measured, and what will determine whether they are just or unjust and have been adequately addressed? Which criteria—equality, sufficiency, priority—if any, offer assistance? How might new knowledge about health and its social determinants be marshalled to influence societal values and create health and social systems that benefit all of human kind?

Throughout this journey, I realized the need for the theories and methods of more than one discipline (e.g. philosophy, economics, or political science) or set of disciplines (e.g. the humanities or the social sciences) to address these queries. This work has thus taken a path of connecting and synthesizing perspectives and methods to enlarge our understanding of the justice and performance of health and social institutions examining the equity and efficiency of health system access, financing, resource allocation, policy decision-making and reform, and the social determinants of health. In essence, this work has sought to build bridges among philosophy, economics, and political science and to transcend and navigate the boundaries that traditionally separate them; both in terms of theoretical analysis and empirical studies. Thus, even though this book is about health and social justice, I consider it as much a treatise in the classical political economy of health.

The research programme that has culminated in this book began during my doctoral studies at Harvard University where I wrote two essays (Ruger 1995a; 1995b) and a doctoral dissertation (Ruger 1998) under the supervision of Amartya Sen and subsequently also Joseph Newhouse and Jerry Green. The first essay, 'Health, Health Care, and Incompletely Theorized Agreements', was submitted in satisfaction of the term paper requirement for Social Choice Theory and Welfare Economics (co-taught by Eric Maskin, Robert Nozick, and Amartya Sen), and the second, 'Value Formation, Democratic Choice Process, and Health Care Rationing', was submitted in satisfaction of the term paper requirement for Rational Choice Theory (taught by Amartya Sen). In this work I argued from an Aristotelian perspective of social justice that, in contrast to libertarian, communitarian, equal opportunity, and utilitarian perspectives, we should give special moral importance to health and to what is here called health capability, and I examined the trade-offs between efficiency and equity in health (Ruger 1995a; 1997; 1998). Health capability has a distinct advantage over outcome or liberty-based themes alone because it incorporates all three—health capability, health functioning (health), and health agency—in its ethical perspective. This has the advantage of both assessing justice in terms of health outcomes (what health is actually achieved) and what health outcomes people are able to achieve, while at the same time accommodating liberal and political considerations of choice and paternalism (the extent to which people choose, or would have chosen a health achievement), and health agency or the bringing about of health outcomes incorporating individual responsibility. I argued for several key principles of what justice requires, with respect to health and health capability, that remain the core principles of the theory of health and social justice presented in this book. These include, but are not limited to, formulating and justifying the theoretical construct of central health capabilities, as developed through partial agreement on a dominance partial ordering employing incompletely theorized agreements, as a universal criterion of justice in health and health policy; measurement and interpersonal comparability of justice in health and health policy through the use of shortfall equality from the optimal average and a hybrid sufficientarian and prioritarian standard of what justice requires in terms of shortfall inequalities; and the application of economic evaluation to equity goals so as to guide resource allocation as efficiently as possible (Ruger 1998).

Since that time, I have expanded this line of reasoning to offer theoretical insights to determine what it means for health inequalities to be unjust and how efforts to reduce them are morally justified, how much priority disadvantaged groups should receive, and whether a health intervention merits societal resources (Ruger 2006b). I have taken the pragmatic turn of applying methods of medical appropriateness and cost-minimization to more efficiently reduce health and health care disparities (Ruger 2006d; 2008d). With respect to health care access, I have argued that it is not enough to provide adequate health care without efforts to influence health norms and expand what is here called health agency, the ability to engage with and navigate one's environment and the health care system to prevent mortality and morbidity and to meet health needs (Ruger 2007a). For finance and insurance, I have offered an alternative to neoclassical economic and traditional bioethics perspectives, providing a philosophical justification for risk management and risk pooling *per se* through health insurance (Ruger 2007c) and social risk management (Ruger 2008b) as ethically desirable.

My work on resource allocation and rationing and the social determinants of health, culminating in this book, stretches back over a decade, where early on I struggled with questions of how to incorporate both a consequentialist focus on health outcomes and costs and a proceduralist respect for autonomy in human agency and also strike a balance between paternalism and autonomy (Ruger 1995b; 1998). I settled on a need to respect both the health and economic consequences individuals face and their agency, resulting in a joint scientific and deliberative process, integrating substantive and procedural principles as a resource allocation framework (Ruger 1995b, 2006d). My empirical research both in economic evaluation (Ruger and Emmons 2008) and in emergency medicine (Ruger et al. 2003; 2004; 2006; 2007) has proved invaluable in attempts to better understand micro-allocational decisions in which both time and resources (human, financial, physical) are of the essence (and thus limited). Efforts to understand the appropriateness/inappropriateness and urgency of emergency department visits have improved my understanding of what criteria are at play in setting priorities in the emergency room. Based in part on this experience, my view has evolved to place considerable priority on efforts to continue to triage individuals based on disease/injury severity and need with priority given to the worse-off. In other words, in addressing the aggregation problem delineated in Chapter 1, in the context of such micro resource allocation decisions, it is clear that efforts to address a common cough would rarely, if ever, supersede in priority to a gunshot wound or laceration. While some would argue that principles for allocating resources and rationing in micro-allocation and macro-allocation contexts are dissimilar (Kamm 1994) and while I agree with this to a certain extent, I contend that empirical and practical applications of such principles in either setting offer useful insights for the other.

On the social determinants of health and the 'separate spheres of justice' question, I have argued for the need to distinguish between supplementing and replacing domain-specific criteria in policy assessment and to keep the domain of health policy distinct from other policy domains (Ruger 1998; 2004b). This approach has allowed the assessment of a wider range of injustices, beyond the distribution of resources or liberties, to include attributes and conditions affecting individuals' freedoms—social norms and relations, self-management, decision-making ability, skills, knowledge, and competence, as well as structures within which resource distribution takes place. Despite the need to take supra-individual factors into account, however, I have argued and contend in this book that any analysis of the social determinants of health must come together at the *individual* level.

Even as I focused on principles of justice and health and health policy from a theoretical perspective, I have been concerned over the years with the process by which policy gets made at the national and sub-national level, how to work toward achieving health equity in a democratic society, and the extent to which norms and values play a role. My academic interests were bolstered by my practical policy experience as a member of Governor William Weld's Task Force on the Health Care Industry (Safran and Ruger

1994), where the state government sought to, and subsequently succeeded in, achieving universal health insurance coverage at the state level in Massachusetts. In health policy decision-making, my queries have aimed to move beyond prior work on public values in health policy, which has overlooked the ways in which values of different levels of specificity connect to create a coherent rationale for health reform (Ruger 1995a; 2007b). For health system reform, I have offered an approach to understanding health reform that analyses the role of values and norms, particularly their level of generality, in health policy decision-making, and the extent to which different policy actors internalize norms themselves and attempt to produce coalitions around them (Ruger 2007b; 2008d). My intuitions are reinforced by Christine Korsgaard's assessment in a volume edited by Martha Nussbaum and Amartya Sen (1993), in which she states that any theory of the good should seek to address three questions: (1) what is the philosophical idea of what constitutes the good life (moral legitimacy)? (2) does the idea have political legitimacy? (3) does the theory provide the more practical armoury for assessing policy reform and evaluation? This book stands apart as an effort to address all three questions.

Taking a wider view of health and social justice opened up a path in which it was clear that issues of *governance* were critical. Health, perhaps somewhat differently from some other goods, rests on factors influential to, and influenced by, both society and individuals. Thus, for a theory of health and social justice, we must examine more than the design of basic social institutions and include various other influences as well. In what is here called *shared health governance*, in order to address health inequalities and externalities, responsibility must be shared among national governments and institutions, non-governmental organizations, the private sector, communities, families, and individuals themselves. A shared health governance model incorporates individuals' decisions for themselves and for their society at large. I argued that ethical commitments are required for social organization and action for redistribution of resources, legislation and policy, public regulation and oversight, and the creation of public goods. Unlike much health disparities research that has come before, which through epidemiological and philosophical inquiry is highly descriptive, this approach probes deeper into the theoretical foundations of health disparities, their measurement and causal factors, and also demonstrates that an insightful understanding of this critical public health problem must examine the ethical underpinnings and causes of collective choice and policy implications in addressing it.

Through the research programme that has led to this book, I have tried to reconcile respect for individual rights with the need for collective decision-making. The individual right that bears most centrally on a theory of health and social justice is the right to health. While the United Nations declared a right to health in 1948, sixty years later, nations around the globe, including the United States with all its wealth, have failed to make it reality. In an article I wrote several years ago, I offered a philosophical justification for a right to health (Ruger 2006a). I made a case for the right to health as a meaningful and operational right and discussed the degree to which this right is necessarily justifiable and enforceable as prescribed in international law. I argued that sustaining the effort to realize a right to health requires individual and societal commitments to what is here called *public moral norms*—treating the right to health as an ethical demand for equity in health. This approach claims that working towards achieving equity in health requires social organization in the form of redistribution of resources, and related legislation and regulation. This obligation requires an ethical commitment as the effort to do so must be voluntary, not coercive. This ethical commitment is an ethical claim to redistribute resources to help meet the health needs of others and of our future selves. Presenting this case and shaping positive norms are key features of a theory of health and social justice.

This vision and strategies of my research programme over the last decade and a half are brought together in this book, where I offer a new theory addressing complex issues at the intersection of economics, philosophy, and political science in health. In so doing, I attempt to bridge the divide between procedures and consequences, between the collective and the individual, between personal freedom and social welfare, equality and efficiency, science and economics. In this book, I offer a theory of health and social justice that weaves together these disparate constructs and original insights to produce a foundational new paradigm for health. This vision is the *health capability paradigm*.

Notes

1. This framework pertains to health policy, public health, and health-related research. In previous work, the term 'health policy' has been used to include health care, public health, and health-related research. I continue to use this terminology here despite its limitations in not directly mentioning public health or health-related research.

2. As opposed to an "ideal" theory in the Rawlsian sense of a conception of a fully just society (Rawls 1999). That said, it is ambitious to present a theory of justice in the Rawlsian sense and this work provides a theoretical framework of justice for health, health policy, and public health. The book will continue to use the term theory to represent the bringing together of ideas expressed in these chapters into a coherent view.

3. In the sense of characterizing the human good in terms of human development and seeking to promote objectively good human lives, not in the sense of achieving a perfect life or a perfect society.

Acknowledgements

This book would not have been possible without the contribution of several of my colleagues over the years. For helpful discussions and comments, I thank Henry Aaron, Jarrad Aguirre, Sudhir Anand, Allan Brandt, Robert Brook, Dan Callahan, Marion Danis, Rebecca Dresser, Ezekiel Emanuel, Edwin Epstein, Richard Epstein, Ruth Faden, John Graham, Jerry Green, Jacob Hacker, James Hammitt, William Hogan, Kenneth Ludmerer, Jane Mansbridge, Theodore Marmor, Michael Marmot, Eric Maskin, Joseph Newhouse, Robert Nozick, David Paltiel, Theodore Ruger, Mark Schlesinger, Amartya Sen, Jody Sindelar, Cass Sunstein, Al Tarlov, and Milt Weinstein. I also thank personally and especially Ted Ruger and Sharon and Harry Prah for their help and support.

I am grateful for comments and input on my work from participants in various lectures, seminars, and workshops, the following in particular:

'Toward a Theory of a Right to Health: Capability and Incompletely Theorized Agreements', Ritsumeikan University, March 2008;

'Moral Foundations of Health Insurance: Implications for Health Reform', University of Texas Southwestern Medical Center Grand Rounds, January 2008;

'Disability and Capability', Yale University Interdisciplinary Center for Bioethics, Institute for Social and Policy Studies, Working Research Group on Disability, February 2006;

'How Health Works Out: Healthcare Challenges Throughout the Lifecycle', Yale Women Faculty Forum and Yale Office of WorkLife, Working Lives: Renegotiating Public and Private Series, Yale University, November 2005;

'Access to Health Knowledge', Yale Law School Information Society, Access to Knowledge Watch List Brainstorming Meeting, June 2005;

'Cost-effectiveness of Motivational Interviewing for Smoking Cessation and Relapse Prevention among Low-income Pregnant Women', Department of Epidemiology and Public Health, Joint Colloquium in Health Policy and Health Services Research and Mental Health Services Research, Yale University, December 2004;

'Ethics of the Social Determinants of Health', 4th Conference on the Capability Approach: Enhancing Human Security, University of Pavia, September 2004;

'Economic Evaluation in Health and Medicine', for 'Designing Outcomes and Clinical Research', Washington University School of Medicine, December 2003;

'Health and Social Justice', presented at Rights, Dignity and Inequality Workshop, Trinity College, University of Cambridge, October 2003;

'Capability and Health Policy', 3rd Conference on the Capability Approach: From Sustainable Development to Sustainable Freedom, University of Pavia, September 2003;

'Economic Evaluation of Addiction Services', in the General Medical Sciences Seminar Series, Washington University School of Medicine, August 2003;

'Aristotelian Justice and Health Policy: Capability and Incompletely Theorized Agreements', Harvard School of Public Health, Department of International Health, August 1998;

'Aristotelian Justice and Health Policy: Capability and Incompletely Theorized Agreements', doctoral dissertation presentation at Harvard Graduate School of Arts and Sciences, Harvard University, 1998;

'Social Justice and Health Policy: Aristotle, Capability and Incompletely Theorized Agreements', Health Policy Doctoral Seminar Series, Harvard University, November 1997.

For research support, I am indebted to The Health Institute, the Henry J. Kaiser Family Foundation, the National Library of Medicine (NIH), the Mark De Wolfe Howe Fund, the Brookings Institution, the Patrick and Catherine Weldon Donaghue Medical Research Foundation, and the George Warren Brown School of Social Work at Washington University. I have been supported by grants from the National Institutes of Health (National Cancer Institute and National Institute on Drug Abuse) and a Career Development Award from the National Institutes of Health (National Institute on Drug Abuse).

I am grateful for institutional support from Oxford University, Harvard University, Washington University School of Medicine and Center for Health Policy and Yale University Schools of Medicine, Public Health, Law and the Graduate School of Arts and Sciences. I thank Tendai Chizana, Sarah Humphreys, Christina Lazar, Laura Mannes, Haley McCarthy, Nora Ng,

Betsy Rogers, Linda Sage, and Takudzwa Shumba for research and editing assistance. I thank several anonymous reviewers for comments.

I would like to thank co-authors, journals, and publishers for granting permission to make use of previously published material in this book:

Ruger JP. 'Health, Health Care, and Incompletely Theorized Agreements', 1995, mimeographed Harvard University.

Ruger JP. 'Aristotelian Justice and Health Policy: Capability and Incompletely Theorized Agreements', 1998, Ph.D. dissertation on file with Harvard University Library.

Ruger JP. 'Catastrophic Health Expenditure', 2003, Lancet 362, pp. 996–7.

Ruger JP. 'Ethics of the Social Determinants of Health', 2004, Lancet 364, pp. 1092–97.

Ruger JP. 'Health and Social Justice', 2004, Lancet 364, pp. 1075–80.

Ruger JP. 'Measuring Disparities in Health Care', 2006, British Medical Journal 333, p. 274.

Ruger JP. 'Health, Capability and Justice: Toward a New Paradigm of Health Ethics, Policy and Law', 2006, Cornell Journal of Law and Public Policy 15 (2), pp. 403–82.

Ruger JP. 'Toward a Theory of a Right to Health: Capability and Incompletely Theorized Agreements', 2006, Yale Journal of Law and the Humanities 18, pp. 273–326. Reprinted by permission of the Yale Journal of Law and the Humanities, Vol. 18 (2008).

Ruger JP. 'Rethinking Equal Access: Agency, Quality and Norms', 2007, Global Public Health 2 (1): pp. 78–96.

Ruger JP. 'Moral Foundations of Health Insurance', 2007, QJM: An International Journal of Medicine 100(1), pp. 53–7. Reproduced by permission of Oxford University Press.

Ruger JP. 'Health, Health Care, and Incompletely Theorized Agreements: A Normative Theory of Health Policy Decision Making', Journal of Health Politics, Policy and Law, Vol. 32, Issue 1, pp. 51–87. Copyright 2007, Duke University Press. All rights reserved. Used with permission of the publisher.

Ruger JP. 'Governing Health', 2008, Harvard Law Review Forum, 121, pp. 43–56.

All reasonable effort has been made to contact holders of copyright in materials reproduced in this book. Any omissions will be rectified in future printings if notice is given to the publisher.

Table of Contents

Contents

Part III: Domestic Health Policy Applications

Contents

List of Figures

List of Tables

List of Abbreviations

ADA   Americans with Disabilities Act
AHRQ   Agency for Healthcare Research and Quality
ASD   Autism Spectrum Disorders
CBA   Cost-benefit analysis
CDC   Centers for Disease Control and Prevention
CEA   Cost-effectiveness analysis
CESCR   Committee on Economic, Social, and Cultural Rights
CHP   Community Health Program
CMA   Cost-minimization analysis
CMH   Commission on Macroeconomics and Health
COI   Cost of illness
CSDH   Commission on Social Determinants of Health
CUA   Cost-utility analysis
CV   Contingent Valuation
DALYs   Disability Adjusted Life Years
DRG   Diagnostic Related Group
EEOC   Equal Employment Opportunity Commission
FDA   Food and Drug Administration
FEO   Fair Equality of Opportunity
FFS   Fee-for-service
GDP   Gross Domestic Product
HMO   Health Maintenance Organisation
HSA   Health Security Act
HSC   Health Services Commission
ICESCR   International Covenant on Economic, Social and Cultural Rights
IOM   Institutes of Medicine
ITA   Incompletely Theorized Agreements

MSUD	Maple Syrup Urine Disease
NIAID	National Institute of Allergy and Infectious Disease
NICE	National Institute for Health and Clinical Excellence
NIH	National Institutes of Health
NORC	National Opinion Research Center
OC	Overlapping Consensus
OECD	Organization for Economic Co-operation and Development
QALYs	Quality Adjusted Life Years
SAVE	Saved Young Life Equivalent
SCCMETF	Society of Critical Care Medicine Ethics Task Force
S-CHIP	State Children's Health Insurance Program
WHO	World Health Organization
WTA	Willingness to Accept
WTP	Willingness to Pay

Introduction

Health systems throughout the world offer mixed results for their populations, both in terms of health outcomes and access to the conditions enabling individuals to achieve good health. Many health systems throughout the globe, the American health system most particularly, paradoxically produce both therapeutic gains and major discrepancies in access to quality care. Medical advances have improved patients' lives dramatically, yet stark inequalities in access, quality, financial burdens, and resource priorities undermine the impact of technological and scientific progress. The cost of health care is also on the rise (G. Anderson et al. 2000). Although providers, ethicists, health-policy experts, and government officials have attempted to address these issues many times, few proposals for reform have succeeded in many countries, notably the United States. In the United States, the failure of the Clinton Administration's 1993–1994 health reform efforts illustrates the problem's complexity. Physicians increasingly face the ethical dilemma of restricting access to necessary medical care when health insurers, state governments, and managed care organizations make, or require them to make, rationing decisions. Moreover, a 2004 United States Supreme Court ruling denies many patients any real recourse in suing their health maintenance organizations (HMOs) for denial of care (Aetna Health Inc. v. Davila, 2004). There is little consensus in the American health system[1], as in health systems in many other countries, about how to ensure equal access, finance health care, allocate scarce resources, or define a benefits package.

Traditional bioethics and public health ethics offer numerous approaches to address these issues, which have generally, though not exhaustively, fallen into five categories—welfare economic and utilitarian schemes, libertarian theories, communitarian approaches, procedural or democratic frameworks, and egalitarian theories. These broad categories have begun to form a collection of approaches to bioethics and public health ethics, each with advantages and limitations when applied to the problems health systems face.

This book proposes an alternative theoretical framework for the more comprehensively defined area of health ethics, policy, and law, integrating both substantive criteria and procedural mechanisms—a joint scientific and deliberative approach—to guide health system development and reform and the allocation of scarce health resources. This theory incorporates a particular vision of the good life rooted in the capability approach[2] and Aristotelian philosophy (Irwin 1999; Lord 1984; Nussbaum 1990b; 1992; 1998). It builds on and integrates both Aristotelian and capability perspectives to develop a theoretical framework for health ethics, policy, and law, and to elucidate its public policy implications. The capability approach is, however, vastly underspecified (Pogge 2002b), so this book moves significantly beyond the roots and the minimalist interpretation of the capability approach and specifies and brings together numerous disparate ideas into a coherent view of health and social justice.

In this view, the ethical principle of 'human flourishing' underlies society's obligation to maintain and improve health capabilities. This principle holds that society should enable human beings to live flourishing lives (Nussbaum 1990b; Irwin 1999). Flourishing and health are essential to the human condition. Certain aspects of health, in particular, undergird other areas of human flourishing, because without life itself, no other human functioning is possible. Therefore, public policy should focus on individuals' ability to function. Health policy should support individuals' capability for health functioning, enabling individuals to meet health needs, and creating conditions for health agency (Ruger 1997; 1998; 2004a).

From this perspective, expanding freedom is both the primary end and principle means of public policy; consequently, public policy should focus on removing barriers to freedom that leave people with little choice to exercise their reasoned agency. Freedom entails both processes of action and decision-making and actual opportunities available to people, given their personal and social circumstances (Sen 1999, p. 17). In what follows, I will argue that both the process and opportunity aspects of freedom are essential to developing individuals' health capabilities and a just health system. Public policy should also be efficient, requiring the wise and prudent use of resources. The primary goal for health systems is to reduce disparities in health capabilities using the fewest resources. Therefore, some limits must be set in allocating resources, and individuals and experts must decide how to make these trade-offs.

This theory offers several unique features and principles for health ethics, policy, and law.

Theoretical foundations

Human flourishing and health capability

First, this theory is rooted in a particular view of the good life: human flourishing, which values health intrinsically and more highly than non-intrinsic or solely instrumental social goods, such as income. This view gives special moral importance to a concept here called 'health capability'. Health capability, a person's ability to be healthy, includes health functioning and health agency (Ruger 1997; 1998; 2004a). It also implies that certain aspects of health are prerequisites for other types of functioning, including one's agency, or the ability to lead a life one has reason to value. Capability describes what individuals are able to do and be, offering a realistic sense of their real freedom to pursue the lives they value. Health capability broadens the scope of social justice and health policy to include health functioning and health agency, but it does not broaden it so much as to include all of what quality of life or well-being might entail.

Social choice theory and health capability

A second major difference between this theoretical framework and those of others centres on the theoretical and methodological approach to collective choice. There is considerable focus in the bioethics and public health ethics literature on democratic procedures for decision-making about health and health care. In espousing a substantive end of health capability in this theory, I address two significant questions:

(1) how to obtain actual collective agreement on a dominance partial ordering of health capabilities; and
(2) what type of social decision-making might apply in such an exercise.

This phase of the work draws on social choice theory and argues that incompletely theorized agreements (ITA) hold promise as a complementary framework for the Aristotelian and capability views and provides a useful approach to collective decision-making in health and health policy. Here I build on previous work in legal decision-making by extending ITA in at least three respects: moving beyond judicial decision-making to broader societal and public policy decision-making; specifying the framework to health and health care decision-making; and combining ITA with the capability approach to advance the operationalization of the capability perspective. ITA thus picks up where the capability approach leaves off, and provides a framework for resolving conflict among divergent views. More specifically, health and health capabilities are multidimensional concepts about which different people have different and sometimes conflicting views. No unique view of health exists as the basis for all evaluations of health and social justice. The incomplete ordering of the capability approach, in combination with the incompletely theorized agreement on that ordering, allows for reasoned public policy development and analysis in the face of plural goods and different, even conflicting, views.

Trans-positionality and prioritization among health capabilities

A third unique aspect of this theory is the development of a model that values 'central' health capabilities above those that are secondary. Central health capabilities are, simply, the capabilities to avoid premature death and escapable morbidity. This model reflects an incompletely theorized agreement on core dimensions of health capability. Agreement on the importance of providing such core health capabilities offers guidance in prioritizing health resources (Ruger 1998; 2004a; 2006a). These central features represent universally valued elements of health capability and offer a clear, grounded, and agreed upon view. This model includes both *potential* health and *actual* health—a duality embedded in health capability. It provides a middle ground or shared standard for health assessment. As such, it is useful in determining how we might go about assessing health policies and interventions and making comparisons among different individuals and groups. This model of health capability, which forms the foundation for prevention and treatment, provides a workable distinction between health-related needs and the goods and services that address those needs. This book offers a universal conception of health capability, while still maintaining room for further specification. This approach can help determine whether a particular public health or health care intervention or technology merits societal resources.

Inequality and health: equality as the standard

Fourth, while theories of justice have put forward a number of normative principles (equality, sufficiency, and priority) for treating people as equals in society and there are a number of different approaches to conceptualizing and measuring equality in bioethics and public health ethics, this approach employs 'shortfall equality' to judge public policies affecting health. The shortfall notion has been used in welfare economics and holds promise for the conceptualization and measurement of health inequalities. Shortfall equality compares *shortfalls of actual achievement from the optimal average* (such as typical longevity or physical performance). Alternatively, the concept of shortfall equality can also assess health capabilities, especially when equalizing achievements for different people is difficult. Human diversity is so pervasive and consequential, and can prevent some people from achieving maximal health. This approach might be particularly relevant for assessing the health capabilities of people with disabilities because it accounts for differences in the maximal potential for health functioning without 'levelling down' achievement goals of the entire group. Moreover, shortfall can be measured in either absolute or proportional terms, allowing proportional weighting for people with severe disabilities or, at the international level, weighting for countries with significant health deprivations. Shortfall equality is also more consistent with the emphasis on health as optimal functioning, 'a group's capacity to cope with all the circumstances of living . . . at an optimum level' and with 'freedom from the risk of disease' (Stedman 2000, pp. 789–90). This approach can also justify having good health as an end goal of public and health policy if we acknowledge that it is impossible to guarantee good health or equal health to everyone. The philosophical and pragmatic task of constructing an equality standard and measure for comparing individual advantage and disadvantage has been neglected in prior work on justice and health care.

Ethical commitments and public moral norms

Fifth, because the achievement of equity in health requires social organization in the form of a redistribution of resources, and related legislation and regulation, this obligation requires an ethical commitment on the part of everyone, those most fortunate and those in need, to the end goal of providing health capability to all. Without this ethical commitment, redistributing resources from the wealthy to those less fortunate and from the well to the sick will not be possible, because the effort to do so must be voluntary, not coercive. As such, individuals must internalize the public moral norm that health is worthy of social recognition, investment, and regulation to the point of successfully operationalizing it. The ethical imperative of health equity provides strong grounding for individual and state action to respect, protect, and fulfil health equity through institutional change. The primary means for achieving justice and actualizing a right to health are both legal and non-legal instruments. This ethical commitment to health equity is an ethical claim, in this case on all individuals, especially the wealthier, to redistribute some of their resources to help meet our own needs and those of others, today and in the future.

Ethics of the social determinants of health

Sixth, there has been much discussion of how social factors or determinants that bear on health fit within an overall theory of bioethics or public health ethics. Efforts have generally either supported or opposed a 'separate spheres of justice' view, whereby it is legitimate to focus on justice in bioethics or public health without reference to justice in other domains of public policy. Those who reject this view claim that justice in bioethics or public health ethics cannot focus specifically on health, but must also address the many overlapping determinates affecting overall well-being, not just health. This approach is much more nuanced than these alternative perspectives. While recognizing that a number of policy domains influence health, I argue that we are far from understanding the precise societal mechanisms that influence health or how to weight different social objectives. Thus, even in light of existing information on social determinants of health, it is unwise to attempt to improve health with broad non-health policies, such as completely flattening socio-economic inequalities, as prescribed by some. Such prescriptions cloud rather than clarify the means and ends of health policy and our ability to evaluate the impact of public policy on health. Moreover, the social determinants of health must come together at the individual level.

A joint scientific and deliberative approach

Seventh, the health capability paradigm involves a joint scientific and deliberative process, integrating substantive and procedural principles, as a resource allocation framework. This public process combines the evidence base of health care and public health with input from individuals, physicians and public health experts to assess the value of treatments, medications, and other health care and public health interventions. Under this view, health care and public health are special (and therefore socially guaranteed) because they play a dominant role among determinants of health capability. It is important to assess both the necessity and the appropriateness of a health intervention. Medical appropriateness is a key principle of this approach. Although individuals have primary authority for health care decisions that affect them directly, physicians can help determine 'medical appropriateness' and 'medical necessity'. In this framework, individuals employ their health agency, and physicians seek their patients' best interest. Physicians and public health experts share knowledge and resources (e.g. benefits, risks, costs) with each other and with lay persons to achieve ethical rationality and practical reasonableness, balancing technical rationality with ethical rationality in collective choice—a more expansive account of rationality incorporates both. This approach provides for public deliberation through collaborative problem solving among physicians, public health experts, and citizens. These formulations focus especially on reasoning—whether at higher levels of abstraction or lower levels of particulars—and on mutual respect among citizens and experts. This approach stresses that participatory decision-making is instrumentally important for forming values and setting priorities when policy choices are difficult, but it does not rely on 'fair procedures' to determine fair outcomes. Rather, this theoretical approach is substantive in nature, incorporating participation and voice, but ultimately evaluating health policy in terms of its consequences and effects on health capability. This framework integrates both consequential and procedural elements of justice, unlike allocation theories resting on procedural justice alone. When policies and law require even greater specification, further iterations of public discussions could be necessary to make difficult choices about which health services merit societal investment.

Public policy cannot result from narrow technical blueprints. Rather, this theory envisions a stepwise process that reviews scientific evidence about the consequences of polices on health. Individuals must therefore have the capability to participate in such deliberations and decision-making and know the risks, benefits, and costs of health prevention and treatment and various health policy options. The deliberative process should also update its recommendations continually to account for changes in medical knowledge, technology, and costs when determining what probability of success would make an intervention worthwhile.

Shared health governance

Eighth, in this theoretical approach, decisions are made by appealing to a shared concept of ability for health functioning. When disagreements occur, practical models of agreement or consensus facilitate workable solutions. The resolutions that flow from these deliberations offer guidance in standardizing prevention and treatment decisions and developing health policies and health laws. This view contrasts with paradigms in which consumers alone, physicians or public health experts alone, strict algorithms or cost-benefit calculations, shared decision-making within an informed consent model, fair procedures, or third parties (such as insurers) make health decisions. The underlying framework is *shared health governance*, a construct in which individuals, providers, and institutions work together to empower individuals and create an environment enabling all to be healthy (Ruger 1998; 2004a; 2006b). The shared decision-making of other approaches focuses narrowly on individual decisions in isolation, but a shared health governance model incorporates individuals' decisions for themselves and *for their society at large*. Shared health governance extends beyond the individual patient–doctor relationship to the institutions that oversee the health sector. This paradigm promotes consensus on substantive principles and procedures of distribution; offers a method for achieving that consensus (incompletely theorized agreements) (Ruger 1995a; 1997; 1998; 2004a); places importance on the results of health policies and laws (costs and effectiveness) in judging them; and promotes deliberation through collaborative problem-solving. Thus, the framework integrates both consequential (substantive) and procedural (democratic) elements of justice, and focuses on both health functioning and health agency. Both decision-making processes and achieved outcomes are important for evaluating justice. Neither fair procedures alone nor desired outcomes alone foster a just system.

Applications

Rethinking equal access: agency, quality, and norms

Ninth, a shared health governance model takes a different tack on the issue of equal access (Ruger 2007a). Equal access should mean equal access to high-quality care, not a 'decent minimum', 'adequate care', or 'tiered health care'. Equal access on this view does not imply equal outcomes or equal results. Nor is it enough to provide health care without efforts to expand individuals' health agency—their ability to engage with and navigate the health system and their environment to avoid mortality and morbidity and to meet health needs (Ruger 2004a; 2007a). Furthermore, shared health governance means shared responsibility—individuals, providers, and institutions have respective roles and responsibilities in achieving health goals. A major emphasis of the health capability paradigm is that institutions and providers are morally obligated to provide as high quality health care as resources permit to all individuals (Ruger 2007a). It is unfair to deny any one individual, or group of individuals, access to quality care if doing so could substantially decrease their chance of a significantly improved health outcome. In policy terms, reaching this goal would require continuous efforts to standardize medicine, reduce medical errors, and move towards a gold standard of care (IOM 2001). High-quality care is not a modest universal criterion of social justice. It is a demanding criterion because it is necessary from a moral point of view for helping people to function at their best, given their circumstances. Its ambitiousness reflects the need to evaluate the impact of equal access policies on health (functioning and achievements) and health agency, taking into account individuals' health needs and disabilities. Such a view would not condone the significant disparities in health care quality that exist in the United States, for example, and in many developed and developing countries.

Responsibility and health: voluntary risk and paternalism

Tenth, this theory seeks to enhance individual responsibility through improving health agency, as both are essential for achieving optimal health outcomes and creating a fairer health system for all. Any theory of health and social justice must address concerns of personal responsibility and voluntary risk. At first glance it appears that some people are not voluntarily risk averse to health consequences—smokers unconcerned about lung cancer, for instance. Some think people who knowingly take risks with their health should pay additional sums of money or be solely responsible for paying for health insurance and health care. Such a system, it is argued, would:

(1) help raise additional financing for services caused by bad health habits; and

(2) help mitigate the moral hazards of such situations by giving people incentives to change their habits.

However, these perspectives suffer from several shortcomings. It is difficult at this juncture to understand the respective causal determinants (including genetic determinants) of, and differences between, voluntary versus involuntary contributors to health risk. As such, it is unjust to always blame individuals for their health problems. That said, improved health agency and health functioning—through public policies that rely on principles ranging from paternalism to libertarian paternalism to free will—at one point in time and over time can impose greater responsibility on individuals to make healthier choices and ultimately improve their health.

Moral foundations of health insurance: preventing, mitigating, and coping with risk

Eleventh, understanding that universal health insurance is essential for human flourishing opens up an alternative moral framework for analysing health insurance. The United States and numerous developing countries do not provide universal health insurance coverage to their populations. Academic approaches to health insurance have typically adopted a neo-classical economic perspective, assuming that individuals make rational decisions to maximize their preferred outcomes, and businesses (including insurance companies) make rational decisions to maximize profits. In that approach, individuals who are risk averse will purchase health insurance to reduce variation in the costs of health care between healthy and sick periods. In empirical studies, however, individuals do not always make rational choices. They also find it difficult to assess their health risks and to know how much insurance they need. In contrast, bioethics and public health ethics have focused on the issue of equal access to health care, but provide little in the way of philosophical justification for risk management through health insurance *per se*. Nor has either bioethics or public health ethics shown how risk-pooling, in which many at-risk individuals pay premiums to cover one individual's expensive health outcome, is ethically desirable, except insofar as it ensures equal access to health care and equal income to purchase it for all contributors. The central ethical aims of universal health insurance coverage are to keep people healthy, and to enhance their security by protecting them from both ill health and its economic consequences, issues not adequately considered in the bioethics and public health ethics literature to date. Universal health insurance that is community-rated and progressively financed is critical because equal access cannot be separated from equity in health care financing.

Market failures, public goods, and the role of the public sector

Twelfth, health care and public health financing, delivery, and organization can involve either private (profit or non-profit) or public entities or a mix of the two. The approach taken in this book is that society must compare the advantages and disadvantages of the free market with those of the government and other political and social institutions. This view transcends systems that are either primarily capitalist or socialist. In the health care and public health sectors, numerous market failures have created a rationale for public sector involvement. Epidemics are one of the most common causes of health care market failure; preventing and controlling them requires public health programmes. Public goods—those whose benefits should extend to everyone and whose consumption by one person does not preclude consumption by another—also require public financing, because private markets typically will not produce goods they cannot sell exclusively to one person. There are also mixed goods that benefit specific individuals but have societal benefits as well. Rehabilitation services, for example, improve patients' physical functioning but also enhance economic progress through better labour productivity. Another market failure in health care is information asymmetry, in which health providers or insurers have significantly more information about a patient's condition than the patient does or vice versa. The drawbacks of an entirely public health sector or an entirely private health sector suggest that mixed public-private systems might be optimal. Market failure types suggest a greater role for public financing and private provision through non-profit institutions. The health capability paradigm proposes a blended approach to create an integrated and multifaceted system, in which different types of institutions work together to improve health capability. To create and maintain equitable and efficient health systems, governments must offer significant direction, oversight, regulation, financing, and, in some cases, provision of care. In many settings, however, the private sector can provide goods and services effectively in conjunction with a supportive and regulatory public sector. In virtually every area of the health sector, public-private collaboration and investment are critical, especially in generating medical knowledge, technologies, goods, and services.

A robust concept of opportunity costs: incorporating efficiency

Thirteenth, this paradigm takes a stepwise approach to resource allocation whereby economic considerations follow and complement clinical input, not vice versa. Evaluation of health policies, laws, and technologies must consider costs because we live in a world of scarce resources. Moreover, every resource has an alternative use, so its expenditure corresponds with an opportunity cost. Therefore, some limits are necessary, and individuals and society, through shared health governance, must use these resources parsimoniously by evaluating efficiency. Efficiency measures include cost-minimization analysis (CMA) and economic incentives for high-quality care. Cost-effectiveness analysis (CEA) can also be useful in comparing interventions for a single population, such as AIDS patients, by weighing the marginal benefits and marginal costs of two alternative interventions. For example, evaluating the cost-effectiveness of combination antiretroviral therapy for HIV infection, or of preventing AIDS-related opportunistic infections (Freedberg et al. 1998; 2001), or simulation modelling of lifetime costs and life expectancy to inform clinical guidelines for the treatment of HIV-related *Pneumocystis carinii* pneumonia (PCP) can help identify the additional costs society must pay for the additional benefits of each intervention.

Most approaches to bioethics and public health ethics fail to consider opportunity costs and efficiency adequately. The consideration of costs under this theory resembles a utilitarian welfare economic perspective in that costs and outcomes are both valued. However, it contrasts with the utilitarian aggregation methodology and recommends the use of cost-minimization analysis and cost-effectiveness analysis in combination with equity-oriented allocations (as opposed to incorporating equity weights into CEA). In addition to helping physicians and patients judge whether a particular medical intervention or technology merits investment, CMA and CEA can reveal financial reasons for basic health care inequalities. For example, some American oncologists profit by purchasing chemotherapy agents and dispensing them at a much higher price, which leads to inefficiency through higher pricing and over-use, particularly at the end of life (Emanuel et al. 2003). This practice also compromises a physician's duty to act in a patient's best interest.

Disabilities and reasonable accommodation

Bioethics and public health ethics have struggled to address disabilities and severe physical and mental impairments in societal decision-making about health care and public health. The health capability paradigm argues for basing judgements on joint patient–physician decision-making (at the policy and individual levels), using medical necessity, medical appropriateness, and medical futility as criteria, rather than attempting to estimate specific weights for severely disabled individuals, as other frameworks do. Thus, this paradigm aims to protect disabled people from discrimination while limiting exorbitantly costly care that would deprive others of necessary health resources.

Normative theory and health policy decision-making

Norms and values in the public's assessment of policy

Another unique aspect of this theory of health and social justice is the extent to which it grapples with domestic health reform and the question of the interplay between political and moral legitimacy. A theory of health and social justice must not only present a morally legitimate conception of the good, but also offer a convincing framework for its political legitimacy and thus ultimately its implementation through political processes and social institutions. Thus, while the theory of health and social justice presented here claims that justice requires relieving shortfall inequalities in central health capabilities as efficiently as possible (as a demand and principle of justice), it also seeks a balance between state interference to achieve these goals and individuals' freedom from interference (right to non-interference). As such, this theory also commits to the idea that, through public reasoning and democratic practice, individuals internalize public moral norms of redistribution and state oversight and willingly embrace ethical commitments to offer political legitimacy to this goal. The final part of this book examines the role of norms and values in public policy decision-making and offers a normative theory of health policy decision-making. This work is based on the premise that in order to achieve changes in health policy at the national level in any country through a politically legitimate democratic process, citizens must be willing to pass federal legislation with moral legitimacy that ensures equity in health for all. This final part of the book presents a normative theory for analysing federal health policy decisions, with specific application to the United States. The goal is to advance a health reform approach that analyses the role of values and norms, particularly their level of generality, in health policy decision-making, and the extent to which different policy actors (political and non-political) internalize norms themselves and attempt to produce coalitions around them. Prior work on public values in health policy has overlooked the ways in which values of different levels of specificity connect to create a coherent (or incoherent) rationale for health reform. This book aims to address these gaps by using a more accurate framework of social agreement, which reflects the fact that values and norms operate at multiple levels of generality and degrees of internalization. In so doing, it provides a better understanding of how norms and values work together to form a coherent (or incoherent) basis for reform. This alternative framework, social agreement theory, builds on political philosophy and legal theory.

Public moral norms and domestic health reforms

The normative framework presented here is unique in that it integrates public moral norm internalization and the social agreement model of incomplete theorization. A 'public moral norm' is a moral value that pertains to our individual and collective morality in the public sphere; an example of such a norm would be collective organization to achieve common goals. A public moral norm contrasts with an individual moral norm in that the moral value pertains not just to individual action but also to collective action regarding the public sphere (e.g. norms about procedural justice, rules of accuracy, trust, ethicality, and neutrality). A particular type of public moral norm, a distributive justice norm, determines the distribution of societal resources. The consistent failure of health care reform efforts in the United States can be understood by first analysing the extent of individual, societal, and political internalization of necessary public moral norms—for instance, that one has an ethical commitment to make financial sacrifices to support the expansion of health insurance— and then determining the extent to which social agreement about this ethical commitment has occurred. This agreement could occur even without consensus on abstract higher-level principles and on principles in other domains of social life (e.g. welfare). When this norm does become internalized, domestic legislation can follow. The failure of health care reform in the United States shows that it will be difficult for America to adopt universal health insurance coverage until this norm of willingness

14

to pay for others' health care coverage gains acceptance at the social and political level. Without this norm's acceptance, efforts to achieve public consensus on abstract principles (e.g. equality) or on 'universal coverage' will continue to be stymied because they create more disagreement than agreement. Americans, especially liberal Americans, experience considerable ambivalence and conflict among the abstract higher-level principles invoked in debates about universal coverage. The theoretical framework developed here illustrates how these cleavages and uncertainties work and how they allow opponents of reform to launch value-based arguments that disrupt reform-supporting coalitions.

Internalization and agreement on moral values

The theory developed here offers promise for analysing health reform efforts in many countries, especially pluralistic constitutional regimes. Drawing attention to coalitions around, and internalization of, values and norms offers insights and prescriptions distinctive from those that prevailing analyses provide. From this perspective, pluralistic constitutional regimes are composed of individuals and their representatives, whose diverse beliefs create social tension and make social agreement difficult to achieve. Therefore, attempts to make collective decisions—for example, through the legislature—must emphasize shared values to achieve stability and social unity. It is necessary to determine shared values, even values that are shared for different reasons, to achieve social agreement for political and legal decision-making. From this perspective, legitimate political authority is not just a matter of political philosophy; it has pragmatic advantages in forging consensus and coalitions amid pluralism. In this way, this theoretical framework helps further traditional political process and bargaining arguments because it illuminates how political actors can undermine the conditions for reasoned agreement on common interests. It challenges the current scope of public opinion research in that it calls for research probing aspects not addressed in most prior studies, aspects connecting values to support for policies. Furthermore, it calls for research to examine whether the conditions of public communication help produce an informed, reasoning, and deliberative public that can come to agreement on norms and values for policy. Moreover, this framework relies on popular sovereignty and political leadership to enhance deliberative public debate and public reasoning in order to agree on the common good. Finally, this approach recognizes that efforts to address health problems in developing and developed countries alike will probably require norms and values to be restructured in a fundamental way—globally, but most importantly, at the national level. Social movements at the national level, such as the civil rights and feminist movements in the United States, for example, have provided momentum and principles for such restructuring.

Collective reasoning about public policy requires a truthful deliberative process and a sincere and dedicated effort to achieve consensus on both the ends (values) and means (acceptable policy solutions) of public policy. These efforts are critical to citizens' ability to 'rule themselves' (Richardson 2002). Public opinion can be manipulated and distorted, so the challenge in a constitutional democracy is to create the conditions under which individuals can agree on a political conception that governs health and health care. Such a conception is likely latent in the political culture and might well emerge through public deliberation and social consensus. Efforts to involve national governments in improving the health of their populations and to ensure access to quality health care for all require more than fragile agreement on mid-level principles. These efforts require invoking principles, values, and norms, as well as honest discussion about the consequences of denying necessary and appropriate care for people's health and security.

Notes

1. Health system includes health care, public health, and health-related research.
2. Martha Nussbaum and Amartya Sen provide different versions of the capability approach. Here both perspectives are drawn on, although I focus more heavily on Sen in developing theory. See generally Sen (1992; 1999). For more on the differences between Nussbaum's and Sen's versions of the capability approach, see generally Nussbaum (2000b).

Part I

The Current Set of Ethical Frameworks

1

Approaches to Medical and Public Health Ethics

Inequality in access to health insurance and health care, exacerbated by cost constraints, has spawned many frameworks of health ethics, policy, and law. These fall into several categories, including: welfare economic and utilitarian schemes that rely on cost-effectiveness, cost-utility, or cost-benefit analyses to aggregate costs and benefits and maximize overall social welfare; communitarian theories that adhere to principles developed through community traditions; egalitarian perspectives that focus on equal opportunity, equal welfare, and equal resources; libertarian theories that emphasize individual rights and typically promote free-market solutions or quasi-market approaches such as *ex ante* choices and advance contracting; and procedural or democratic approaches, which set forth right procedures or random processes to prioritize care. These frameworks have varying advantages and disadvantages. The following discussion reveals the profound need for an alternative paradigm.

1.1. Welfare economic and utilitarian approaches

One of the leading frameworks for health ethics, policy, and law is utilitarianism, which arguably serves as the standard framework for health policy analysis (Weinstein 1990, pp. 93–4; Weinstein and Stason 1977, pp. 716–21) and was endorsed by the Panel on Cost-Effectiveness in Health and Medicine. The United States Public Health Service created the panel in 1993 to review the state of the field and develop guidelines for standardizing cost-effectiveness analyses in health and medicine (Gold et al. 1996). The panel comprised thirteen non-federal scientists and scholars with experience in cost-effectiveness analysis (CEA), medical ethics, health law, and health outcomes measurement (Gold et al. 1996). The panel recommended a system that captures individual preferences for different states of health, and recommended Quality-Adjusted-Life-Years (QALYs) as the metric for ranking health interventions.

Utilitarian frameworks require allocations that maximize social utility. However, rights have an 'indefinite and tenuous foundation' (Beauchamp and Childress 1994, p. 335) because they rely upon overall utility maximization, and thus only improved net social utility would justify a right to health care (Buchanan 1984). Cost-utility analysis (CUA) is the primary method for evaluating health policy under a utilitarian ethic. CUA values health status in terms of health preferences, desires, or utilities; the QALY index combines preferences for length of life with those for quality of life. Like most utility measures, QALYs rest on the premise that utilities of different individuals and health conditions can compare on a single quantitative scale.

Other welfare economic techniques use different outcome metrics and include CEA and cost-benefit analysis (CBA) as well as CUA. CBA translates all benefits into monetary units through various techniques such as Cost of Illness (COI) studies, which value health outcomes by direct (medical and non-medical expenses) and indirect (lost productivity measures) costing methods (Rice et al. 1989). Willingness to Pay (WTP) and Willingness to Accept (WTA) methodologies use questionnaires to assess individuals' willingness to pay for risk reduction or accept additional risk (Mishan 1976; Tolley et al. 1994, p. 6, 24, 74). Cost benefit analysts also assess individuals' preferences for changes in risk, based on their purchasing decisions; and they ask people to assign a monetary value to various health states and associated risks, using Contingent Valuation (CV) surveys (Viscusi 1992, p. 51).

The various welfare economic techniques are not without their weaknesses, however. One common concern about CBA is that respondents' income levels skew monetary valuations. Critics have faulted COI for not including pain and suffering in its calculations. WTA and WTP have raised objections because extrapolations from market transactions and individuals' hypothetical assessments might not accurately reflect individuals' valuations of health benefits and risks. Risk and survival are difficult to quantify. Moreover, the cost per QALY methodology also does not recognize that health care evaluation must assess both the severity of a patient's initial state *and* the effect of treatment (Nord 1993a, p. 227). To account for the trade-offs between severity and treatment effect, Nord proposes a mathematical model and index (cost per Saved Young Life

Equivalent (SAVE)). SAVEs allow expression in numerical terms of the social value of saving a young person from dying, and allowing him or her to live a healthy life. They are a reference outcome related to costs in the same way as QALYs (Nord 1993a, p. 227). However, these methods of health valuation yield widely disparate estimates of the 'value of life', and it is unclear which method best applies the principles of welfare economics.

The application of welfare economic and utilitarian principles to health ethics, policy, and law raises several concerns. First, accounting for only aggregate welfare without considering the distribution of benefits and burdens in society is problematic. CUA, CBA, and CEA tolerate significant inequalities in order to increase total or average social utility. In response to this concern, there have been attempts to incorporate a distributional ethic (equity weights) into the utilitarian approach (Nord et al. 1999). Kantian and libertarian ethicists, however, would be concerned about the attempt to aggregate across persons (Kant 1898; Rawls 1971). Such an attempt conflicts with the principle that each individual is an end in herself and cannot be used instrumentally to assist other individuals. 'People will differ', Nozick observes, 'in how they view regarding natural talents as a common asset . . . and they will wonder whether any reconstruction of Kant that treats people's abilities and talents as resources for others can be adequate' (Nozick 1974, p. 228).

The Oregon Medicaid experiment illustrates the problems that can result from strict application of utilitarianism and cost-utility analysis. In an 'aggregation problem' resulting from weighing a small benefit for many individuals against a large benefit for a few (Daniels 1994, p. 28), the experiment's algorithm counter-intuitively ranked tooth-capping ahead of surgery for ectopic pregnancy (Brock 1995; Hadorn 1991, pp. 2218–19). Moreover, strict CUA discriminates against disabled people by assigning less weight to their health benefits than to those of non-disabled individuals (Brock 1995). This strategy relates to the 'priorities problem' in health care rationing, or determining how much weight to give to society's most needy members (Daniels 1994, p. 28).

Using utility measures to the exclusion of other measures also raises concerns. Sen (1987a; 1999) has identified three main limitations of the utilitarian framework:

(1) it omits freedom and focuses on achievements;

(2) it omits certain achievements that are not reflected in the utility measure; and

(3) it fails to measure accurately situations of persistent deprivation and adversity, in which people with significantly reduced functioning might not appear to be so deprived because they have adapted to their adverse environment (Letiche 1987; Hawthorn 1988; Nussbaum 1997).

Entrenched inequalities highlight the difficulty of comparing interpersonal utilities and different utilities on a single quantitative scale. Commensurate measures of utility, satisfaction or desire fulfilment cannot assess well-being in functional terms. '*Incommensurability occurs when the relevant goods cannot be aligned along a single metric without doing violence to our considered judgements about how these goods are best characterized*' (Sunstein 1994, p. 796). In terms of health, this means that different health conditions, such as deafness, blindness, cardiovascular disease, diabetes, depression, cystic fibrosis, autism, and loss of limb, cannot be compared because differing values cannot be reduced to a unitary quantitative scale. Critics of commensurability differ in the degree to which different values can be compared. Sunstein, for example, does not rule out the ordinal or qualitative ranking of values, though he sees no ethical foundation in their cardinal comparison. He also believes, as do Anderson and I, that individual and collective rational choices can be made among incommensurate alternatives (Anderson 1993, p. 59–64; Ruger 1998; 2006a; Sunstein 1994, p. 809). Raz holds a similar view—that incommensurability does not preclude choice, and the choices made between incommensurate options appear rational because the actor has assigned comparative values to the options (Nussbaum 1990a; Raz 1986, p. 339).

In an extension of the commensurability problem, CEA, CBA, and CUA assume that saving life and extending life are commensurable with changes in health status or quality of life. For example, in employing QALY maximization, two years of additional life with a 0.5 reduced quality adjustment is deemed equivalent to one year of additional life with no quality adjustment (e.g. a fully healthy life). In addition, saving the lives of twenty-five people for one year is deemed equivalent to saving the lives of five people for five years or one person for twenty-five years. Kamm argues that individuals' judgements regarding aggregation differ when saving lives is at issue because any other change in health status (increase or decrease) cannot compete with life saving as a health outcome (Kamm 1993). Hadorn discusses the 'Rule of Rescue' and the symbolic value of saving 'identifiable lives'—specific, flesh and blood individuals as opposed to the faceless abstractions of statistics. He argues for the need to incorporate this altruistic value into any health-related assessment and for guidelines that would balance quality of life-based benefits with the value of saving identifiable lives (Hadorn 1991, pp. 2223–4). However, life-saving interventions have drawbacks when expensive technology keeps people alive temporarily, or even for extended periods of time (Schiavo ex rel. Schindler v. Schiavo, 2005), regardless of the resulting quality of life. The challenge, then, is to respect the unique value of saving lives while recognizing the need to assess treatment efficacy.

There are two issues here. The first is whether there is a real and significant higher-order value in saving 'identifiable lives' over both saving 'statistical lives' and providing other health benefits. The second is whether there is a real and significant higher-order value in saving all lives (both identifiable and statistical) over providing other health benefits (Hadorn 1991). Tolley and Eddy both believe that saving identifiable lives has 'symbolic' or 'altruistic' value, even 'vicarious utility' that providing other health benefits does not (Eddy 1991a; 1991b, p. 2135–40; Tolley et al. 1994). Gibbard argues that although these values are irrational and will not maximize life due to the higher-order ranking of identifiable lives over statistical lives, symbolic or expressive values embody 'compassion' and strengthen the 'social fabric' of a society (Gibbard 1982, pp. 399–428). Hadorn, however, argues that saving identifiable lives should not be traded for other health benefits (Hadorn 1991, pp. 2219–25). My view aligns closely with those of Pildes, Anderson, and Sunstein, who support higher-order values but do not endorse lexical ordering that protects certain values against *all* trade-offs (Pildes and Anderson 1990, p. 2145–61; Ruger 1997; 1998; 2006a; Sunstein 1994). This view accords with the culture and ethics of the health profession (Beauchamp and Childress 1994).

Other critics of CUA argue that QALYs disfavour individuals with a diminished capacity to benefit, people with disabilities (Powers and Faden 2000, pp. 112–13), and older individuals with fewer years to live (Harris 1985, pp. 88–90). Still, many defend the maximization principle behind CEA and the *ex ante* rationale that accepts trade-offs (Nord 1999, pp. 123–7; Powers 1995, p. 147, 159). 'We who do cost-effectiveness analyses aren't coldhearted accountants who take pleasure in depriving people of health care...', Eddy writes. 'We think that we are responding to a national call for help' (Eddy 1992, p. 1675). CUA proponents argue for its more limited role, for example, as an input to policy decision-making (Russell et al. 1996). Nonetheless, it tends to be monistic—evaluating health programmes or policies by one measure of cost per QALY, typically in maximizing QALYs.

Some argue that cost-value analysis should replace CUA altogether, precisely because it incorporates social values (Nord et al. 1999; Powers and Faden 2000, p. 117). Cost-value analysis proponents propose that the public's preference for interpersonal trade-offs should guide resource allocation rather than an aggregation of individuals' preferences for health states. 'What ultimately is needed in resource allocation decisions is not utilities for health states per se, but rather societal values for different health improvements relative to each other', Nord argues (1999, pp. 115). And according to Menzel, 'CEA needs to incorporate a broader set of values—social or societal values—than the individual utilities incorporated by the conventional . . . form of CEA' (Menzel 1999, p. 258). Indeed, empirical research reveals that most people favour a system of resource allocation that prioritizes severely ill individuals, even if their capacity to benefit is limited and the cost of treating them is relatively high, over utility maximization (Nord 1999, pp. 30–37). This finding illuminates the importance of social values and individual preferences for interpersonal trade-offs (distributive preferences) that look beyond individual utility; from this perspective, CUA elicits the wrong type of preferences when it prioritizes individual preferences for health states.

There are, however, critics of the cost-value paradigm who question whether so-called societal preferences actually represent the majority view. They wonder how one can know whether such judgements are 'sufficiently reflective or sufficiently informed'; how to reflect political and moral disagreement about social values in a public and transparent manner; and argue that the cost-value paradigm fails to account for the significance of a patient's history and life circumstances (Powers and Faden 2000; pp. 118–19).

The Disability Adjusted Life Years (DALYs) approach attempts to address some of these concerns. It advocates a process for establishing group preferences on disability weights, which are aggregated using DALYs to measure the health of different population groups. 'We do not take into account health satisfaction of individuals at all; the task is to isolate health conditions and limit the relevant non-health contingencies to determine the impact of health conditions on individuals', Murray and Acharya note (1997, p. 723). While the effort is laudable, concerns remain regarding the use of such data for policy purposes due to the bias towards the able-bodied over disabled persons (Anand and Hanson 1997, pp. 700–702) and the limited ability to incorporate additional moral criteria into decision-making (Powers and Faden 2000, pp. 120–21).

1.2. Communitarianism and liberal communitarianism

Communitarian theories of justice argue that the provision of health care is an expression of community values, and therefore, the justification for health care varies by community (MacIntyre 1981; 1988; Sandel 1982; 1984; Walzer 1990). Under communitarian theory, each society constructs its own principles as it evolves politically; morality is a cultural rather than abstract concept (Walzer 1990). Cultural or moral relativism is the predominant claim and there are no universal principles or standards. Taken to the extreme, this viewpoint could threaten the sense of common humanity that is a basis for morality, and could also undermine political and social cooperation in societies that respect individual liberties and diversity. Buchanan, for example, argues that 'reliance on the judgment of virtuous individuals...is no substitute for principled public debate about the ethical character of our common institutions.' (Buchanan et al. 2000, p. 378).

Ezekiel Emanuel proposed a communitarian approach that incorporates aspects of libertarianism. In an ideal system, he proposed, deliberative, democratic communities could develop shared conceptions of justice and the good life (Emanuel 1991, pp. 156–7). However, Emanuel is critical of non-communitarian democratic political procedures, arguing that it is difficult to agree on a substantive conception of distributive justice in a liberal polity. He would also designate the current level of federal health spending as the national health care budget and give patients vouchers so they could choose among community health programmes (CHPs) offering different levels of services (Emanuel 1991, pp. 184–7). He rejects utilitarianism as a framework in which to analyse medical ethical issues and eschews cost-benefit, cost-utility, or cost-effectiveness methodologies because they bypass the need for collective reflection on values (Emanuel 1991, p. 156). His proposal has been criticized on impracticality and moral grounds because CHPs might be tempted to select benefit structures that favour some citizens over others (Beauchamp and Childress 1994).

1.3. Egalitarian theories: equal opportunity and equal welfare

Egalitarian theories, a third framework, focus on the equal distribution of certain societal goods, one of which is health care. They do not support 'equal sharing of all possible social benefits' (Beauchamp and Childress 1994, p. 339). The most noteworthy egalitarian theory of justice is John Rawls's view that justice requires the fair distribution of 'primary goods'. 'As a first step', Rawls proposes, 'suppose that the basic structure of society distributes certain primary goods, that is, things that every rational man is presumed to want' (Rawls 1971, p. 62). Rational agents behind a 'veil of ignorance' (Rawls 1971, p. 12) about their personal circumstances would choose principles of justice that maximize the minimum level of primary goods. 'This ensures that no one is advantaged or disadvantaged in the choice of principles by the outcome of natural chance or the contingency of social circumstances' (Rawls 1971, p. 12). While Rawls did not initially apply his theory to health care, he did include health care in later works (Rawls 1999), as others have also done. Those who have analysed Rawls's approach in the context of health care, particularly Rakowski, have concluded that hypothetical choosers would prioritize resources randomly (Rakowski 1991).

Norman Daniels and colleagues also apply Rawls's theory of justice to health care and argue that health care is a right because it provides 'equality of opportunity' (Daniels 1985)—the Fair Equality of Opportunity (FEO) account. Gerald Cohen (1989) has drawn on Rawls's theory and expanded the Rawlsian view through an 'equal opportunity for welfare' and 'equal access to advantage' approach which supports rights for those disadvantaged by poor talents and skills, as well as by disease or disability (Arneson 1989; Cohen 1989; Cohen 1993). Daniels (2001) counters that this interpretation places too little emphasis on choice or responsibility and raises problems for public policy including access to interventions that go beyond ameliorating disease (Buchanan et al. 2000; Sabin and Daniels 1994). He supports the 'level playing field concept of equal opportunity' (Buchanan et al. 2000, p. 65; Roemer 1995), which requires 'efforts to eliminate or ameliorate . . . social factors that limit opportunity over and above discrimination' (Buchanan et al. 2000, p. 16).

Drawing on Rawls, Daniels adopts the 'veil of ignorance' concept (Rawls 1971), which suggests that individuals should attempt to formulate hypothetical allocation standards for a 'potential future self', without knowledge of their current or future health status. Under these conditions, people would choose allocations that would enable them to achieve an age-relative normal opportunity range at each stage of life (Daniels 1985).

The FEO account does not distinguish between the different types of health care that society should provide its citizens under the 'equality of opportunity' principle, nor does it consider the trade-offs between health care and other social goods or adequately consider the costs of health insurance, goods, and services. Moreover, Daniels and others later extended the FEO approach to social determinants of health, claiming that health results largely from social conditions (Daniels 2001, p. 5; Cohen and Rogers 2000). Many have criticized this expansion, asserting, in particular, that the reduction of socio-economic inequalities might not necessarily diminish health inequalities. Marmot, for example, argues that flattening social hierarchies altogether may not lead to a reduction in health inequalities (Marmot 2000). To solve rationing problems in the realm of health care, Daniels and colleagues argue for 'fair procedures' that solve rationing problems reasonably (Daniels and Sabin 2002), although they have paid less attention to how individuals make rationing decisions and how to evaluate the outcomes such procedures generate.

The critiques of FEO tend to cluster around a few themes. First, The FEO account relies too heavily on statistical averages (Stern 1983), which fluctuate with changes in the distribution of health and disease. Second, it does not include the alleviation of pain and suffering as a goal of health care (Folland 1990; Kamm 2001, pp. 17–19; Stern 1983). Third, it appears to exclude 'sicker' or 'socially isolated' individuals. Green (2001, pp. 22–3) and Kamm (2001), for example, challenge a Rawlsian understanding of FEO and argue that Daniels's notion of species-typical normal functioning is a vague concept that might not justify the right of beneficial health care for non-productive or socially isolated individuals. With such a fundamental objection, the theory has limited universal appeal. Fourth, it fails to clarify the concept of 'fair equality of opportunity' and its link with health care. Fifth, indeterminacy and subjective valuation are implicit in the FEO account. A sixth area of criticism focuses on the absence of guidance in Daniels' approach on weighing health care against other types of resources (Rai 1997, pp. 1023–24). A seventh points to insufficient consideration of 'hard cases', such as patients with intractable and exorbitantly costly disabilities, who might receive unlimited medical services (Emanuel 1991, p. 135). Eighth, some critics argue that Daniels' notion of 'adequate care' is too vague to be effectively implemented (Elhauge 1994; Emanuel 1991; Rai 1997). Ninth,

FEO is criticized as being too circular because the opportunity range is not distinct from the process of determining social investments in health care and other sectors (Buchanan 1984, p. 64; Folland 1990). Tenth, even more recent attempts (Daniels 2008) to include health as a focus in the FEO account do so indirectly, for example, in terms of fair equality of opportunity. Despite efforts to show how the FEO account has similarities with other views (e.g. capability and other opportunity based accounts), this line of reasoning, by failing to provide a constitutive account of human flourishing or well-being, cannot offer justification for health for its own sake. One critique notes about Daniels's more recent attempts, 'would it not be more compelling to argue directly for health, or its social basis, as an object of justice?' (Rid and Biller-Andorno 2009, p. 1); while another argues that Daniels's approach to justice in health and health care is deeply flawed and health matters only indirectly for its effect on opportunity (Wilson 2009). Eleventh, there are concerns about theoretical coherence in the sense that the more recent extension of FEO to the social determinants of health recommends action inconsistent with Rawls's difference principle. Moreover, the relationship between fair opportunity and accountability for reasonableness is unclear. The latter is 'not clearly anchored in Rawls' principles of justice that Daniels's theory is otherwise based on', (Rid and Biller-Andorno 2009, p. 1), nor does it necessarily produce fair processes or decisions (Rid 2009). By linking health to fair equality of opportunity, the FEO, even in modified form, will not address persistent adverse health outcomes that do not affect one's opportunities. A direct justification for health as constitutive of human flourishing and on its own grounded, for example, in Aristotelian justice and health policy is necessary (Ruger 1998). It is critical to underscore that a Rawlsian approach to social justice is a liberal one that does not define the good and does not evaluate states of affairs based on their consequences. Moreover, Rawls's fair equality of opportunity concept was designed to ensure that individuals with the same talents could compete equally for success in positions and offices—Rawls did not, and had no intention of, extending his theory to such conceptions of the good.

Responding to these concerns, Daniels acknowledges that both his approach and those of his critics fail to meet many of these challenges. He identifies four unsolved rationing problems:

(1) the fair chances/best outcomes problem (how to balance best outcomes with chances for a given benefit);

(2) the priorities problem (how much priority to give to the most disadvantaged);

(3) the aggregation problem (how to weigh small benefits for many against large benefits for a few); and

(4) the democracy problem (when to use fair processes that rank democratic preferences over substantive principles).

'My "fair equality of opportunity" account of just health care', he concedes, 'fail[s] to yield specific solutions to these rationing problems', adding that consensus about distributive justice and rationing problems is unlikely (Daniels 1994, p. 27).

A number of scholars have worked on these issues (Baily 1994; Broome 1994; Kamm 1994; Nord 1995; Nord 1999; Rakowski 1994; Raz 1986). Kamm, for example, has studied the aggregation and priorities problems, using hypothetical case studies to develop agreement on mid-level principles (Kamm 1994; 2001). But because these mid-level principles supplement highly contested theories of distributive justice, Daniels believes that even with this method, broad moral disagreements will prevent consensus on principles (Daniels 2001, pp. 2, 10). Nord has proposed an empirical approach based on person trade-off questions, a way of estimating social values of different health care interventions (Nord 1995), in order to reveal moral principles in a given population and provide potential guidelines for decision makers (Nord 1999). Others have argued for random allocation of health care to those with equal 'capacity to benefit' (Orentlicher 1994; Taurek 1977). Despite these laudable efforts, Daniels notes that broad moral disagreements will prevent consensus on principles, and we must retreat to a process—'accountability for reasonableness' upon which all can agree as a fair way to resolve disputes (Daniels 2008). A number of approaches favour procedural mechanisms of justice and democratic deliberations for resolving such disputes (see below).

Ronald Green has applied Rawls's theory to health care differently from the FEO account. Instead of deliberative decision-making, Green envisions an income-adjusted price system that enables consumers to establish their priorities for health care (Green 2001, p. 23). Finally, a major concern with the Rawlsian approach is that it focuses on means (resources) rather than ends and fails specifically to address human diversity (Sen 1992). Even Rawls's recommended adjustments in primary goods for 'special needs' are inadequate, I argue (below), to address societal failures in ensuring the conditions for individuals' health capability.

Some theories of justice that focus on equal welfare attempt to address the concern about focusing on resources rather than ends. In the context of health care, Robert Veatch advocates consideration of ends in his resource-based distributive theory via a 'capacity to benefit' principle of distribution (Veatch 1978). Some critics of this approach argue that the capacity to benefit (likelihood, length, and quality of benefit) is difficult to define, both in theory and practice (Kilner 1990); while others maintain that it would be quite similar to a QALY methodology (Rai 1997, pp. 1065–70). Veatch emphasizes autonomy, cautioning society to 'permit only certain consequences to be balanced against autonomy', such as helping the disadvantaged or promoting equality (Veatch 1996, p. 43). Similar equal welfare accounts employ principles of comparable opportunities and argue for equal opportunity for welfare. 'When persons enjoy equal opportunity for welfare in the extended sense', Arneson asserts, 'any actual inequality of welfare in the positions they reach is due to factors that lie within each individual's control' (Arneson 1989, p. 86).

1.4. Libertarian and market-based approaches

Proponents of the fourth framework argue that a market mechanism is the ideal way to distribute health care. This approach generally stems from an overarching libertarian philosophy (Engelhardt 2000; Lomasky 1981, p. 69; Nozick 1974, pp. 167–74) in which individual liberties and autonomy are the predominant societal values, and in which the government's role is to protect individual rights—especially property rights. This framework does not support a right to health or to health care because efforts to guarantee such a right could infringe on individual liberties, by requiring people to pay taxes, for example. 'If it would be illegitimate for a tax system to seize some of a man's leisure (forced labor) for the purpose of serving the needy,' Nozick wonders, 'how can it be legitimate for a tax system to seize some of a man's goods for that purpose?' (Nozick 1974, p. 170). Individuals are autonomous agents who may freely choose to purchase or forgo health insurance or health care. 'Those who place a premium on present consumption should be free to devote only a minimal amount of income to health care coverage', Lomasky argues (Lomasky 1981, p. 87). Thus, a strict market-based approach would allow the more affluent and those with strong preferences for certain goods and services to receive more and better health care, regardless of need or capability.

Havighurst, who believes that current health plans are essentially alike, argues for a market-oriented approach that would allow consumers to choose among different plans according to the benefit level they desire. 'If consumer choice is to serve consumers and the economy well, competing health plans must be free to establish alternative standards and requirements by contract', he asserts (Havighurst 1995, p. 3). Lomasky would give consumers the 'opportunity to make informed purchases in a genuine medical marketplace' (Lomasky 1981, p. 88). Whereas strict libertarian views deny that society has a political obligation to provide health resources to its citizens, more moderate adaptations support some form of income transfer. Lomasky and Engelhardt, for example, favour cash vouchers for health insurance (Engelhardt 2000; Lomasky 1981, p. 86), while Fried sanctions income transfer for health care; 'What if ... each person were assured a certain amount of money to purchase medical services as he chose?' (Fried 1976, p. 33). These more moderate libertarian views recognize a very limited role for the state in improving welfare while maintaining their primary focus on individual autonomy. Engelhardt, for example, has emphasized medicine's role as a secular profession in a pluralistic society in which people disagree on a common substantive morality (Engelhardt 2000). He focuses on the peaceful settling of moral differences, with respect for personal autonomy as the utmost societal value. Engelhardt is critical of hypothetical choice procedures, arguing that they result in decisions that reflect a thin theory of the good based on antecedent choice (Engelhardt 1986).

More recently, market-based approaches, such as managed care, have become more prevalent in the United States. This model attempts to allocate health services through capitation payments to physicians, financial incentives based on quantity of health care goods and services, gatekeeping, and longer waiting periods. Although managed care might lower health care costs in certain contexts (Cutler and Zeckhauser 2000, p. 526), many argue that financial incentives have put doctors in an unethical position (Council on Ethical and Judicial Affairs, American Medical Association 1995, pp. 330, 333), by encouraging them to avoid diagnostic tests, hospitalizations, and expensive referrals that might benefit their patients. Such financial incentives erode patients' confidence and break down 'the foundation of the patient-physician relationship ... the trust that physicians are dedicated first and foremost to serving the needs of their patients' (Council on Ethical and Judicial Affairs, American

Medical Association 1995, p. 331). There are also concerns about other quasi market-based reforms, such as *ex ante* contracting for insurance plans with rationing protocols that leave patients insufficiently insured for interventions they might need (Hall 1997). In the United States, for example, the Emergency Medical Treatment and Active Labor Act (EM-TALA) requires emergency room personnel to treat even uninsured or underinsured individuals in medical emergencies, including people who would have contracted to forgo treatment for certain conditions (Emergency Medical Treatment and Active Labor Act 2005, 42 USC. § 1395dd). The unpredictable nature of many adverse health events and society's obligation to address health needs can make contractual approaches impractical and unethical.

One of the main concerns with the libertarian perspective is that the conditions for efficient supply and demand market allocation do not exist in the health care or health insurance markets. Health care is unique among commodities in the marketplace (Arrow 1963, pp. 941, 948–54). Although individuals have the right to make their own treatment decisions in many settings, they often defer to providers and insurance companies because of information asymmetry, uncertain health risks, and limits on benefits. Moreover, consumers do not necessarily pay the full cost of health care or receive the full value of the goods and services they choose to purchase. Additionally, the market fails in key ways—such as the public goods aspects of medical knowledge (Chen et al. 1999), the externality effects of communicable diseases, the failure to serve vulnerable populations, uncertainty, asymmetric information, moral hazard, adverse selection, and equity concerns. These failures argue against a market-based approach and for public intervention in financing (and sometimes provision) of health care.

Another approach based on the free-market view is 'rationing through choice', which claims to '[accommodate] diverse individual health and allocational preferences and thus respects autonomy' (Rai 1997, p. 1032). In this model, individuals ration health care at the micro-allocational level through *ex ante* choices among various health plans. The 'rationing-through-choice' system, designed to use existing market mechanisms for health care delivery, requires all individuals to contribute to a publicly funded health care system, which would fund health plans or provide vouchers for purchasing private or public plans. Plans that exceeded a certain government-allocated amount per capita would be more expensive to purchase (Rai 1997, p. 1036).

This allocation model is similar to a 'prudential insurer' system, in which initial resources are equal (Dworkin 1981a; 1981b), information on costs, benefits, and risks is widely accessible, and health care and insurance markets function freely. Thus, individuals' choices would define the fair and final allocation of health resources. Dworkin, in particular, has focused on this approach, drawing on Rawls's 'veil of ignorance' concept. Dworkin argues that the needs of a 'representative individual' should shape the health care budget and the distribution of health care resources (Dworkin 1981a; 1981b). The 'representative individual' has an average income, full knowledge of the costs and benefits of health interventions and the prevalence and incidence of disease, but no knowledge of his or her own genetic or medical disposition. Rakowski applies a hypothetical choice mechanism for individuals to make *ex ante* resource allocation choices and consent to certain rationing principles, such as life maximization (Rakowski 1991; 1993). Elhauge argues, however, that 'consensual theories cannot offer a complete moral justification for health care allocations' (Elhauge 1994, p. 1456).

In opposition to the free-market view, one finds the widely discussed bureaucratic, technocratic, or legislative protocol approach to allocating resources (Fleck 1992). This category of views are sometimes called 'controlled' or 'regulatory rationing' because legislators take primary control of allocating resources and weighing social costs and benefits to set priorities (Blank 1992). Conceptually, regulatory approaches to rationing merge with technocratic models. Technocratic allocation is managed by a group of experts and is authoritatively designed. The main criticism of the technocratic approach is that it is too centralized and does not involve enough public input or fair procedures.

1.5. Deliberative democratic procedures

Given the persistent disagreement about principles governing resource allocation, some argue that we must retreat to fair democratic processes. Democratic approaches ensure widespread public input and encourage local and national dialogue about distributing health services and goods, especially where fair terms of deliberation are ensured. This approach abandons 'direct appeals to theories of justice', using instead 'a finely honed understanding of the democratic process...to reach decisions about priorities' (Beauchamp and Childress 2001, p. 258). Fleck supports the use of democratic political procedures to make micro-allocational decisions (Fleck 1992, p. 1617). Daniels and Sabin (2002) advocate publicly accessible decision-making for managed care decisions, while Amy Gutmann and Dennis Thompson have identified certain procedural and substantive principles to ensure fair deliberative processes (Gutmann and Thompson 1996).

In some democratic approaches to allocating resources, citizens, as payers of insurance and consumers of health care, are involved in democratic deliberation and allocation decisions (Daniels and Sabin 2002; Fleck 1992; Leichter 1992; Morone 1992; Nagel 1992). Such approaches are considered fair because they are determined by patient choice. Anderson (1993), for example, argues that individual autonomy is realized on a collective scale through democratic institutions.

One democratic decision-making model is the 'informed democratic consensus model' (Fleck 1992, p. 1617), which proposes a district health council composed of about fifty citizens. Each council would elect one person to serve as its representative to a national health congress, which would oversee a single comprehensive health plan. The national legislature would set the overall budget for the plan, and the national health congress would establish priorities and rationing protocols.

All of these prototypes espouse the principles of autonomy, political equality, political legitimacy, deliberation, and explicit public processes. Fleck also proposes 'constitutional principles of healthcare justice' that would 'avoid . . . giving political legitimacy to results of the deliberative process that are seriously unjust' (Fleck 2001, p. 20). Patients have the highest stake in health allocation decisions, Fleck argues, because they are the recipients of care as well as the payers for health care, in taxes, insurance premiums, copays, deductibles, user fees, and other charges. The endpoint would be a set of rationing protocols, such as a list of services covered to which all would have to adhere (Rosenbaum 1992).

Though they might provide for deliberation, these proposals have been criticized for providing little guidance on the 'rightness of the rationales put forward . . . [or] any assurance of substantively just outcomes' (Powers and Faden 2000, p. 115). A number of other criticisms have emerged in the literature. For example, some argue that neither Daniels's approach nor other theories of just processes are ever entirely culture free, abstract, or universal (MacIntyre 1988; Waymack 2001). Others criticize Daniels's account of the conditions of procedural fairness on the grounds that the 'relevance condition' is too normative (Gorovitz 2001, p. 29). Since accepted reasons in a democratic process might be 'theory-laden, or embedded in particular conceptions of justice', it might be difficult for participants to choose among competing principles of justice 'in a particular distributive context' (Powers and Faden 2000, pp. 115–16). Emanuel argues that Daniels's use of democratic political procedures as a 'last resort' to 'resolve all remaining problems' when defining policy is based on a conception of democratic political procedure that is practical, not philosophical. Currently, these frameworks have provided little guidance on how to agree on principles of justice or what the content of those principles should entail. They also provide little guidance on the evaluation of the outcomes of such procedures. Often, there is even considerable disagreement on what procedural alternatives and elements would comprise politically legitimate fair democratic procedures. As a result, deliberative democratic approaches raise objections about indeterminacy (Emanuel 1991, pp. 32–4), given the 'risk that no solution will emerge from the deliberation because the depth of moral disagreement is so great' (Powers and Faden 2000, p. 115).

Still others argue that using democratic procedures at the micro-allocational level to ration health care affords less respect for autonomy than does *ex ante* choice (Rai 1997, p. 1096). Emanuel criticizes collective political procedures for not permitting an agreed-upon, substantive conception of the 'good life' (Emanuel 1991, p. 144). For Beauchamp and Childress, it is 'relatively unclear about what makes democratic procedures fair, how to protect against unfair outcomes, whether citizen deliberators could ever satisfy the demands of true deliberative democracy, and how much real agreement they could reach' (Beauchamp and Childress 2001, p. 258). Additionally, Hadorn (1991), referring to the 'rule of rescue', has noted that deliberative democratic decisions tend to be most difficult to implement, given the tendency to 'rescue' suffering patients, even if their condition is not covered. Moreover, such deliberations would have to consider the costs and benefits of thousands of treatment options for thousands of diseases, a task too onerous to produce fair rationing policies. Another criticism is that 'majority preferences, no matter how well informed and fair, will sometimes eventuate in unjust outcomes' (Beauchamp and Childress 2001, p. 258). Therefore, a purely, or even primarily, procedural mechanism could 'return us to the same failures of justice that we have already encountered in health care' (Beauchamp and Childress 2001, p. 258). Deliberative democratic procedures run the risk of producing no acceptable options, and certainly no acceptable rationales or reasons, to the extent that one can assess reasonableness without substantive moral principles.

While all of these approaches strive for a just distribution of health care resources, one medical ethicist has noted that 'discordant positions, irresolution, and an exhausted uncertainty seem the only conclusive products of three decades of discussion on medical ethics' (Emanuel 1991, p. 6).

1.6. Summary of problems with the current set of frameworks

Major themes emerge in this discussion of the current set of frameworks in health ethics, policy, and law. These issues impact the health debate in important ways.

- Existing theories, even those that include health assessment, have typically justified health care as a special social good. Universal concerns of social justice with respect to health itself have received less attention. Over a decade ago, I offered a justification for the special moral importance of health from a capability point of view (Ruger 1997; 1998; 2003b) and argued that the traditional bias seems to stem from at least one assumption: that health is not an appropriate focal variable for assessing social justice or rights, whereas utilities, community values, liberties, opportunities, resources, and primary goods are. In earlier work, Daniels argued, 'health is an inappropriate object, but health care, action which promotes health, is appropriate' (Daniels 1985, p. 6). He and others emphasize that 'a right claim to equal *health* is best construed as a demand for equality of access or entitlement to health *services*' (Daniels 1985, p. 7). Such reasoning illustrates a bias against health as a focal variable in existing theories. The focus on health care has led one to believe the major inequity in health policy has been differential access to care, not differences in health (Brock 2000, p. 21; Evans et al. 2001). Even recent equality of opportunity efforts to extend the justification of health care to health needs that promote equality of opportunity (Daniels 2008) fall short in the liberal social structural fashion (see above). One must ask whether health care and the social determinants perform other functions beyond preserving equal opportunity. The Rawlsian project not only did not attempt to define the good life, but was quite sceptical of such an exercise. This emphasis left a void in the literature on the philosophical foundations of health and its distribution, which some of my work over the last decade and a half has aimed to address (Ruger 1997; 1998; 2003b; 2006a). Other recent work in social justice more broadly has underscored the importance of health, but is quite underspecified in this regard (Powers and Faden 2006).

- Efforts to establish fair procedures for allocating resources have claimed more attention than the development of substantive and procedural principles for prioritizing health-related goods and services. This imbalance stems, in part, from the way in which medical ethics has evolved. Establishing a right to health care has been central for decades and has thrust the field into a plethora of efforts to determine the existence and content of this right (Buchanan 1984; Daniels 1985; Ruger 2006a). But despite the emphasis on fair procedures, there is little agreement on how and whether to specify such a right (Powers and Faden 2000). And the focus on democratic procedures as a way of distributing health care leaves scholars without a moral theory of prioritization and resource allocation. It also leaves the field without a principled approach to the needs of the most disadvantaged and improving the overall health of the population (Brock 2000).

- There is a need for workable frameworks to guide collective choices about valuable social ends and their trade-offs. It is clear that purely procedural strategies are limited in their application to health ethics, policy, and law. However, it is less clear which methodology might best elicit individual preferences for health states and incorporate them into a collective choice (Menzel 1999), or whether this is the direction to pursue at all. CEA, CUA, and CBA have encountered criticism on a number of grounds, including their indifference to distributional effects and the plight of the worse off (Brock 2000). Although there have been efforts to quantify equity concerns and include them in cost-utility models (Nord 1999; Ubel 2000), such approaches still lack a deliberative component that enables groups to reach 'reflective considered judgments' (Brock 2000, p. 29).

- A fourth theme involves the question of whether individual or social preferences and values should prioritize social goals and interventions aimed at reaching those goals. While preferences based on societal values should be included in CEA as the public's distributive choices (Menzel 1999, pp. 258–9; Nord 1999), it is unclear what role these preferences might play in the development of public policy.

- Existing frameworks fail to ensure justice in rationing because they are indeterminate and do not solve the four rationing problems Daniels identifies (above) (Daniels 1992; 1994; 1996).

- Public reasoning should receive more emphasis than formal quantitative, aggregative, or purely procedural methods for making health policy. There has been more focus on 'accountability for reasonableness' than on understanding how individuals and groups value different aspects of health and agree upon decisions. Eliciting an acceptable public response about resource allocation requires greater clarity about shared moral values. The interdisciplinary field of health ethics, policy, and law has much to learn from work in the fields of social choice and public choice theory. Over the last ten years, an alternative substantive and procedural framework for resource allocation has begun to emerge (Ruger 1998; 2006d).

Related to these issues are more specific concerns:

(1) Using maximum benefit, utilities, or best outcomes as a basis for resource allocation confers lower priority to those who might benefit less from the use of a limited resource. This effect runs counter to widespread preferences in the public, where individuals tend 'to emphasise equality in value of life and in entitlement to treatment rather than level of health after treatment' when asked about their ethical preferences in prioritizing among health programmes (Nord 1993b, pp. 37).

(2) A strong focus on helping those in greatest need must acknowledge and deal with the so-called 'bottomless pit problem'; researchers such as Nord have increasingly found that individuals are reluctant to deny benefits to patients who have less potential for health than others (Nord 1993b; Nord et al. 1995).

(3) Theory is lacking to justify the well-established practice and intuition to allocate resources to those in worse health (sicker or severely ill individuals) even if utility or health-related utility is not too low (adaptation), or primary goods thresholds have been met. Neither welfare economic (CUA or extra welfarism) nor Rawlsian (primary goods) approaches can justify this prioritarian intuition.

(4) Summation techniques fail to respect individuality. The utilitarian notion of maximizing collective or social benefit disregards the separateness of persons. By measuring utility on a single

quantitative scale, it posits global population utility as being experienced by one individual. Korsgaard in particular argues that one cannot apply a principle of 'moral addition' by combining the respective assessments of happiness of two different individuals (Korsgaard 1993).

(5) Incommensurability poses problems in health and health care. All benefits are not equal and therefore cannot be assessed according to a single metric (money in CBA, and utilities in CUA) (Anderson 1993; Nussbaum 1990a; Raz 1986; Ruger 1998, 2006a; Sunstein 1994).

(6) Aggregation techniques can produce results that defy clinical judgement by, for example, ranking life-saving treatments below those that improve quality of life (Beauchamp and Childress, 1994; Eddy 1991a, 1991b; Hadorn 1991; Tolley et al. 1994). Nord (1994, p. 89) notes that the QALY concept does not 'work in comparisons of life saving interventions with interventions that improve health or increase life expectancy.'

(7) The indeterminacy of distributive principles for guiding resource allocation is especially problematic in pluralistic environments where participants cannot agree about moral constraints on rationing.

(8) If preferences are used to allocate resources, there is some disagreement as to whose preferences should take priority (Nord 1994; Richardson and Nord 1997) (e.g. those of citizens, medical experts, patients, payers, regulators, etc.). Those with particular health conditions and disabilities have been found to modify their preferences to cope with their conditions; different preferences can result in underestimating or overestimating treatment benefits.

(9) Methods for eliciting preferences, costs, and benefits differ and produce different results (e.g. Willingness To Pay, Willingness To Accept, Contingent Valuation, standard gamble, rating scale.) In the Oregon experiment, some argue that concerns over the accuracy of measured costs and benefits discredited the cost-utility methodology (Eddy 1991a; 1991b). The Panel on Cost Effectiveness in Health and Medicine (Gold et al. 1996) was convened in part to answer some of these questions and standardize CEA in health and medicine. Still, over a decade later, variation in analytical methods remains.

(10) Decisions about benefits packages are unresolved: whether to guarantee and/or mandate a benefits package, which services to include and exclude, whether to provide a floor and/or a ceiling for benefits, whether to guarantee a decent minimum, a basic benefits package, or a comprehensive benefits package.

(11) Differences exist about information to consider in resource allocation (McIver 1995) (e.g. prevalence, incidence, effectiveness in terms of quality of life, life extending, life saving effects, overall economic impact on society, medical necessity, costs, and some measure of economic efficiency such as CEA, CUA or CBA).

(12) There is considerable disagreement about how to consider choice and responsibility and some accounts fail altogether to address personal responsibility for health.

(13) If open and democratic processes determine resource allocation, then the decisions might or might not be just or consistent with clinical judgement. Should they be accepted as a matter of procedural justice or be evaluated for substantive content?

(14) Some liberal theories (e.g. equality of opportunity) do not adequately address scarcity and efficiency, set limits, or incorporate costs into their frameworks. A robust concept of opportunity costs is necessary.

The academic area of health ethics, policy, and law is at a crossroads, oscillating between two dichotomous paradigmatic positions—consequentialism and proceduralism. Consequentialists argue that we should assess health policies and laws by their consequences; proceduralists believe that fair processes will yield fair decisions. Adherents often present them as mutually exclusive. Thus far, neither end of the spectrum has promised, nor delivered, a plausible solution, and attempts to incorporate both positions have been unsatisfactory. As a result, the field is at a standstill. Any movement forward involves elements of both the consequentialist and proceduralist frameworks.

It is time for an imaginative new theoretical model, one that addresses these issues and bridges the divide between procedures and consequences, between the collective and the individual, between personal freedom and social welfare, equality and efficiency, science and economics. It is time for a model that weaves together disparate constructs and original insights to produce a foundational new paradigm for health. It is time for a vision of human flourishing. It is time, in short, for the health capability paradigm.

Part II

An Alternative Account—The Health Capability Paradigm

Part II of this book argues from an Aristotelian/capability perspective that what are here called health capabilities should be the central focal variable for assessing the justness and efficiency of health policy. This part proceeds in four stages. The first, in Chapter 2, draws on moral and political philosophy to argue that the Aristotelian/Capability view provides the basis for the special moral importance of health capabilities as the central focal variable for assessing equality and efficiency in health policy. These lines of thought take a universal view of humans' capability to flourish as an end of political activity and provide an analytical framework to address questions of justice and human rights in a way that other philosophical schools do not. More specifically, it is argued that in certain evaluative exercises, universal attention to central health capabilities—people's capability to avert premature mortality and escape morbidity—should be the morally central or prior objective of health policy, to which we have a special social obligation above and beyond our obligation to the provision of non-central health capabilities. This obligation is universal, applying to all human lives, irrespective of class, gender, race, ethnicity, or community. The focus in some evaluative exercises on central health capabilities as morally central in the evaluation of health policy stems from the need to separate out the ability to satisfy certain critically important functionings up to certain minimally adequate levels. Central health capabilities are indisputable categories of moral and practical importance. The application of the central health capabilities idea, in terms of what premature mortality and escapable morbidity mean, is taken up in Chapter 4.

The second stage, explained in Chapter 3, draws on social choice theory. Here incompletely theorized agreements (ITA) are proposed as an approach to collective decision-making in public policy and human rights. Previous work in legal decision-making is built on by extending the ITA framework in at least three respects: moving beyond judicial decision-making to public policy and human rights; specifying the framework to health and health care decision-making; and combining ITA with the capability approach to operationalize the capability view. The ITA framework helps extend the capability approach when 'dominance partial ordering' and incomplete specification fail to provide reasonable procedures for resolving conflict among different views. The capability approach needs such a framework for social choice. ITA thus picks up where the capability approach leaves off, providing a structure for resolving conflict among divergent views. Health and health capabilities are multidimensional concepts about which different people have different and sometimes conflicting views. No unique view of health exists as the ideal for all evaluations. The incomplete ordering of the capability approach, in combination with the incompletely theorized agreement on that ordering, allows for reasoned public policy development and analysis in the face of plural goods and different, even conflicting, views.

The third stage, in Chapter 4, aims to provide a workable operationalization of health capabilities. It seeks an agreed upon or shared standard of health because the demands of social justice and the right to health according to the capability view necessitate a universally shared norm of health to establish a framework for interpersonal health comparisons. In the health capability paradigm, the challenge is to construct a conception of health that reflects the 'view from everywhere'. This paradigm identifies which dimensions of health might require prioritization when resources are scarce and establishes the scope and content of a right to health. Moreover, it identifies a standard of equality to judge public policies affecting health, and argues for a robust concept of opportunity costs and assessing how to examine health capabilities in the context of other policies.

Finally, the fourth part, in Chapter 5, applies this ethical framework to the right to health. It focuses on the need to understand the corresponding duties and obligations of individuals, states, and non-state actors. It also provides a framework for state health reform efforts, based on the belief that the underlying goal of health policy is fulfilling the right to health. Such efforts would place health and human flourishing at the centre of health policy, law, and practice in all states.

2

Health and Human Flourishing

2.1. Aristotle's theory

Invoking an Aristotelian point of view as a basis for social justice involves applying his principles in a more universal way than he himself did more than two thousand years ago (Nussbaum 1990b). Sen's capability approach, rooted in and yet departing from Aristotle's work, provides a good example of the various ways in which Aristotle's writings can apply to modern scholastic purposes. For scholarship focused on health, Aristotle's humanitarian emphasis—that human flourishing is the end of all social activity—has great appeal. Several major components comprise the Aristotelian view.[1]

2.1.1. Human flourishing

The first is that human flourishing[2] is the end of all political activity. This is Aristotle's theory of the good, the supreme good, the good that is the aim of 'every action and decision' (Irwin 1999, p. 1: 1094a 1). 'It belongs to the excellent legislator to see how a city, a family of human beings . . . will share in the good life and in the happiness that is possible for them' (Lord 1984, p. 201: 1325a 7–10), Aristotle says. This conception also expresses the idea of 'capability'—what humans are able to do and be and what 'is possible for them', and it suggests that our social obligation involves enabling all to live flourishing lives.

The political goal is defined, then, as Martha Nussbaum puts it, in terms of 'the capability to function well if one so chooses' (Nussbaum 1990b, p. 165). This formulation is important for justifying capability's central role in political activity.[3] This formulation also distinguishes between achievement and the freedom to achieve. By focusing on the capability to achieve valuable functionings, the theory secures differential allotments of goods and circumstances needed to produce capabilities and also respects the central importance of freedom and reason in enabling humans to make choices. On this, Nussbaum makes the point that while functioning should be 'held in view' by government—that we should use functionings as indicators of how people are doing—capability is the political goal. This point recognizes the importance of respecting humans' abilities for practical reason and choice—once capabilities are assured people must be free to make the choices they like (Nussbaum 1990b; 1993).

This component of Aristotelian theory is especially important for health ethics, policy, and law. It requires the government to distribute sufficient goods, services, and conditions to achieve human functioning, while re-specting human dignity by giving individuals the freedom to choose the life they want to lead.

To allow for choice, for example, the state would need to provide the resources and circumstances for good nourishment, while respecting the right to fast for religious purposes (Nussbaum 1998; Sen 1992, p. 8). This distinction is important for understanding both the state's role in distribu-tive justice and the difference between the malnourished and those who are intentionally fasting. In short, this first component of Aristotle's theory is important for securing different allocations to people who need varying levels of resources to lead a flourishing life.

2.1.2. Appropriate ends of political activity

A second major component of the Aristotelian view is that resources, such as wealth, medical care, and income, do not constitute appropriate ends of political activity. 'Clearly wealth is not the good we are seeking,' Aristotle argues, 'since it is [merely] useful, [choiceworthy only] for some other end' (Irwin 1999, p. 5: 1096a 6–8).

Instead, resources are merely a means to an end, each having instrumen-tal rather than intrinsic value. Resources, Nussbaum observes, 'are not good in their own right; they are good only insofar as they promote human functioning' (Nussbaum 1992, p. 233). This formulation is important be-cause individuals' ability to function, rather than resources, should be the primary goal of public policy.

2.1.3. Enabling functioning as a measure of political arrangements

A third major component of the Aristotelian view concerns the evaluation of political arrangements—namely, that political arrangements aim at enabling people to function best, and 'it is evident that the best... is that arrangement... according to which anyone whatsoever... might do best... and live a flourishing life' (Nussbaum 1990b, p. 153), given their natural circumstances. Individuals will inevitably face natural and social barriers that can impede optimal functioning. This claim acknowledges the difficulty of equalizing achievements and the role of human diversity in conceptualizing political distribution. Aristotle's conception judges a political arrangement as best 'provided that it secured to the people involved a good life up to the maximum permitted by circumstances' (Nussbaum 1990b, p. 155). Aristotle regards an arrangement as best if it 'brings the people as close to good functioning as their natural circumstances permit' (Nussbaum 1990b, p. 155). When these formulations are combined, a conception of political distribution derived from Aristotle implies that the:

aim of political planning is the distribution to the city's individual people of the conditions in which a good human life can be chosen and lived. This task aims at producing capabilities. That is, it aims not simply at the allotment of commodities, but at making people able to function in certain human ways... The task of the city is, then, to effect the transition from one level of capability to another (Nussbaum 1990b, p. 152).

2.1.4. Other ends for political action

Although Aristotle's theory of political distribution rests on his theory of the human good 'as what everything seeks' (Irwin 1999, p. 1: 1094a 3), a fourth major element is that it also acknowledges the existence of other ends for various actions: 'Since there are many actions, crafts, and sciences, the ends turn out to be many as well; for health is the end of medicine, (Irwin 1999, p. 1: 1094a 7–8). This passage is particularly instructive for justifying health as a primary objective of health policy. Thus, health has both intrinsic and instrumental value (Ruger 2003b, p. 678).

2.1.5. Defining flourishing

A fifth major claim of the Aristotelian view is its emphasis on the need to define 'human flourishing' in order to determine whether political arrangements promote it. Aristotle argues that 'concerning the best regime, one who is going to undertake the investigation appropriate to it must necessarily discuss first what the most choiceworthy way of life is. As long as this is unclear the best regime must necessarily be unclear as well' (Lord 1984, p. 197: 1323a 14–17). This formulation calls for a 'substantial account of the human good and what it is to function humanly' (Nussbaum 1990b, p. 152) to assess a society's success or failure in meeting the goal of functioning and well-being. It places the Aristotelian view in the realm of theories that emphasize an 'appeal to conceptions of the good life' (Emanuel 1991, p. 8) in justifying public policies and laws. Aristotle also argues that it is possible to specify functionings that constitute a good human life (Nussbaum 1990b, p. 154).

An attempt to completely specify the list of functionings that constitute 'human flourishing' has followed from these Aristotelian principles. There has been some controversy over this attempt, which typically concerns whether there exists a 'true' or unique or culturally defined view of human flourishing. Some cultural or moral relativists argue that even such basic human experiences as reasoning and happiness are culturally or socially constructed. A strict Aristotelian view might suggest that human flourishing is unique, while a less strict view would focus purely on objectivity—that human flourishing entails certain objective elements. Between these polarities lie intermediate positions. For the purposes here, this distinction is important but, as discussed in subsequent chapters, the resolution of this issue is less important than the practical policy solution. This offers not a resolution to the definitional question of what human flourishing or health are, but a framework for establishing the important aspects of health regardless of epistemological positions. To evaluate health-related goods and services meaningfully for policy purposes, incomplete theorization on matters about which there is significant agreement will be a key component of this framework.

In an Aristotelian view, an account of the human good involves identifying a list of functionings at a certain level of generality, allowing more local and personal specificity for practical application. Under this view, the processes of specifying the list of functionings and assessing the most effective means of enabling people to achieve them should be a rational, empirical investigation, deliberative in nature. Deliberation, according to Aristotle, involves an investigation and analysis, 'for a deliberator would seem to inquire and analyze...as though analyzing a diagram' (Irwin 1999, p. 35: 1112b 20–22). He also stresses that deliberating citizens might require help from experts, emphasizing the need for those with experience to take part in decision-making, since they are the best judges of what they know well. Reinforcing this idea, he argues: 'Further, each person judges rightly what he knows, and is a good judge about that; hence the good judge in a given area is the person educated in that area' (Irwin 1999, pp. 2–3: 1095a 1–3). At the same time, Aristotle warns against exactitude and precision in decision-making, stating that 'the educated person seeks exactness in each area to the extent that the nature of the subject allows' (Irwin 1999, p. 2: 1094b 24–5).

A key aspect of successful deliberation, Aristotle argues, is the virtue of practical wisdom or prudence which 'must be a state grasping the truth, involving reason, and concerned with action about human goods' (Irwin 1999, p. 90; 1140b, p. 21–2). Through use of practical wisdom, deliberators will be able to judge wisely what is good and expedient for humans and what can effectively be brought about. Thus, practical wisdom must concern itself with particulars as well as with broader, universal concepts. Justice, like the other Aristotelian virtues, involves a balance between general ethical rules and particulars in which both are subject to assessment and revision. This formulation supports social decision-making as an ongoing, iterative process, which incorporates new information as it becomes available. It also asserts government's responsibility for developing individual capabilities for participation and deliberation. Applying these formulations to health, health policy, and law offers a framework for deliberations among citizens and experts that range from broader decision-making about laws and policies to discussions of specific medical treatments. Further discussion of reasoned consensus through scientific and deliberative process for allocating health care resources follows in Chapter 8.

Aristotle also recognizes the difficulty of choosing among items that cannot readily be compared. Solving disagreements and making effective choices is a critical element of the Aristotelian view, and it has practical implications. Deliberation is concerned, by its very nature, with indeterminate things; 'the right way to act is undefined' (Irwin 1999, p. 35: 1112b 10). For 'if we encounter an impossible step—for instance, we need money but cannot raise it—we desist; but if the action appears possible, we undertake it. What is possible is what we could achieve through our agency [including what our friends could achieve for us]' (Irwin 1999, p. 36: 1112b 25–8). Although Aristotle emphasizes the importance of making definitive decisions and taking actions as a result of deliberation, he provides less guidance about how to come to agreement on principles and particulars. Chapter 3 shows how an incompletely theorized agreements framework for resolving disagreements when making practical decisions can extend these principles.

Finally, Aristotle's principle of proportional justice provides guidance on distributing limited resources to promote flourishing lives. Aristotelian justice treats like cases alike and different cases differently. Chapter 4 applies this principle of proportional justice to health and argues for reducing barriers to equal health capability, especially by giving significant weight to the needs of the worse off as compared to those of the better off, in proportion to their difference. Aristotle introduced the concept of 'disproportionate' effort, which aims to bring disadvantaged individuals as close to a threshold level of functioning as is possible for them.

Ultimately, Aristotle's principle of proportional justice applied to health would support allocation of resources to those in greater need to bring them as close to a certain level of health functioning as their circumstances permit. Aristotle's efforts to qualify this principle to accommodate the constraints some individuals face help illuminate the limits on our social obligation to allocate resources. Aristotle emphasizes practical reasoning, arguing that one person's agency cannot be sacrificed to improve another person's functioning, even if the latter still falls short of normal functioning. For health care, these formulations would generally imply that the government should bring each individual's health functioning as close to a threshold level of functioning as possible for them without diminishing others' functioning below that level. There is currently considerable discussion about how much priority society should give to its most needy, and efforts to craft a flexible compromise between strict maximization and prioritization are necessary (Chapter 4).

2.2. The capability approach

Amartya Sen has formulated a capability approach that links closely to the Aristotelian conception of social and political ethics (Sen 1985; 1999). Like Aristotle, Sen asserts the importance of freedom, attaching value to choice and opportunities for individuals to live the life they choose given their personal and social circumstances.

The capability approach rests on several major claims. The first is that equality can be judged in numerous ways and that other approaches, while all being egalitarian, differ by the focal variable used to assess equality. Income egalitarians demand equal incomes, for instance; welfare egalitarians require equal welfare levels; classical utilitarians demand equal weights for all utilities; and pure libertarians demand equality of rights and liberties. In critique, Sen asks: 'Equality of what?'

Both Sen's approach and the Aristotelian view hold that resources such as wealth, income, and health care are not appropriate standards for ethical evaluation. They make individual capability to achieve valuable functionings the focal variable for social evaluation. The capability approach, like the Aristotelian view, focuses on the capability to lead a worthwhile life. It seeks capabilities for all members of society, irrespective of race, class, gender, community, sexual orientation, or ethnicity. Capability to function, Sen argues, incorporates both well-being and the freedom to pursue well-being. Functionings are a person's achievements: what they are able to do or be, their activities and states of being. Capability is a person's freedom to achieve functionings that they value. Capabilities thus address both actual and potential functionings (Sen 1992), taking into account individuals' abilities to function even if they are not actually functioning at that level at a given time. For example, someone who is convalescing typically retains the capability for work (a functioning) even though he or she cannot work right now, whereas someone who is seriously injured might lose that capability.

2.2.1. Capability sets

Capability relates to well-being in two ways. First, if a set of functions, such as the ability to feed oneself and walk unaided, constitutes a person's well-being, then the capability to accomplish those functions will constitute the person's freedom to achieve well-being. This is important if freedom is valued for itself, not just for instrumental purposes. Because the capability approach regards freedom as an intrinsic value, it defines a good society as one that aspires to freedom. Second, well-being depends on the capability to function. The opportunity to exercise freedom can itself be valuable (Sen 1992, p. 7).

Sen notes that a set of capabilities provides information about the vectors of functioning within a person's reach. This information is important, regardless of how well-being is characterized. The 'amount or the extent of each functioning enjoyed by a person may be represented by a real number, and when this is done, a person's actual achievement can be seen as a *functioning vector*' (Sen 1999, p. 75).

Sen has provided mathematical formulations to illustrate capability (Sen 1985, pp. 11–14). For judging the well-being of a person, it is necessary to think beyond analysing the characteristics of the goods possessed, and functionings of persons must be considered, as they indicate what a 'person succeeds in *doing* with the commodities and characteristics at his or her command' (Sen 1985, p. 10).

If the person chooses the utilization function $f_i(\cdot)$, then with his or her commodity vector x_i, the achieved functions will be given by the vector b_i,

$$b_i = f_i(c(x_i)).$$

[V]ector b_i (represents a) person's *being*, (therefore) '[w]ell-being' ... can plausibly be seen as an evaluation of this (vector), indicating the kind of being he or she is achieving.

(And) the happiness that he will then enjoy is given by u_i

$$u_i = h_i(f_i(c(x_i))).$$

(where) $h_i(\cdot)$ (is) the happiness function of person i related to the functionings achieved by i. ... The function h_i (only provides information about) how happy the person is with the functioning vector b_i, (but not a valuation of the person's life).

If $v_i(\cdot)$ is the valuation function of person i, then the value of that vector of functionings b_i is given by

$$v_i = v_i(f_i(c(x_i))).$$

For a given commodity vector x_i, the functioning vectors feasible for the person are given by the set $P_i(x_i)$,

$$P_i(x_i) = [b_i | b_i = f_i(c(x_i)), \text{ for some } f_i(.) \in F_i].$$

(where) F_i (is) the set of 'utilization functions' f_i, any one of which person i can ... choose. ...

If the person's choice of commodity vectors is restricted to set X_i, then the person's feasible functioning vectors are given by the set $Q_i(X_i)$,

$$Q_i(X_i) = [b_i | b_i = f_i(c(x_i)), \text{ for some } f_i(.) \in F_i \text{ and for some } x_i \in X_i].$$

$Q_i(X_i)$ represents (a person's freedom) in terms of the choice of functionings, given his personal features F_i ... and his command over commodities X_i. ... Q_i (represents) the 'capabilities' of person i given those parameters (Sen 1985, pp. 11–14).

Capabilities and functions occupy the same categorical 'space', but a functioning combination or vector is a *point* in space whereas a capability is a *set* of such points. 'Capability is a *set* of such functioning n tuples, representing the various alternative combinations of functionings from which the person can choose one combination' (Sen 1992, p. 50). The concept of capability is expressed as a set of vectors of functionings reflecting the person's freedom to lead one type of life or another. The capability set is not directly observable, but it is similar to a budget that is constructed from empirical data.

A person's 'capability' refers to the alternative combinations of functionings that are feasible for her to achieve. Capability is thus a kind of freedom: the substantive freedom to achieve alternative functioning combinations (or, less formally put, the freedom to achieve various lifestyles) (Sen 1999, p. 75).

Sen argues that the 'evaluative focus' of the capability approach 'can be either on the *realized* functionings (what a person is actually able to do) or on the *capability set* of alternatives she has (her real opportunities)' (Sen 1999, p. 75). In terms of social evaluation of public policies, Sen asserts that 'individual functionings can lend themselves to easier inter-personal comparison than comparisons of utilities . . . These are advantages in using the capability perspective for evaluation and assessment' (Sen 1999, p. 76). The range of capabilities can vary from elementary to more complex.

The Aristotelian view as well as the capability approach allow for people to make choices in accordance with their own conceptions of the good. Both Sen and Nussbaum distinguish between functioning and capability by employing the example of starving versus fasting: the two conditions represent different capability sets. 'It is possible to attach importance to having opportunities that are *not* taken up', Sen notes (1999, p. 76). More-over, the capability set, rather than happiness, desire fulfilment, utilities, income, primary goods, liberties, etc., serves as the central focal variable for evaluation.

2.2.2. Heterogeneity

The capability approach's second major component is that considering human heterogeneity (Sen 1992, p. 1) is central to assessing equality. Sen argues that humans have diverse internal characteristics (e.g. age, sex, physical stature, and mental attitude) and external characteristics (e.g. geographical environments, social norms, familial levels of wealth, income, and education) that should inform the assessment of equality, especially because equality requires society to aid those in proportion to their degree of disadvantage. This point is particularly important for justifying claims to positive freedoms that all should enjoy and the societal obligation to provide individuals with needed resources to improve their capability to function. This notion contrasts with the Rawlsian focus on primary goods, which fails to consider the different effects of the same bundle of goods on different people.

2.2.3. Measures of well-being

A third major component of the capability approach is that preferences or desires, in and of themselves, are not suitable indicators of well-being. Instead, the capability to achieve valuable functionings should be the main variable for evaluation. In particular, employing utilities to judge consequent states of functioning is problematic because 'the mental metric of pleasure or desire' (Sen 1999, p. 63) is subjective and changeable. These metrics are not robust measures of deprivation and disadvantage. Others have expressed concerns about the subjectivity of utilitarianism. In health policy, Dan Brock, in particular, has focused on how different health states should be valued, differences in evaluations among different groups (e.g. disabled versus non-disabled), methods for preference elicitation, whose values to use, and whether or not to discount utilities (Brock 1993; 1995).

2.2.4. Freedom: opportunity and process

A fourth major component of the capability approach is that freedom involves at least two elements: opportunity and process. The opportunity aspect judges public policy in terms of its impact on individuals' substantive freedoms. Thus, public policy must be concerned with the opportunities individuals have to achieve valued outcomes.

The process for articulating this goal and agreeing on how to achieve it constitutes the second aspect of freedom. Process freedom involves the ability to choose freely embodying 'autonomy of decisions' (Sen 2002, p. 512). The process aspect makes public participation and deliberation in political decisions and social choice a constitutive part of public policy. Sen argues that such participation has three main roles: direct, instrumental, and constructive. It is direct because participation is associated with basic capabilities and the reasonable, inherent value we attach to having 'unrestrained participation in political and social activities' (Sen

1999, p. 152). It is instrumental, he argues, because 'informed and unregimented *formation* of our values requires openness of communication and arguments' (Sen 1999, p. 152). It is constructive, he continues, because public discussion and debate help participants understand needs and conceptualize solutions. 'These processes are crucial to the formation of values and priorities', Sen notes, 'and we cannot, in general, take preferences as given independently of public discussion' (Sen 1999, p. 153).

The process-oriented emphasis of the capability approach stems in part from the fundamental focus on individuals' 'agency' or ability to understand and 'shape their own destiny and help each other' (Sen 1999, p. 11). The approach focuses primarily on 'the individual as a member of the public and as a participant in economic, social and political actions' (Sen 1999, p. 19).

Freedom can also be categorized in the capability approach as *control* freedom and *effective* freedom. The former refers to the realization of certain freedoms when they are all brought about by the individual who experiences them, whereas the latter refers to the realization of certain freedoms (by an individual) that are brought about or generated by another person or external entity (for example, when a person is free from hunger when they are fed under a food stamps programme sponsored by the government).

2.2.5. Selection and valuation

The capability approach requires selecting and valuing capabilities to assess public policy. This approach leaves the specification of valued objects (selecting and determining relative weights of functionings) partly open because the deliberative process must be explicit and open. It requires agreement among individuals on the selection and weighting of different functionings and capabilities, thus involving them in decisions that affect them and generating a reasoned consensus on a specific range of weights. It does not necessarily require an unique list of functionings or an unique system of weights. However, the capability approach is not fully indeterminate either. It acknowledges some *universally shared objectives*, but resists a single unique social ordering. Sen offers the option of defining certain functionings contextually. One example is social functioning, because the capabilities for "being able to appear in public without shame" vary greatly from one community to another' (Sen 1993b, p. 47).

On valuation and weighting, Sen's primary criterion is well-being as measured by functioning and capabilities:

It is in asserting the need to examine the value of functionings and capabilities as opposed to confining attention to the *means* to these achievements and freedoms (such as resources or primary goods or incomes) that the capability approach has something to offer (Sen 1992, p. 46).

The capability approach espouses variations in weights that different people attach to different functionings. It leaves partly open (1) the choice of value-objects (the class of functionings for measuring capabilities) and (2) the relative weights or range of weights given to functionings in evaluating capabilities. This process is a social choice exercise, requiring public discussion and democratic agreement. Sen does, however, emphasize that operationalizing the approach requires identifying valuable capabilities and ranking them.

In some evaluative exercises, the capability approach does separate out a subset of 'basic capabilities' enabling elementary and crucially important functionings up to minimally adequate levels. Sen has argued for his own selection and partial ranking in assessing equality in terms of fulfilling certain 'basic capabilities' in environments of elementary deprivation, although the capability approach is not confined to 'basic capabilities'. Sen's notion of 'basic capabilities' argues that justice requires raising people above a certain threshold level. In later works he defines a set of five categories of fundamental freedoms: social opportunities, economic facilities, political freedom, transparency guarantees, and protective security (Sen 1999, p. 127).

Other major claims of the capability approach—incomplete specification and partial ordering—are important for understanding the demands of equality in public policy and law. Both tend to be more procedural than substantive, focused primarily on achieving consensus in identifying and prioritizing valuable capabilities and the means to achieving those capabilities. The focus on basic capabilities that are essential or fundamental to human flourishing is an example of incomplete specification. It helps us to prioritize certain capabilities and to determine which are universally accepted objectives, even though other capabilities are unspecified.

The second aspect—partial ordering—asserts that not all dimensions of a construct need be fully ordered and weighted for every social evaluation. Here, employing the procedure he calls 'dominance partial ordering', Sen shows that the capability approach can identify a certain subset of functionings or capabilities as valuable, without requiring agreement on the relative weights to be attached to those capabilities.

The selection and weighting of capabilities should be, however, an iterative process for providing a certain level of basic functioning before addressing inequalities in less important capabilities. Fine-tuning a complete ordering with exactitude is unnecessary. As Sen notes, 'Partial agreements still separate out acceptable options (and weed out unacceptable ones), and a workable solution can be based on the contingent acceptance of particular provisions, without demanding complete social unanimity' (Sen 1999, p. 253). The ideas of incomplete ordering and partial agreement apply to the selection of social arrangements, policies, programmes, and interventions as well. 'It is also important to recognize that agreed social arrangements and adequate public policies do not require that there be a unique "social ordering" that completely ranks all the alternative social possibilities' (Sen 1999, p. 253).

Chapter 3 applies the incompletely theorized agreement framework to extend the capability approach when 'dominance partial ordering' and incomplete specification fail to provide reasonable procedures for resolving conflict. The capability approach needs such a framework for social choice. ITA thus picks up where the capability approach leaves off, providing a means of resolving conflict among divergent views. No unique view of health or health capabilities exists. The incomplete, partial ordering of the capability approach combined with incompletely theorized agreement on that ordering allows for reasoned public policy decision-making.

2.2.6. Basic capabilities

To distinguish between varying capabilities, Sen finds it useful, as we have seen, to identify a subset of capabilities 'dealing with... "basic needs"' (Sen 1993b, p. 40). These capabilities are critical because if they are unavailable, most other capabilities are inaccessible. They are essentially prerequisites to other capabilities. There is a 'fair amount of agreement' on the 'extreme urgency of a class of needs' (Sen 1992; 1993b; World Bank 1990; 1997), claims with 'particular moral and political importance' (Sen 1993b, p. 40). Nussbaum also uses the term basic capabilities, but in a different sense, referring to them as innate capabilities such as practical reason and imagination (Nussbaum 1990b). In contrast, the basic needs literature focuses more on resources than on human beings (Streeten et al. 1981), a focus that hinders the assessment of how resources affect people's ability to function. The capability approach accepts the basic needs concept but stresses choice and individuals' ability to make their own decisions (Nussbaum 1998). However, the use of the capability approach is not confined to basic capabilities only.

Nor is the capability approach confined to a total comparison that ranks all capability vectors. The health capability paradigm constitutes a distinguished capability comparison in which health capabilities are the focus of health policy.

2.2.7. An underspecified theory

The capability approach is a broad normative framework for evaluating the social state of affairs and policies, and individual well-being. It is, however, drastically underspecified as a theory of social justice (Pogge 2002b). It provides very little in the way of guidance for social justice. The capability approach is highly minimalistic, specifying only an evaluative space and no particular combining rule (e.g. maximization), distributional principles (e.g. sufficiency or priority), or quantitative measures for diversities in conversion factors (Pogge 2002b). Moreover, the capability approach provides little guidance on the weighting or prioritization of different capabilities and functionings; the approach is deliberately open and underspecified and requires specification before operationalizing it. While this book builds on and integrates both Aristotelian and capability perspectives, it moves significantly beyond the roots of these foundations and the minimalist interpretation of the capability approach. It attempts to specify and bring together the ideas that follow into a coherent view of health and social justice.

2.3. Capability and health policy

There are several principles expressed in both Aristotle's theory and the capability approach that have relevance to justice in health policy[4] and public policy more generally.

First, the capability approach expresses the idea of human heterogeneity—that individuals have varying needs for resources in order to achieve the same level of capability—and its importance to assessing equality. This point is particularly important for justifying the positive freedoms that all should enjoy and the societal obligation to provide individuals with the different resources that they need to enhance their capability to function. This idea expressly contrasts with the Rawlsian focus on 'primary goods'—an idea that does not consider the different effects that a similar bundle of goods has on diverse people. The Rawlsian approach does not account for the barriers to capability and functioning that may exist in people's lives.

This point is relevant to health policy because the focus on human heterogeneity provides reasons for treating individuals differently. Not only does this recognition help us to understand how different determinants of health capability work differently in different contexts, but it ensures we take account of differences in assessing inequality in health capability for social justice. Under Rawls's theory, by contrast, even if wealth and income are maximized for the worst off under the application of the difference principle (maximin), we would still face significant health deficits without remedy.

Acknowledging heterogeneity provides a rationale for treating individuals differently under a health capability paradigm. For example, children require different resources from adults to achieve optimal physical and mental functioning. Thus, a newborn with pneumonia may require hospitalization, antibiotics, and defensive monitoring, whereas an adult would likely regain full pulmonary function with no hospitalization and low dosages of antibiotics. Similarly, a person with a disability would require more resources than one without a disability to achieve the same capability to function—a ramp to access the workplace, for instance. Consider also the nutritional requirements of children, who need different types of vitamins and minerals than adults because they are growing, and pregnant women, who must take in adequate quantities of certain vitamins (e.g. folic acid) to ensure normal fetal development. As Dreze and Sen show, the relationship between food intake and nutritional adequacy varies greatly with metabolic rate, body size, gender, pregnancy, age, climate, epidemiological characteristics, and other factors (Dreze and Sen, 1989). Thus, individual and social variations affect the relationship between resources and capabilities.

A second idea expressed by both Aristotle's theory and the capability approach that has importance for health policy is the concern that preferences or desires are unreliable indicators of well-being, quality of life, and of health—utility should not be used as the sole basis for social evaluation. Instead, Aristotelian/capability perspectives focus on the capability to achieve valuable functionings as the focal variable for evaluation. This has significance for health policy in that it focuses centrally on human functioning that includes as essential the capabilities related to health.

In the health capability paradigm, using preferences or utilities to evaluate health interventions would not necessarily produce allocations that serve the array of health functionings, health needs, and health capabilities in a given society. Health preferences might be weak or health utilities might be low for certain objectively important health functionings; for example, in some cultures, devaluation of women might diminish preferences for maternal health during and after pregnancy.[5] In these cases, utilitarian allocations will differ from those based on health capabilities, which invoke health functionings and health needs as objectively important criteria for resource allocation. In the health capability paradigm, safe motherhood in all countries is valued as an essential human functioning. Functionings, as opposed to utilities or preferences, might also lend themselves better to interpersonal comparison.

As Figure 2.1 demonstrates, it matters what perspective or view of life we take regarding people's existence because we get a very different accounting of how people are doing when we look at different variables. The focal informational space thus has policy relevance for three primary reasons:

(1) for assessing individual advantage and disadvantage, by telling us whether people are well off or worse off, which is important for matters of justice in order to assess inequalities and externalities;

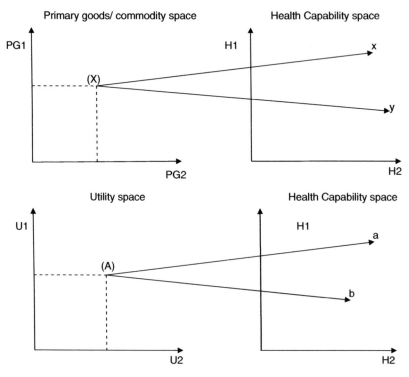

Figure 2.1 Focal Informational Space

(2) for policy evaluation, health planning, defining a basic benefits package and resource allocation; and

(3) for policy decisions to design and implement public policies through interventions or incentives to reduce inequalities in health capabilities.

Perspective matters because public policies are developed and evaluated based on different variables and assessments and different policies are thus implemented. Therefore, if we work backward from health capability as our objective, our focal variable, then we must assess the instrumental effectiveness (and cost-effectiveness) of the respective determinants of health capability (medical care and non-medical resources) and the associated public policies aimed at improving health capability.

The third and fourth aspects of the capability approach that are particularly important for understanding the demands of equality in health policy are:

(1) the emphasis on 'basic capabilities'; and

(2) incomplete specification.

The focus on basic capabilities—those capabilities that are essential or fundamental to human flourishing—is important to health policy because it helps us prioritize among the various health capabilities that are the goal of health policy. This point will be returned to in the following chapter in which it is argued that two health capabilities are central—the capability to avoid premature mortality and the capability to avoid escapable morbidity—and these capabilities should receive priority in assessing both justice and efficiency in health policy because they are valuable in their own right and in many respects are prior to other health capabilities— without them many other capabilities are unattainable. The second aspect, which emphasizes incompleteness, is important for health policy because it guides us in thinking about how we might resolve the specification and weighting of non-central health capabilities in the midst of disagreement about the 'true' nature of these capabilities. A suitable method for selection and valuation is discussed in the next chapter.

Fifth, the process aspect of decision-making bears particularly on health policy due to the role of agreement on individuals' capabilities and functionings and the necessary requirements for a flourishing life. Developing institutions to maintain and improve health should reflect the influence of the public participating in social choice and decision-making. Applying this to health, health policies would be evaluated by their impact on individuals' health capabilities and health functionings, selected and rated according to generally accepted standards, as discussed in Chapter 4. The health capability paradigm also assigns value to the patient's role in decision-making. In this regard, it is important to account for information asymmetry. Physicians would necessarily play a role in decision-making with patients. Enabling patients to make their own decisions as agents of their own health, however, is essential. Chapter 4 provides further discussion on the extent to which society supports what is here called health agency so that individuals can convert health care resources into health functionings.[6] A sixth idea expressed in the capability approach is the need to balance the demands of equity and efficiency. From the capability perspective, goals of equality should not be pursued without taking note of efficiency concerns, and this is an important factor in the assessment of health policy. In addition to our concern for equality in policy assessment, we must also keep the demands of efficiency central. This aspect will be returned to in Chapter 4.

In summary, the contrast and connections between the Aristotelian and capability approaches provide useful analytics for health ethics, policy, and law. Aristotle's ethical and political theory takes us a very long way in that human flourishing provides justification for taking health capabilities as the objective of health policy[7] (as opposed to the means—e.g. medical care—to this end); it requires as an approach to justice that government distribute a fair share of those capabilities taking note of human diversity; and it provides guidance on assessing equality in terms of shortfalls, rather than achievements.

However, Aristotle's ideas and the open and unspecified nature of the capability approach do not help us in efforts to prioritize central health capabilities for assessing justice; on the one hand, equity, and on the other hand, efficiency, in health policy. Additionally, the Aristotelian view and capability approach are not broad enough to include other routes, which allow for alternative specifications and weighting schemes to prioritize among the non-central health capabilities for health policy assessment in different communities. Thus, both Aristotle's theory and the capability approach focus on the distinction between the means and ends of practical policy—a distinction that is important to health policy and health ethics. The Aristotelian view that instruments (or resources such as health care) do not have intrinsic value is particularly useful for providing reasons for prioritizing the ends of good and free human lives over the means to health. Both theories imply that the primary goal of public policy should be to enhance people's capabilities. Finally, both approaches also demonstrate that translating the focus on enhancing human capabilities into practical policy raises important issues regarding the development, organization, and delivery of health policy.

Notes

1. For translations and discussions of Aristotle, this project relies on Irwin (1999) (for a translation of *Nicomachean Ethics*) and Lord (1984) (for a translation of *The Politics*), Nussbaum (1990b; 1992; 1998). Only several relevant components of the Aristotelian view are discussed herein. For a more exhaustive exposition, see the voluminous work of Martha Nussbaum on the subject.
2. There has been some question about this translation of Aristotle's work in addition to concern over the internal inconsistency in Aristotle's writings that would lead one to question whether he actually held this view. For the purposes here, it is assumed that Aristotle did hold this view and the translation and discussion presented in Nussbaum (1990b) is accepted to this effect.
3. Nussbaum's view is that there are three types of capabilities on which politics should be focused: basic capabilities, internal capabilities, and combined capabilities. Basic capabilities are innate capabilities that are the necessary basis for developing more advanced capability. Basic capabilities include practical reason and imagination. Internal capabilities are those capabilities that are within a person and are sufficient conditions for the exercise of the pertinent functions. An example is the case of sexual expression. A person who has not suffered genital mutilation, for instance, has the capability for sexual pleasure. Combined capabilities are internal capabilities combined with suitable external characteristics for functioning. A woman who is not genitally mutilated but is nonetheless prevented from sexual expression by enforced seclusion, for example, would have internal but not external capabilities for sexual expression. On the relationship between justice and capabilities, Nussbaum says that the aim of public policy is the production of external capabilities. This means promoting the states of the person by providing the necessary education and care; and it also means preparing the environment so that it is favourable for the exercise of practical reason and other major functions (Nussbaum 1998, p. 316). Nussbaum has come up with a list of capabilities for constitutional design; although it has been criticized for being utopian, omitting income and wealth, and lacking attention to efficiency.
4. Health policy includes health care, public health, and health-related research (as it relates to health functioning and health agency, this is not a complete theory of the ethics of health-related research).
5. For an alarming picture of lack of access to obstetric care in many developing countries see Farmer and Kim (2008).
6. Other approaches to medical ethics and bioethics have also emphasized a major role for choice (Engelhardt 1986; Havighurst 1995; Lomasky 1981; Menzel

1990). Theorists emphasize choice primarily because it embodies a respect for individual autonomy. But individual choice must be assessed in the context of aggregative well-being, and the challenge is how to compare and weigh small benefits for many with large benefits for a few. The health capability paradigm is unique in the manner in which it integrates, rather than dichotomizes, individual autonomy and aggregative well-being. In this sense, it brings together both deontological and consequentialist views. The account also considers the impact of external and internal characteristics on individual choice.

7. And, as an end to other policies too, as discussed in Chapter 4.

3

Pluralism, Incompletely Theorized Agreements, and Public Policy

As the preceding chapters have shown, the Aristotelian view and capability approach differ on the question of selecting and weighting capabilities and functionings for the capability set. Determining what valuable functionings constitute human flourishing, and grounding such an account in light of plural views about it, is an essential step in operationalizing either approach for practical use. The Aristotelian view requires in the extreme an unique account of capabilities—that there is 'just one list of functionings...that do in fact constitute human good living' (Nussbaum 1988, p. 152; Sen 1993b, p. 46). The Aristotelian view is thus unique and singular and many have criticized it on precisely those grounds. Yet Aristotle was right in his conviction that we must be clear about our objectives in order to assess policy in terms of those objectives. The capability approach, on the other hand, has been criticized for not fully specifying the valuable functionings that constitute human flourishing.

This chapter focuses on developing a systematic, definable framework for determining what valuable capabilities and functionings inherently constitute health. Here, new territory is charted between an Aristotelian perspective that claims uniqueness and singularity, and a capability approach that does not aim to specify valuable functionings for practical use. In this way, the health capability paradigm furthers the capability approach for operationalization. By grounding this analysis in ethical and political theorizing, this book also aims to avoid some of the arbitrariness in other approaches (Daniels 1994; 2001). In its use of the ITA method, it seeks to further the capability approach by picking up where the capability approach leaves off—the ITA method is complementary to the capability approach and can help to extend it.

The capability approach ends with two critical analytical components:

(i) the selection and weighing of capabilities and functionings is left partially (not fully) open—it does not provide a substantive account of the 'good life' and in this way is incomplete; and

(ii) the theory promotes the idea of dominance partial ordering in that some capabilities can be given priority over others without fully specifying all capabilities at once. This chapter will also analyse how to extend this aspect of the approach through distinguishing between central and non-central health capabilities.[1]

The ITA social choice method is complementary to the capability approach because it provides a systematic framework for decision-making that enables agreement on a core set of human values that are necessary conditions for human existence. It does so without requiring agreement on non-core values *and* without requiring a fully epistemological theorizing of that agreement. The ITA method allows us to move forward in operationalizing the capability approach to health policy without a full epistemological understanding, or a fully theorized agreement, on *why* this class of fundamental health needs should be so prioritized. The health capability paradigm also sets out procedures for evaluating non-central health capability sets where such assessments are at issue.

This chapter analyses the problems of plurality, fuzziness, and social choice in order to demonstrate the value of a method like ITA in the health capability paradigm. In particular, the ITA is valuable in operationalizing the capability approach—and other multidimensional theories of well-being—for use in social evaluation.[2,3]

This chapter develops and argues for ITA as an approach to collective decision-making in public policy, thus furthering[4] the capability approach.[5]

3.1. Social choice theory, collective rationality, and Arrow's impossibility result

3.1.1. Problems in social choice

In his classic book *Social Choice and Individual Values*, Kenneth Arrow set out to study whether any method of aggregating individual values can imply social rationality and be satisfactory in other ways. In defining social rationality, Arrow states that:

rational behavior on the part of the community would mean that the community orders the three alternatives according to its collective preferences once for all,[6] and then chooses in any given case that alternative among those actually available which stands highest on this list (Arrow 1951, p. 2).[7]

Throughout his analysis, Arrow assumes that individuals are rational—capable of ordering alternatives to satisfy Axioms I and II (completeness and consistency).[8] The primary goal of his study was 'to construct an ordering relation for society as a whole that will also reflect rational choice-making so that R may also be assumed to satisfy Axioms I and II' (Arrow 1951, p. 19).

Arrow attempted to integrate diverse individual preferences into a social preference that satisfied four seemingly reasonable conditions. However, he obtained only an impossibility result—that it usually is not possible to 'construct a procedure for passing from a set of known individual tastes to a pattern of social decision-making' (Arrow 1951, p. 2).

3.1.2. Arrow's impossibility theorem

Arrow set out to formally define a social welfare function that specified a social ordering, R, over all social states of affairs for every set of individual preference orderings that also satisfied the following four conditions:

(1) Universal Domain (U)—a social ordering must be yielded for every possible combination; any complete and transitive ordering is permissible, with no restrictions on individual preferences.

(2) Independence of Irrelevant Alternatives (I)—a social ranking of x and y should depend only on the individual preferences over x and y and not on how other alternatives (a, b, c, d, etc.) are ranked.

(3) Non-Dictatorship (D)—no individual should make the decision.

(4) Pareto Principle (P)—all individuals taken together should be decisive (Arrow 1951).

Arrow discovered and proved that it was impossible to achieve such a result. Arrow's impossibility theorem demonstrates formally that it is impossible to obtain a social welfare function that satisfies all four conditions. His work has helped define social choice theory, which includes any exercise in which people aim to make collective decisions and especially pertains to politics and policy.

Many other scholars have attempted to explain and modify Arrow's impossibility result. Amartya Sen has focused on plurality, ambiguity, and informational constraints as key problems in social choice theory, attributing the impossibility result to two factors: the combination of the four conditions; and the absence of information that is necessary for interpersonal comparisons. The required information is a metric for making interpersonal comparisons; this metric must include 'non-utility, non-welfare information' (Sen 1992). The main issue is to broaden the relevant information to shape more appropriate criteria for social choice. This could be achieved, partly by incorporating the fulfilment of basic liberties, which are both intrinsic and instrumental. Utility, on the other hand, is an inappropriate measure of the intrinsic value placed on freedom in many choice situations.

The capability approach, by contrast, illustrates that basic liberties can be incorporated into the states of affairs in social choice formulations. While integrating non-utility, non-welfare information may address the plural value structure of the decision problem, it does not deal with the inherent fuzziness that occurs when multiple values must be considered during individual or collective decision-making and on which Arrow's impossibility theorem sheds light. For instance, the 'impossibility of a Paretian liberal' that stems from efforts to integrate minimal liberties in social choice exercises illustrates that, when a plural value structure exists, principles can conflict and preclude completeness in choice. As Sen notes, 'the "impossibility of the Paretian liberal" captures the conflict between (i) the special importance of a person's preferences over her own personal sphere, and (ii) the general importance of people's preferences over any choice, irrespective of field' (Sen 1995a, p. 13). A central difficulty in Arrow's social choice formulation is that the Pareto principle conflicts directly with the libertarian principle of Universal Domain—that an individual can have any ordering. Thus, Universal Domain allows any individual ordering, whereas the Pareto Principle allows only individual orderings that do not worsen anyone's condition. This means that if everyone prefers x to y, then x must be chosen in the presence of y (on one occasion or on multiple occasions, according to the internal consistency requirement). In trying to address the impossibility of the Paretian liberal, various attempts have been made to weaken the conditions of social choice—I, U, and P—failures of which confirm that the combination of the conditions leads to an enduring impossibility. This impossibility, however, need not detain us in our quest for social agreement.

Much of the optimism about social choice stems from the potential to obtain partial agreements 'without demanding complete social unanimity' (Sen 1999, p. 253). While social choice theory has incorporated a plural value structure in theoretical formulations, the field has not entirely addressed the residual ambiguities and conflicts that exist in theoretical and practical exercises with plural views. One type of analysis that has not been extensively explored to deal with the demands of reasoned decision-making and that offers significant promise of partial accord is that of incomplete theorization. The following sections set forth incomplete theorization and the related aspects of the capability approach as a feasible and practical solution to the difficulties involved in plurality and unresolved conflicts.

3.2. Incompletely theorized agreements

The preceding section noted how classic social choice theory, that demands complete agreement and complete reasoning, has faced difficulty in putting forth an effective framework for individual and collective choice. On an individual level, people will rarely be able to completely theorize a decision in situations involving plural concepts and values. On a collective level, the difficulties of individual choice are magnified, and people will rarely agree on all aspects, and at all theoretical levels, of a particular solution. Yet the demands of every day life dictate that individuals make decisions and that members of society reach agreement on a particular course of action, whether or not they agree on all reasons justifying the collective act. To describe this real-world decision-making, a theory must accommodate judgements on human goods that are plural and fuzzy and must allow individuals to take different but convergent paths to a common, though often partial, agreement.

In exploring the theoretical implications of Aristotle's theory and the capability approach to health, health policy, and the right to health, two questions are significant:

(1) how to obtain actual collective agreement on a dominance partial ordering of capabilities; and
(2) what type of social decision-making might apply in such an exercise.

The incompletely theorized agreements approach holds promise for addressing these questions. Indeed, the health capability paradigm is groundbreaking not only because it extends Aristotelian and capability views to health but also because it folds into the mix this third indispensable element.

It is important to note, before moving on, that the ITA framework is applied here *only* to one point of the capability view—that of the social choice exercise of reaching agreement on a partial order of capabilities. ITA is thus one aspect of the theoretical framework advanced here, and its use is distinctly complementary to the capability perspective. It is an additional element, not a substitutional one, and as such provides a critical analytical component of the health capability paradigm—the broader theoretical framework essential for the debate about justice and health, which includes in Chapter 9 domestic health policy reform.

The method of incompletely theorized agreements (Sunstein 1995) has been applied generally in law as a descriptive and normative framework of legal and specifically judicial decision-making, but, until this work, had not been applied to specific policy areas, such as health. An incompletely theorized agreement is one that is not uniformly theorized at all levels, from high-level justifications to low-level particulars. Incompletely theorized agreements fail to produce depth (full accounts of foundations) or width (coherence with other dimensions), an idea that relates somewhat to John Rawls's notion of *overlapping consensus* (OC) (Rawls 1993). Both Rawls and Sunstein attempt to bring about stability and social agreement—the resolution of social disputes—among people who disagree on fundamental matters. Rawls asserts that people who disagree on 'comprehensive views' can agree on certain political abstractions and can converge enough for political decision-making. According to Rawls, social accord can be achieved in a democracy through shared commitment to abstract principles (Rawls 1993, pp. 134–73).

The ITA approach contrasts, in part, with the Rawlsian programme. ITA concedes that agreement on abstract political principles can produce stability, social agreement, and in defining political moments, social reform. But it argues that this type of agreement is less useful for legal purposes and for ordinary politics because of its focus on large philosophical questions. These larger questions, Sunstein argues, are less relevant to ordinary political and legal decision-making than are questions of particulars.

High-level principles can have an important role in democratic political life generally and in major social movements specifically. Decision-making in public policy settings, however, requires reasoned agreement on particular outcomes, regardless of whether there is agreement on political abstractions. As there is rarely agreement on high-level principles, those particular outcomes must be justified by low-level principles. People can disagree on general principles but agree on concrete cases. Lawyers and judges are more likely to converge on lower levels of abstraction than higher ones—dealing with decisions of 'what to do rather than exactly how to think' (Sunstein

1995, p. 1736 n. 8). This approach is therefore more appropriate for well functioning legal systems in democratic societies.

The incomplete theorization typology applies usefully to decision-making about health and health policy. Diagrams of the three types of incompletely theorized agreements—incompletely specified agreements (Figure 3.1), incompletely specified and generalized agreements (Figure 3.2), and incompletely theorized agreements on particular outcomes (Figure 3.3)—illustrate ITA.

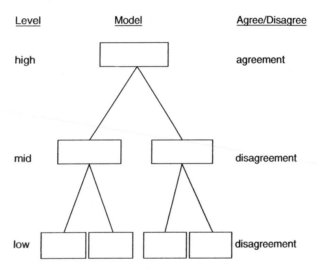

Figure 3.1 Model One: Incompletely Specified Agreements (High-level Agreement)
Source: Ruger (1998, p. 105).

3.3. Incompletely specified agreements

The first type of incompletely theorized agreement occurs when there is agreement on a general principle, accompanied by sharp disagreement about mid-level principles and particular cases. Here, people who accept a general principle—murder is wrong, for instance—need not agree on what this principle entails in particular cases—for example, abortion (Sunstein 1995, p. 1739). Applying this model to health, people who accept the general principle of supporting good health can disagree on what good health requires in provision of health care and other concrete social services.

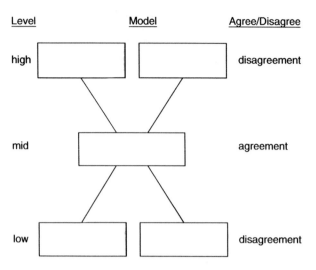

Figure 3.2 Model Two: Incompletely Specified and Generalized Agreements (Mid-level Agreement)

Source: Ruger (1998, p. 106).

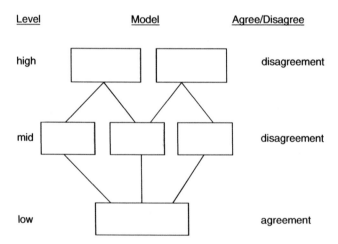

Figure 3.3 Model Three: Incompletely Theorized Agreements on Particular Outcomes (Low-level Agreement)

Source: Ruger (1998, p. 107).

3.4. Incompletely specified and generalized agreements

The second type of incomplete theorization provides agreement on a mid-level principle, but disagreement both about the more general theory that accounts for it and about outcomes in particular controversies. The connections are unclear both between the general theory and mid-level principles and between specific cases and mid-level principles (Sunstein 1995). As a health example, people might agree on universal health insurance coverage without settling on a large-scale theory of equality or on a specific health plan. In this model, there is a great deal of uncertainty and ambiguity leading to more divergence than convergence.

3.5. Incompletely theorized agreements on particular outcomes

Incompletely theorized agreements on particular outcomes involve, in a public policy and human rights context, decisions and agreement on particular policy options. In this model, parties reach agreement on low-level principles and/or policies or outcomes that do not necessarily derive from one particular high-level theory. In other words, low-level principles may be compatible with more than one high-level principle. People might agree on individual judgements while disagreeing on the level of general principle.

3.6. Incompletely theorized agreements and public policy

While the ITA framework has been applied generally in law, it also has promise as a normative and prescriptive analytical framework for public policy (Ruger 1998, pp. 88–107) and for human rights (Ruger 2006a). It is well suited to human goods that are plural and ambiguous; and it allows for different but converging paths to the same agreement. In matters of political philosophy concerning inherently plural and indistinct concepts, and in dealing with collective choice involving numerous views and disagreements, ITA can help bring actors to agreement on certain specific outcomes.

In social decision-making about health capabilities, health policy, and a right to health, the ITA framework is particularly useful and advances the capability approach in at least three important respects. First, health, and thus health capabilities, are multidimensional concepts about which different people have different and sometimes conflicting views. No unique view of health or health capabilities exists. No view is ideal or unanimously agreed upon for all evaluative purposes. Complete theorization is thus difficult to achieve. Second, the incomplete, partial ordering of the capability approach combined with incompletely theorized agreement on that ordering allows for reasoned public policy decision-making in particular situations. Third, given the demands of certain evaluative exercises, particularly in public policy and human rights contexts, the flexibility of these approaches allows reasoned agreement on central aspects of health and health capabilities, without requiring agreement on non-central aspects. It also allows for different paths to the same conclusion.

3.7. Pluralism, ambiguity, and incompletely theorized agreements

Often in decision-making settings 'people can know that [something] is true without entirely knowing why [this something] is true' (Sunstein 1995, p. 1742). Consider these instances: people might agree that murder is wrong, that the government should prevent famines, that society should not let people starve and die in the streets, that we should try to prevent the spread of communicable diseases, and that people should not be subject to forced genital mutilation. People can hold these views without knowing why exactly. For example, in Oregon's Medicaid experiment (US Congress Office of Technology Assessment 1992), there was substantial agreement that cystic fibrosis and viral pneumonia claimed allocational priority in providing medical care over tooth capping, acute headaches, and thumb sucking. However, people did not generally agree on or know exactly why this should be the case. In hospital emergency rooms, physicians will agree on triage decisions prioritizing life-saving interventions over quality of life enhancements, without fully theorizing why. And in certain applications of the capability approach, there is considerable agreement on urgent basic capabilities without a full comprehension of the reason.

The need for effective public policy in the face of these ambiguities makes the ITA approach compelling, especially in the context of public policy and human rights. Like many concepts in public policy and human rights, 'health' and 'human flourishing' are multidimensional and ambiguous. People can understand the concepts of 'health' or 'human flourishing' or 'capability' without fully articulating their details.

Through partially theorized concepts, humans can evaluate policy as desirable or undesirable. The ITA approach allows people to agree on an outcome despite their ambiguities. Decision-makers need not comprehensively share a common set of foundations for their beliefs and are allowed to leave unarticulated the 'right' reasons for their respective convictions. When their convergence over a human right is incompletely theorized, it enables them to obtain some clarity and decisiveness in the result without precisely specifying their reasons for it.

3.8. Incompletely theorized agreements and health capability

Collective agreement on the selection and weighting of health capabilities is necessary to achieve a common understanding and to operationalize it. A better understanding of what justice requires for health necessitates a response to the question of what set of health capabilities might be included in evaluating social justice. This raises both substantive and procedural issues. The ITA framework complements the capability approach in this phase because it allows for collective agreement on a dominance partial ordering of capabilities without requiring that political participants agree on other capabilities. It can thus obtain agreement on central health capabilities without requiring agreement on non-central or secondary health capabilities.

The ITA framework also assumes pluralism in many forms. Plural value structures and plural agents do not upset the framework as long as there are at least some areas of consensus. In this sense it allows the capability approach to apply more widely. 'People value things not just in terms of weight but also in qualitatively different ways', Sunstein observes. 'Human goods are plural and diverse, and they cannot be ranked along any unitary scale without doing violence to our understanding of the qualitative differences among those very goods' (Sunstein 1995, p. 1748).

Applying the ITA framework to questions of health, health capability, and health policy, one sees that people can agree on particular outcomes. Individuals can agree, for instance, on those health capabilities that are critical to a right to health and the low-level principles that justify them without agreeing on complete answers to metaphysical questions, such as 'what is human flourishing?' or 'what is health?'

In summary, in the context of a political or social discussion, the ITA framework allows for complete decisions on agreed and theorized *incomplete* orderings, a central aspect of the capability approach. In a liberal democratic society, it is important to see the essential connection between the exercise of civil liberties through political participation and practical policy decisions. The ITA framework illuminates that connection and holds promise for health policy and for defining a right to health.

3.9. Health capability set: central and non-central health capabilities

Extending this concept to health policy, I set forth a distinction between central and non-central health capabilities. Central health capabilities are a particular subset of health capabilities, which take priority over non-central capabilities in evaluating health policies (Ruger 1998, pp. 108–12). These capabilities can be seen as prerequisites for other capabilities, such as developing abilities, using talents, and carrying out plans. These central health capabilities may be seen as prerequisites to other health capabilities and other capabilities more broadly because, for example, in terms of treatable heart disease, one's heart must beat and pump blood properly in order to breathe, and one must breathe in order to obtain oxygen for the brain, and the brain requires oxygen to function in practical reasoning. Without oxygen to the brain, even for a few minutes, the brain will cease to function normally. The central health capabilities, which include the capacity of our organs and systems to function, are necessary conditions for humanity, regardless of social context. Meeting the health needs and health agency deficits associated with central health capabilities must precede addressing other health capabilities; the selection and weights among non-central health capabilities can await further specification (selection and weighting) through social agreement (Ruger 1998, pp. 108–12) at the next stage. These essential elements of health are universally shared objectives.

To evaluate health policy and effectuate a right to health, determining how to measure capabilities and at what levels to provide them is necessary. Health capabilities evaluation can use '*realized* functionings' (what a person actually does) and their possible alternatives (real opportunities or what a person is free to do) (Sen 1999, p. 75). Capability, in its *potential* sense, is thus not directly observable or measurable, but constitutes an ability for functioning represented by options for alterative functionings. To evaluate health policy in the health capability paradigm, one may still assess *realized* health functionings (e.g. physical and mental functionings) to view individuals' health capabilities and health agency evaluation is also necesssary. Measures for assessing realized health functionings linked to central health capabilities in many respects already exist. These include life expectancy, infant and child mortality, and prevalence and incidence rates of disease (e.g. tuberculosis and polio), dysfunction (e.g. infertility), and physical and mental functioning and disability (e.g. paraplegia, inability to climb stairs, manic depression).[9] However, one must also assess a person's *potential* health achievement, which is especially relevant when considering pre-existing illness and disability. Health capabilities constitute individuals' *abilities* to achieve health functionings; the aggregated set of health capabilities represents a person's overall freedom to achieve health functionings. Chapter 4 returns to these issues, while health capability (health functioning and health agency) measurement and operationalization is examined elsewhere (Ruger in press).

Notes

1. Dominance partial orderings differ from a complete ordering in the sense that we can have a subset of health capabilities such as the central health capabilities that are prioritized as a group higher than other health capabilities (e.g. non-central health capabilities). Thus, the central health capabilities dominate or are partially ordered above the non-central health capabilities. In this sense there are two orderings—one for central health capabilities and one for non-central health capabilities. At this point no specific orderings within non-central health capabilities is determined—hence the approach is partly open. A completely invariant ordering, on the other hand, would require all health capabilities to be ordered and weighted at this stage and every stage of evaluation, thus the difference in process between allowing partial and complete orderings.
2. Such problems run through nearly any multidimensional theory that requires selection and weighing of its dimensions. Utilitarianism faces this challenge as does the fair equality of opportunity account noted in Chapter 1.
3. Many social choice frameworks face difficulties in dealing with central problems of fuzziness and plurality. Ideas of fuzziness—when not every aspect of a problem or prioritization is clear—and plurality cut across many aspects of human choice and behaviour. These include: (1) the concepts at issue (e.g. health, capabilities, quality of life, well-being, or equality); (2) agency (e.g. one or multiple decision makers); (3) motivations and criteria of choice (e.g. conflicting principles such as libertarianism and Pareto optimality or multiple

determinants of human behaviour such as balancing self-interest and empathy in social contexts); (4) assessment of uncertainty (e.g. the ambiguity of uncertainty); and (5) ways in which we measure and interpret criteria.

4. Despite the considerable interest in Sen's capability approach, there are relatively few operationalizations or applications of the approach. As noted earlier, there have been no other applications that have systematically applied the approach to health policy.

5. While this chapter discusses the promise of incompletely theorized agreements in public policy, there is further work to be done to apply them in this setting.

6. This approach takes preferences as fixed—not influenceable by the decision-making mechanism itself.

7. On the question of whether to incorporate individuals' tastes or values, Arrow notes that, 'we must look at the entire system of values, including values about values, in seeking for a truly general theory of social welfare' (Arrow 1951, p. 18).

8. Arrow is more permissive on the homo economicus condition—leaving the objective function unspecified in his work.

9. For further discussion of indicators to employ in measuring realized functionings linked to central health capabilities, see Ruger (1998, pp. 111–12).

4

Justice, Capability, and Health Policy

Due to the fact that health capabilities are not directly observable we must examine health functionings and health agency that lead us to issues of conceptualizing, defining, and operationalizing health.

4.1. Trans-positionality: a global view of health

To provide a workable theory of health and social justice a practical and clear account of health capabilities is necessary. The goal here is not to 'resolve' irreconcilable epistemological differences about health because this is virtually impossible, but rather to lay out the thrust of these different perspectives. This section then offers a conception of health that constitutes an incompletely theorized agreement reflecting a global view on health's core dimensions. The demands of social justice and health require a universally shared norm of health as a framework for such interpersonal comparisons. The capability approach (specifically in its emphasis on basic capabilities) clearly promotes objectively assessed health (e.g. using mortality and morbidity standards) as an universally valued capability. Thus, the challenge is to construct a conception of health that reflects the 'view from everywhere'. The capability approach calls for efforts to construct 'trans-positionally' consistent 'global' points of view on various crucially important functionings (Sen 1993a, p. 130). This paradigm seeks a globally shared standard of 'health' upon which to make interpersonal comparisons of health capabilities.

There has been much discussion in the philosophical, medical, and human rights literature about how to define health and its most important dimensions. General Comment 14 of the ICESCR provides a definition of health and the goal of a right to health as 'the highest attainable standard of mental and physical health' (UN CESCR 2000). It did not elaborate, however, on different accounts of health or the meaning of a 'highest attainable standard' in a world of diverse individuals with variable genetic and biological capacity. While no unanimous or unique account of health exists, it might be possible to isolate certain central agreed upon features for assessing political arrangements. This section focuses on deriving a practical, consensus-driven account of health to shape ethical and social obligations for health policy and with applications to a right to health.

Concepts such as 'health' or 'quality of life' cannot claim to have a unique, unchanging meaning. Such concepts entail a degree of social and cultural construction, with different meanings across time and place. Society must decide which different possibilities are important. Still, as Thomas Scanlon argues about social ethics more broadly, there is merit in searching for a substantive-enough account against which to assess activities so that it can serve as a basis for criticism of injustices and oppression in the world (Scanlon 1975).

This line of reasoning calls for thinking about concepts such as human flourishing and health in a more universal and critical way. Even communitarians like Michael Walzer and others maintain that while absolute 'objectivity' might not exist, it is important to take note of the criticism that exists within a given culture (Walzer 1983; 1993). Here we want to understand what good health or good functioning might entail. And while there may be no unanimous or unique account of health, it is possible to isolate certain primary defining features of health and human life to which we assign priority for assessing political arrangements. Arguments favouring universally shared conceptions of health can define the central features of human health at a practical level. The health capability paradigm uses this viewpoint to clarify the assessment of health policies.

Sen's focus on 'positional objectivity'—the notion that some assessments of social affairs can be made with a certain degree of objectivity once individuals' circumstances are taken into account (Sen 1993a, p. 130)—underscores the need for a more objective account of health. A 'trans-positional' or more 'global' point of view is useful both in assessing equity and efficiency in health policy and in interpreting the right to health. Subjective reports of health can fail to reveal health deprivations. Examining differences in mortality and self-reported illness between men and women in India illustrates this discrepancy. Even though women had higher rates of morbidity than men, they reported poor health less often (Sen 1993a, p. 135). This example underscores the point that 'positional' assessments of health by individuals themselves, resting on inadequate medical knowledge and cultural attitudes devaluing women's lives and women's health vis-à-vis men, could lead to misallocation of resources away from those with bona fide health needs. In the health capability paradigm, health needs map directly to health functionings, which in turn relate to health capabilities. Physical therapy following orthopaedic surgery, for instance, yields restored muscular strength, which in turn fosters the capability for better physical functioning.

4.1.1. Health capabilities: health functionings, health needs, and health agency

Health capabilities represent the ability of individuals to achieve certain health functionings and the freedom to achieve those functionings. As noted above, the difference between health capabilities and health functionings is the difference between achievement and the freedom to achieve, though health functionings do not fully embody autonomy and freedom. Because health functionings or achievements map directly on to health capabilities, they are effective as measuring indicators of health capabilities. Health functionings can be used as a proxy and can be causally linked to health capabilities; for example, the ability to walk is both indicated by and associated with a person's physical functioning. Thus, health capabilities are the abilities that individuals have to achieve health functionings. Impairments in an individual's functionings reduce his or her health capabilities, which ultimately affects a whole host of other capabilities. In a society that is obligated to improve individuals' health capabilities and reduce inequalities in them, it is central to understand the health needs[1] associated with impairments in health functionings. Health agency is another component of health capability and can also be used as a proxy, and can be causally linked both to health functioning and health capability (Figure 4.1). Health agency is taken up further in Chapter 6. Health capability is not directly observable and its operationalization and measurement are beyond the scope of the present book, addressed elsewhere (Ruger in press).

Why, one might ask, should we be concerned, as a matter of social justice, with health capabilities? Why not make the ethical perspective, the focal variable, health or health functionings alone? The author argued over a decade ago and maintains here that health and health capabilities have special moral importance in a theory of social justice. Health capabilities encompass both health functionings and health agency and, as previously argued (Ruger 1998), should be the central focal variable for assessing justice in health policy because:

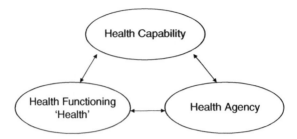

Figure 4.1 Health Capability, Health Functioning, and Health Agency

(1) health capabilities represent *abilities for good health* as the outcome, as opposed to a scheme that justifies functioning or health care *for equality of opportunity or some other societal objective such as utility.* This is because human flourishing, or being capable of functioning as a human being, and health are ends in and of themselves;

(2) taking health capabilities as central throws light on the distinction between achieving a given health outcome (e.g. lower fertility rates) through coercion versus voluntary action. Just looking at health outcomes alone (e.g. fertility rates), while a key component of this theory and helpful for practical policy purposes, will not, in and of itself, demonstrate how these outcomes came about (e.g. through coercive sterilization, pregnancy termination or one-child policy laws);

(3) health capabilities appeal to theories of choice by shedding light on the choices and options individuals have at their disposal in achieving health outcomes;

(4) health capability includes health agency, which provides a picture of an individual's or group's ability to pursue valuable health goals and to effectively bring about health; and

(5) as discussed further in Chapter 6, health capabilities, as opposed to health functionings alone, through health agency, incorporate a role for individual responsibility, a crucial element to any theory of health and social justice. Individual responsibility is critical for a number of reasons, the two foremost of which being: guidance on the limits of social responsibility in the context of irresponsible or imprudent choice, and the causal influence of individual responsibility on health outcomes (e.g. lifestyle and behavioural

determinants of health). The health capability paradigm thus includes health capabilities, health functioning, health needs and health agency in its ethical perspective.

The relationship between health functionings and health needs is a key component.

Health needs are directly ascribable to and map to health functionings, which in turn map to health capabilities.

Health needs, through their relation to functioning, define what is required to improve individuals' health capabilities. For example, a person might be harmed through malnutrition, by having a heart attack or by breaking his leg. Improving individuals' health capabilities requires preventing, curing, and compensating for conditions that curtail their capabilities for health functioning (Ruger 2006d). Thus, meeting health needs is an objective measure of our success in improving health capabilities. The task, then, is to specify health needs as they relate to health functionings and health capabilities. The concept of medical necessity and medical appropriateness (discussed in Chapter 8) is also an essential consideration and helps to clarify the account of health needs under the health capability paradigm (Ruger 2006d).

It is important to emphasize that this analysis does not depend on resolving the dichotomy between normative and non-normative approaches to defining health. For the purposes of resource distribution and policy evaluation, it is usually sufficient to rely on the distinction between health and disease and on scientific knowledge about human anatomy, physiology, and biochemistry. The basic model of health, which forms the foundation for treatment and prevention, provides a workable distinction between health-related needs and the goods and services that address those needs. As the scope of resource distribution broadens, it may be necessary to resolve the conflict over the epistemology of health at higher levels, but such analytical steps should be addressed as needed.

4.1.2. Health and disease

The literature defining health is varied and contentious. On one end of the spectrum are particularly narrow views, adhering to the so-called biomedical model of health, that define health as the 'absence of diseases or abnormalities of the organ tissues or biological processes' (Lerner and Levine 1994, p. 44). Illness represents deviations from biological norms.

Concepts such as wellness, well-being, or functional effectiveness (a person's ability to perform activities of daily life) sometimes, but not always, fall within these narrower views. On the other end of the spectrum are definitions that are so broad as to include all of what might be included in the concept of quality of life.

Disease is defined primarily, but not solely, anatomically through the categorization of pathology. More precisely, disease is defined as:

1. An interruption, cessation, or disorder of body function, system, or organ. Syn. illness, morbus, sickness.

2. A morbid entity characterized usually by at least two of these criteria: recognized etiologic agent(s), identifiable group of signs and symptoms, or consistent anatomic alterations. See also syndrome.

3. Literally, dis-ease, the opposition of ease, when something is wrong with a bodily function (Stedman 2000, pp. 509–10).

For example, cancer, congestive heart failure, manic depression, a broken leg, hypertension, diabetes, cleft palate, hearing impairment, arthritis, and anxiety are all diseases, disabilities, or dysfunctions. This definition is consistent with the one found, for example, in *Webster's Third New International Dictionary, Unabridged* (1981, p. 648), in which disease is defined as:

an impairment of the normal state of the living animal or plant body or of any of its components that interrupts or modifies the performance of the vital functions, being a response to environmental factors, . . . to specific infective agents, . . . inherent defects of the organism (as various genetic anomalies), or to combinations of these factors: Sickness, Illness.

Numerous scholars and practitioners have reviewed the literature and practice on conceptualizing and operationalizing health exhaustively, and in particular look to the health status measurement literature and practice for alternative models. After studying 332 patients over the age of eighteen, one team of researchers postulated that functional status has two dimensions, physical and psychosocial, the latter strongly related to depression and other mental illnesses (Brooks et al. 1990, p. 793). Hays and Stewart (1990, p. 22) surveyed 1,980 patients in the Medical Outcomes Study using a concept of health that also had two dimensions: physical (role limitations due to physical health, physical function, satisfaction with physical ability, and mobility) and mental (depression, behavioural emotional control, positive affect, anxiety, feelings of belonging).

Lohr and Mock (1989) as well as Ware (1991) expanded these conceptions by attributing four dimensions to health: physical, mental and emotional, everyday functioning in social and role activities, and general sense of well-being and vitality. Ware's version emphasizes four health components—physical, mental, social and role functioning, and general health perceptions. Manning et al. (1982, p. 148) delineated the four aspects of health as physical, mental, social, and physiological. Engelhardt (1974) used a more normative approach, regarding poor health and disease as deviations from the social norm as well as from the biological blueprint. In a study of 3,980 elderly people, Whitelaw and Liang (1991) defined three dimensions of health: physical (chronic illness, functional limitation, self-rated health), mental (depression, anxiety, positive well-being, self-rated health), and social (social contacts, emotional support, and instrumental support). Engelhardt (1974) argues that the concept of disease itself can be normative—subject and relative to social norms and values. Christopher Boorse (1975) has defended a mechanistic or biological view of health and disease, arguing that disease is a biological malfunction—a deviation from the biological norm of normal function.

Globally, the World Health Organization (WHO) defined health as 'a state of complete physical, mental, and social well-being, and not merely the absence of disease or infirmity' (Constitution of WHO 1946). Since that time, a number of scholars in health policy and the medical sciences have broadened that definition of health with concepts that are very close to well-being and quality of life. Many note, however, that this trend of making all of human well-being a health issue is something of 'health imperialism'—whereby health policy extends to all of human well-being.

While this sample is not exhaustive, it illustrates the broad variations in concepts of health ranging from narrow anatomical to broader quality of life views. One model of health falls between these extremes, offering the following:

1. The state of the organism when it functions optimally without evidence of disease or abnormality.

2. A state of dynamic balance in which an individual's or a group's capacity to cope with all the circumstances of living is at an optimum level.

3. A state characterized by anatomic, physiologic, and psychologic integrity, ability to perform personally valued family, work, and community roles, ability to deal with physical, biologic, psychological, and social stress; a

feeling of well being, and freedom from the risk of disease and untimely death (Stedman 2000, pp. 789–90).

This model defines health and disease by building on medical research, education, knowledge, and practice. In this view, health is a multidimensional construct that includes psychosocial as well as physical aspects.

This model identifies, diagnoses, and prognosticates over the process of change along a continuum between healthy and not healthy. It rests on the understanding that humans are biological organisms living in social environments. It thus concerns both physical and mental states and recognizes that humans interact as social organisms. For example, one field, occupational therapy, helps people return to work, school, and other social environments. The model typically does not reach beyond these fields to promote social functioning, such as relationship development, except during treatment for mental illness: but neither does it completely reject the social aetiology of health and disease. The third part of the above includes the ability to perform valued family, work, and community roles. It differs from the narrow biomedical model of health, which stands primarily on anatomical and biological facts and excludes psychological and social elements. A narrow biomedical model of disease also fails to specifically address the adaptation and balance required on the part of *society* to enable individuals' health capabililies—for example, the need for norms that value and support the human dignity of all persons, regardless of functioning level, norms that entail an inclusive view of normality and respect all human life. In this regard, this approach addresses societal influences through cultural pluralism.

Though it relates less to particular social norms and values than other concepts of health and disease, this model demonstrates that a more expansive understanding of health contains many core elements, if not everything that might constitute quality of life.

This model reflects an incompletely theorized agreement, or partial consensus, on core dimensions of health. Its definition brings together these overlapping elements toward greater standardization in conceptualizing health. It also fits well with the idea of health capability by including the concept of freedom from the risk of disease or untimely death. Most importantly, it defines individuals' practical opportunities for optimal health in both potential and actual terms—a duality embedded in the health capability paradigm. It can serve as a middle ground or shared standard for health assessment.

Thus, an expanded model of health can define the central features of human health at a *practical* (if not an epistemological) level. These central features represent universally shared beliefs about core elements of health. It is a clear, grounded, and agreed upon view of health, useful in the health capability paradigm for public policy and a right to health. And, it includes two levels of analysis, *potential* and *actual*.[2] In addition to the advantage of this account in providing a consensual view, by grounding the definition of health in the medical sciences, the components of the account are comparable and in a sense commensurable across humanity, embodying a 'global' point of view. It therefore allows, to a certain extent, international and interpersonal comparability providing measures and indicators of health and health capabilities for policy analysis.[3] I return to the health agency aspect of health capabilities in Chapter 6.

This model also has a dynamic and synergistic quality, recognizing the changing interaction of the individual with the broader social environment and the individual's ability to respond positively to changing socio-economic circumstances to achieve health potential. As such, it is useful in determining how we might go about assessing health policies and interventions.

This expanded model of health can form the foundation for prevention and treatment, and provides a workable distinction between health-related needs and the goods and services that address those needs. Central health capabilities require a set of key health-related provisions—individual health care goods and services (prevention, diagnosis, treatment, rehabilitation) promoting the capability for physical and mental functioning and a maximal and achievable lifespan; public health goods and services and social support services; and adequate nutrition as well as sanitary, safe living and working environments (Ruger 1998, pp. 108–12). As the scope of resource distribution broadens, it might be necessary to harmonize conflicting views at different levels, but these steps should occur incrementally.

It is worth clarifying here the difference between health capabilities that relate to health functionings and talents and skills that might be associated with the broader set of capabilities. Talents and skills reflect and impact individuals' accomplishments, overall achievements, and opportunities in life. At some level, talents and skills do affect one's health capabilities, and vice versa, but given the rather narrow focus of this analysis on health capabilities, the issue of differential talents and skills is not highly relevant. This issue did come up, however, in the fair equality of opportunity account (Daniels 1985). In the health capability paradigm, talents and skills are taken to be essentially constant or fixed—neither is the *direct* object of health policy actions or assessments. Health knowledge and health-related skills are appropriate foci, however, and health agency is critical (Ruger in press).

4.2. Equality, sufficiency, and priority

A theory of health and social justice must not only make claims about the central focal variable for equality, but also provide guiding principles (criteria) for the assessment of equality. Theories of social justice have put forth a number of normative principles for treating people as equals in society, which generally, though not exhaustively, fall into three broad categories: equality, sufficiency, and priority. An in-depth discussion of the strengths and weaknesses of these different approaches is beyond the scope of this book, but briefly taking Thomas Pogge's (2004) definitions as a guide, a given theory's correct criterion of social justice is either equalitarian (equality demanding or that a given society treats all people equal and none worse than others) or prioritarian (that gives greater weight to the relative gains and losses for the less advantaged persons or percentiles in a population) or sufficientarian (brings all individuals up to a given threshold, determined by society). Richard Arneson (2006) has similarly discussed these criteria in the context of examining the strengths and limitations of Nussbaum's sufficiency theory, and Rawls's difference principle (priority). He critiques both Nussbaum and Sen stating 'The Nussbaum and Sen approach can usefully be interpreted as sufficientarian... The nub of the difficulty with sufficiency is that it overstates the moral importance of sustaining each and every person at the "good enough" level' (Arneson 2006, p. 20). He refers to the so-called 'bottomless pit' objection (discussed in Chapter 8.8), noting concerns about setting the threshold. Elizabeth Anderson (1999) has focused on advancing a sufficiency oriented capability approach where all persons stand in relations of equality to others. Arneson critiques the capability threshold sufficientarian views for demonstrating little concern for inequalities above the threshold adequate level to function. The rather open and underspecified nature of the capability approach has left it vulnerable to such objections.

4.2.1. A hybrid account: measuring inequality in health policy

The view presented here, while eschewing a call for complete equality, is a hybrid of sufficiency and priority principles, since both are relevant for better understanding claims of justice pertaining to health. Sufficiency applies to health capability thresholds as goals, whereas priority applies to triage in achieving these goals. Shortfall equality is the primary methodology and standard of equality, bringing these together, as discussed in the following sections.

This book has reasoned that health capabilities should be the focal ethical variable for assessing health policy and that a subset of core health capabilities is central to examining the justice of health policies. A subset of functionings and associated health needs can serve both as an indicator and as a causal link to a central health capability set. The task now is to identify a suitable method for measuring inequality to judge public policies affecting health, to evaluate health policy (health care and public health), and to implement a right to health. A major factor in assessing individual disadvantage is how we conceptualize and measure inequality.

4.2.2. Attainment and shortfall equality

Equality can be classified as 'attainment equality' or 'shortfall equality'. For many decades scholars such as Ramsey, Atkinson, Dalton, and Musgrave, among others, have used shortfalls in the welfare-economic literature. The distinction between attainment and shortfall is important when assessing health capabilities. Attainment equality compares individuals according to *absolute levels of achievement*, whereas shortfall equality compares *shortfalls of actual achievement from the optimal average* (such as longevity or physical performance) (Anand and Sen 1994; Sen 1992; World Bank 1990). There are different reasons for taking each approach when assessing equality, and each measure is informative. Because attainment equality compares absolute achievement levels and disregards the maximal potential of individuals or groups, it limits society's obligation to address potential achievement. Additionally, much of the current work in health and health care disparities takes the form of inter group differences in health attainment or health care access. As such, health and health care indicators are stratified by income, education, social class, race, ethnicity, geographic location, and more (Ruger 2006b; 2006c; Ruger and Kim 2006). Attainment equality has the disadvantage of a '"leveling down" of all to the condition of the lowest achiever' (Parfit 2001; Sen, 1992, p. 93) in the group so that the attainment goal will be a '"low level equality" for all' (Sen 1992, p. 92), and many individuals will not realize their full potential.

Alternatively, the concept of shortfall equality can assess health capabilities, especially when equalizing achievements for different people is difficult. Human diversity can prevent some people from achieving maximal health and thus undermine the goal of equalizing maximal health levels potentially achievable by all. This approach might be particularly relevant for assessing the health capabilities of people with disabilities because it accounts for differences in the maximal potential for health functioning without 'levelling down' achievement goals of the entire group. It is also consistent with Aristotle's conception that an arrangement is best if it 'brings the people as close to good functioning as their natural circumstances permit' (Nussbaum 1990b, p. 155). Moreover, shortfall can be measured in either absolute or proportional terms, allowing proportional weighting for people with severe disabilities or, at the international level, weighting for countries with significant health deprivations (U.N. Development Program 2003). Shortfall equality is also more consistent with the emphasis on health as optimal functioning, 'a group's capacity to cope with all the circumstances of living . . . at an optimum level' and with 'freedom from the risk of disease' (Stedman 2000, pp. 789–90). Shortfall equality offers a promising way to evaluate health policies and health equity by whether they promote 'equal use of the *respective potentials*' (Sen 1992, p. 91). Because it illuminates inequities so clearly, this approach can also help justify having good health as an end goal of health policy (health care, public health, and health-related research), so long as we acknowledge that it is impossible to guarantee good health or equal health[4] to everyone. This approach thus resists standard utilitarian prescriptions of the goals of public health as maximizing to achieve as much population health as possible (Kass 2001; Roberts and Reich 2002). By focusing on reducing shortfall inequalities in individuals' health capabilities, this may over the long run lead to improved health at the group level, thus addressing both the maximization and distribution of health.

At the societal level, shortfall equality measures can assess quantitatively how much a given society has realized its health potential and how much remains unrealized, because they compare the actual achievement of a given public policy or health system (or limitations thereof) with the possible maximum. The typical unit of analysis for comparing countries is the nation state, though these measures can also compare groups within countries. This analysis focuses on the accomplishments of health systems and health policies in terms of inequities in health capabilities. It estimates what should be possible and how to prioritize resources in order to reduce the gap between achievements and potential. For example, a high prevalence of preventable death and disease (e.g. high rates of AIDS, TB, and malaria) would clearly imply that a group was falling short of its health potential and that public policies and the health sector were falling short of their obligations. Moreover, this analysis would focus expeditiously on eliminating clear injustices without the need to fully rank order among them. For example, one might say that if freedom from under five mortality and freedom from contracting AIDS are both deemed valuable, it is unnecessary at the first stage of ranking to determine the exact relative weights to attach to those freedoms. Having both freedoms is valuable; quantifying how valuable at this first stage is less important.

Also at the societal level, proportional reduction in shortfall can reveal inequality. Measurements of maximal average achievement would employ some reference points. For instance, the world's highest life expectancy is Japan's, at eighty-three years. This age could become the target against which to measure shortfall. The United Nations used this approach to compare life expectancies in different countries (UNDP 2001; 2003). When the target average life expectancy is eighty-three years, for example, the shortfall is reduced by a larger proportion when a population's average life expectancy changes from sixty to seventy years (a ten year reduction in a twenty-three year shortfall) than when it moves from thirty to forty years (a ten year reduction in a fifty-three year shortfall). Therefore, the proportional reductions in the two shortfalls would be 0.43 (10/23) and 0.19 (10/53), respectively. Such calculations assume that both populations are capable of reaching the target average life expectancy of eighty-three years. Using this standard, Sierra Leone has a shortfall of forty-three years, whereas Uruguay's shortfall is eight years. When the proportion of shortfall reduced is used as an indicator of improvement in life expectancy, it provides a measure of progress toward boosting health capabilities to certain levels. In the developing world especially, the shortfall must diminish considerably to reach the target of eighty-three years. Clearly, many countries are falling far short of their potential to maintain and improve the health of their populations or of different subgroups.

At the individual level, too, there is a case for assessing inequality in terms of shortfall, or even proportional shortfall, to permit functional comparisons between those with and without chronic illnesses or disability. This application must proceed with caution, however. Sen argues that 'in the case of serious disabilities, attainment equality may be hard to achieve, and it may be particularly tempting to opt for shortfall' (Sen 1992, p. 91). Later, he warns against applying the concept of shortfall equality too strictly. He notes that while:

a disabled person cannot, in any way, be given the freedom to enjoy the *same* level of the functioning in question...there is nevertheless a good case—based on fairness—for trying to *maximize* his...functioning ability, rather than settling for the same shortfall (absolute or proportionate) as others have from their—much higher—maximal functioning (Sen 1992, p. 91).

Thus, the goal at the individual level in this case is assessing the maximal potential functioning and reducing the gap or shortfall between realized and potential functioning.

From this perspective, in evaluating health policy and in implementing a right to health, we should be concerned with reducing inequalities in health capabilities among individuals and groups. Such concern accords with Aristotle's conception of political distribution, which requires the state to distribute the conditions allowing each individual to achieve the highest possible level of health functionings in order to choose and live a good life. This task aims to optimize every individual's health functioning. The lower the individual's ability for health functioning the greater the moral importance of raising it is. There is precedence for this type of prioritization in the way, for example, emergency departments triage and match individuals' health needs to services. The shortfall methodology offers a contrast to the utilitarian view, in which a person with a greater preference could have a greater claim than someone with a lower preference or to views where non-health related factors determine allocation priority.

Justice in health policy requires rules that allow a society to maintain and improve health capabilities in accordance with these principles. Thus, political activity should prioritize producing central health capabilities over non-central health capabilities, and this means central health capabilities for all. At the same time, it is also the case that there are limits to our obligations and these limits are manifested in the sense that no individual should be asked to sacrifice his or her own central health capabilities for the sake of another. For instance, one person should not be expected to die for the sake of another, this would be inconsistent with the goal of human flourishing and the central importance that freedom and practical reason play in enabling humans to live a flourishing life. Thus, while the health capability paradigm focuses on reducing shortfall inequality in the central health capabilities and this goal applies to all, it would be inconsistent with that line of reasoning to expect that a person should sacrifice her central health capabilities for the sake of another. In other words, no one person's central health capabilities are more or less valuable than another's, and as such, no one person can be used as a means to another person's ends. This limitation has a primary place in the Aristotelian line of reasoning due to the centrality of the human being as an end, with the capability for practical reason and affiliation. This conception of health and social justice is counter to utilitarian conceptions in which it would be plausible that a person with a higher utility—greater preference or desire—would have a greater claim than someone with a lower utility. Especially in wealthy societies that exist today, resources should be plentiful enough and efficiently allocated such that no individual need sacrifice her central health capabilities for the sake of another, thus deprivations in a person's central health capabilities for the sake of another are not acceptable under this theory.

What does follow from this political conception, however, is that non-central health capability sacrifices will have to be made (e.g. in the form of progressive taxation). These sacrifices are a common aspect of contemporary political economy and are often distributed in a way that is associated with the ability to sacrifice (e.g. progressive taxation in which those at the highest end of the income spectrum are able to, and expected to, pay more taxes in real and percentage terms than are those at lower ends of the spectrum). A comprehensive discussion of the way in which these sacrifices are distributed is beyond the scope of this book. Under this paradigm, however, sacrifices that an individual is expected to make in health policy end at the point at which that person is at risk of sacrificing his own set of central health capabilities. Under this theory, the central health capabilities are non-fungible, inalienable from the self for a price and thus trade-offs between people are unacceptable.

In summary here, the central health capabilities are prioritized with the aim of political planning in the face of scarce resources, over the non-central health capabilities and as such central health capabilities cannot be sacrificed for non-central health capabilities. For example, efforts to enhance the capability of a person to avoid premature mortality *should* receive priority over efforts to enhance the capability of a person to look more muscular (e.g. through cosmetic surgery to implant biceps). It would not be acceptable to prioritize non-central health capabilities, such as the capability to look more muscular, on the basis that someone desires it more than the central health capabilities. It is perfectly acceptable, and indeed in congruence with the Aristotelian/capability respect for human choice, to allow a person, once they have the capability to avoid premature mortality, to spend his own resources on enabling himself to look more muscular. Indeed, the very notion of capability and the underlying emphasis on human agency, respects the individual's choice to make those decisions in line with his view of the good life. Furthermore, justice in health policy requires that an ethical society determines principles and rules by which it is able to meet the obligation of enhancing the central health capabilities and that these principles reflect the non-fungibility of the central health capabilities.

As empirical evidence suggests, according to this conceptual framework, there are many injustices that currently exist in the distribution of central health capabilities. And justice in health requires efforts taken to reduce the inequalities in central health capabilities throughout the world, between regional populations (e.g. the north and the south, developed and developing countries), as well as the disparities that exist between different groups and classes within developing and developed countries, such as the United States.

Each society will have a slightly different set of guidelines for the distribution of resources in accordance with the overarching goal of reducing shortfall inequalities in its population's health capabilities. Each society will have a different ability to pay—a different total budget and different relative costs of necessary services. A poor society might have less to spend on services, but it might also need less to spend due to the lower costs of those services. Each society will have a different number of people who require services for maintaining and improving health capabilities. To the extent that a society has additional funds to allocate to enhancing the non-central health capabilities, it should establish a separate set of principles and rules by which to allocate funds in the domain of health capabilities.

This conception differs slightly from Rawls's maximin Difference Principle (a priority view). With reference to severe conditions (those with very low maximum possible achievements), for example, there is still the case from a shortfall point of view of reducing the gap between potential functioning and realized functioning. Rawls's application of the maximin principle to primary goods, meanwhile, aims to make the worst off as well off as possible (Rawls 1971, p. 153). However, Rawls does not provide guidance on the limits of justice in the face of intractable situations and his view allows health inequalities relative to a given threshold to go unaddressed. This differs from the relativist and proportional principles elaborated above, which in application would require reductions in health inequalities to the extent possible.

In short, this view suggests that our moral intuition about health and the ability to be healthy supports principles of justice focused on reducing shortfall inequalities in health capabilities; that these inequalities are unjust and that this hybrid principle integrating intuitions from commitments to equality, priority, and sufficiency fits suitably with how we ought to think about social justice as it applies in the domain of health policy. This view is likely consistent with those that make less, not more, of the differences among these theoretical alternatives, for example, Thomas Nagel argues that prioritarian views must ultimately take equality into account for social assessment (Nagel 1979).

4.3. Efficiency and health policy

Another key concept in the health capability paradigm is that efficiency concerns should temper the goals of equality. Efficiency guards against waste and effectively promotes objectives. While consistent with welfare economics in its focus on efficiency, this paradigm differs by *allowing efficiency principles to be applied to equity goals*. Thus, the nation state should strive for reducing shortfall inequality in health capabilities as efficiently as possible, using as few resources as possible. When choosing between two services that promote the same level of health capabilities, for example, it should select the least costly. This paradigm thus endorses the dual social obligations of equality and efficiency in health resource allocation. Because many of the necessary conditions for individuals to lead healthy lives are beyond the scope of the market to provide, state intervention and the assessment of state regulation and programmes are necessary.

Attempts to achieve optimal levels of health and reduce inequalities in individuals' abilities to be healthy with the fewest resources will require *a joint clinical and economic solution*. Under a health capability paradigm, risks, benefits, and costs must be weighed on at least two levels. At the societal level, citizens, physicians, and public health experts delineate a package of goods and services to which all individuals are entitled (Ruger 2006d). A stepwise approach first addresses equity, using clinical input to promote equality in individuals' ability to be healthy; then it addresses efficiency by using cost-minimization analysis and, in specific cases, cost-effectiveness analysis[5] as economic input in the decision-making process. This process differs from other efforts to address the efficiency-equity trade-off in health policy. Menzel, for example, argues for securing individual consent for different rationing options (Menzel 1990), whereas Rakowski supports employing hypothetical choice constructs such as the 'veil of ignorance' in making resource allocation decisions, arguing that individuals would choose random selection, with a caveat for age and prognosis (Rakowski 1993). The health capability paradigm's process, by contrast, is iterative and takes a variety of pragmatic turns employing complementary methodologies to address the competing social obligations of equality and efficiency. Empirical studies are finding increasingly that individuals tend to emphasize value of life rather than level of health benefit after treatment (e.g. capacity to benefit) in their ethical preferences. People are reluctant to deny treatment to individuals based on their benefit maximization. Erik Nord proposes an approach called the 'cost-value analysis' in which they employ equity weights to incorporate concerns for health severity in QALY calculations (Nord 1993a; Nord 1999).

At the individual level, individuals decide whether to choose a particular public health or medical intervention on the basis of full information about its risks and benefits. If individual health agency is complete at this level, input from physicians and public health experts can provide objective information for effective choice. Some efficiency gains might also result from expanding shared decision-making, which can decrease costs when individuals decide not to pursue a given treatment after weighing the risks and benefits. For example, use of appropriateness guidelines could reduce cost-ineffective care. A study that compared appropriateness ratings of coronary angiography after myocardial infarction (MI) made by an expert panel, with cost effectiveness ratings predicted by a decision-analytical model, found that the clinical scenarios considered appropriate by the expert panel were more cost-effective (average of $27,000 per QALY gained) than those deemed inappropriate by the panel (average of $54,000 per QALY gained) (Kuntz et al. 1999, p. 2246).

Demanding that resources be allocated in an efficient way reveals opportunities to shift resources within existing health budgets. An example of opportunities to redirect government spending from least to more efficient services arises in studying health policy in developing countries. As discussed above, the amount that a society should spend on health-related services (the total budget) is a function of the economic means of the society in addition to the relative costs of delivering those services and the needs of the population. In developing countries, despite the fact that most countries spend much less on health-related services than do developed countries, much of the burden of death and disease could be prevented, or cured inexpensively, by reallocating resources in a more efficient manner. Some time ago, for example, in a classic study of developing countries that still resonates today, the World Bank found that most government resources were allocated such that too much money 'goes to specialized care in tertiary facilities that provides little gain for the money spent. Too little goes to low-cost, highly effective programs such as control and treatment of infectious diseases and of malnutrition' (World Bank 1993, p. iii). The same report concluded that 'developing countries as a group could reduce their burden of disease by 25 per cent—the equivalent of averting more than 9 million infant deaths—by redirecting to public health programs and essential clinical services about half, on average, of the government spending that now goes to services of low cost-effectiveness', (e.g. interventions that depend on sophisticated hospitals and specialized physicians) (World Bank 1993, p. iii). The report suggested that much of the nearly $2 trillion devoted to health services in the developing world was wasted or used to help the more affluent. The critical and highly cost-effective services that require attention in improving health in developing countries included:

(1) immunizations,

(2) supplements of vitamin A and iodine,

(3) provision of drugs for school-age children suffering from schistosomiasis (bilharzia), intestinal worm infections, and deficiencies of vitamins and other micro-nutrients,

(4) preventing malaria, diarrhoea, respiratory illnesses such as tuberculosis and AIDS,

(5) reducing tobacco consumption, and

(6) essential clinical services.

Similarly, in the United States, a study of the costs of different health policy interventions in terms of life years saved found that primary preventions (e.g. interventions "designed to completely avert the occurrence of disease or injury") were more cost-effective (e.g. a median cost-effectiveness ratio of $5,000 per life year saved) than either secondary prevention (e.g. interventions "intended to slow, halt, or reverse the progression of disease or injury through early detection and intervention" with an incremental median cost-effectiveness ratio of $23,000 per life year saved) or tertiary prevention (e.g. "medical or surgical treatments designed to limit disability after harm has occurred, and to promote the highest attainable level of functioning among individuals with irreversible or chronic disease") (Tengs et al. 1995, pp. 369–90).

Efficiency is an important social concern due to the opportunity costs of misallocation. When resources are misallocated—when public money is spent on health interventions of high cost and low life year gain—the opportunities to reduce premature mortality and escapable morbidity and disability are reduced or are lost. In developing countries, money allocated to health interventions of low cost-effectiveness precludes spending on critical and highly cost-effective interventions, such as treatment of tuberculosis and sexually transmitted diseases (STDs). According to the World Bank, in some countries, 'a single teaching hospital can absorb 20 per cent or more of the budget of the ministry of health, even though almost all cost-effective interventions are best delivered at lower-level facilities (World Bank 1993, p. 4). This information reveals that opportunities exist to reallocate money within existing health budgets in health policy to primary prevention and facilities that are both critical to reducing shortfall inequalities in the central health capabilities—the capability to avoid premature mortality and the capability to avoid escapable morbidity—and is highly cost-effective in the use of valuable resources. Chapter 8 returns to these issues.

Nearly ten years later, the 2001 Commission on Macroeconomics and Health (CMH) report, 'Investing in Health for Economic Development', found that the poorest countries were disproportionately affected by preventable and curable disease. The Commission subsequently recommended massive scale-ups of health investments (WHO 2001). The Commission also found that most of the world's health deficits were attributable to HIV and AIDS, malaria, TB, maternal and infant diseases, tobacco-related illness, malnutrition, and vaccine-preventable childhood diseases such as pneumonia, diarrhoea, and measles, which accounted for 14 million deaths per year for people under sixty years, and mostly occurred in developing countries. The Commission argued that a scale-up of essential interventions and making them available worldwide could save 8 million lives each year, translatable to 330 million DALYs, by 2010 and provide a measurable way of reducing poverty and ensuring economic growth and security (WHO 2003, pp. 13–14).

4.4. Ethics of the social determinants of health

A major goal of the health capability paradigm is to reduce inequalities in individuals' ability to achieve health-related functionings. Although many factors influence health, health policy (health care, public health, and health-related research) continues to be one of its most influential determinants. Therefore, public policy that attempts to address a particular population's and individual's shortfall from optimal health should rest on objective data about factors contributing to that shortfall, and the study should include a number of public policy domains.[6] We have an obligation to enhance the central health capabilities of all individuals and the means and resources by which we are able to do so may very well go beyond the reach of health policies, extending into the realm of other policy domains. Indeed, counter to other approaches that claim that the social determinants of health work through an unique causal pathway such as autonomy (Marmot 2005) and those that criticise such a view for failing to successfully link the social determinants of health to a normative theory (Courtwright 2008), this book's approach recognizes that there are multiple factors and policies that affect health and disparities in health's domains. This obligation is expansive, making health a goal not only of health policy, but also of other policies that affect it. This is a wider-reaching claim that has substantial importance to the assessment of health and other policies. Thus, the central health capabilities should be an objective not only of health policies, but of all policies that affect these capabilities.

The analysis should include the scope, interaction, and policy influence of different policy domains—including education, social welfare, environmental protection, and housing—which influence health. Although a number of additional policy domains impact health, this book does not, however, extend the traditional boundaries of health policy to include, for example, employment policy. Nor does it endorse the adoption of major non-health policy measures whose impact on *all* possible outcome measures is undetermined. It just would not be feasible to attempt to achieve threshold levels on multiple domains of well-being simultaneously as the moral requirements of public health and health policy, nor is it clear that we want to prioritize by socio-economic status or disadvantage in the domain of health care (Powers and Faden 2006). Public health, health policy, and health-related research cannot be responsible for all aspects of well-being: this proposal is too expansive. The health capability paradigm does recognize a relationship between health policy and other public policies affecting health, but it regards these domains as distinct and defines health capabilities as the central goal of health policy. This approach is applicable to all countries, but is particularly relevant to developing countries, where many determinants of health lie outside the health care system. Moreover, we are far from understanding the precise societal mechanisms that influence health or how to weight different social objectives. Thus, even in light of existing information on health's social determinants, it is unwise to attempt to improve health with sweeping non-health policies. For example, arguments for completely flattening socio-economic inequalities, advanced by some (Daniels et al. 2000), cloud rather than clarify the means and ends of health policy, and diminish our ability to evaluate public policy's impact on health. The multilayered complexities of these issues muddy the health policy waters. As Frances Kamm (2001) notes, for instance, it would be necessary to compare health gains from economic growth associated with social inequality with health gains from complete social equality in order to fully understand the net effects of these alternatives. Others have listed a series of problems associated with eliminating all socio-economic inequalities (Anand and Peter 2000; Angell 2000; Emanuel 2000; Gakidou et al. 2000; Marmor 2000; Starfield 2000) and the need for a general theory of distributional justice (Marchand et al. 1998). By distinguishing direct and indirect approaches to justice and social determinants, some critique that, 'this view relies on the premise—not made explicit by the authors—that inequalities in health are unjust if, and only if, they are the result of unjust social arrangements' (Anand and Peter, 2000, p. 50). For evaluations that include the social determinants of health, a complete comparison of a number of different objectives in addition to health is in order. Such evaluations are beyond the scope of the current work.

Several distinctions can help clarify how these complex matters should be considered within an overall theory of social justice (Ruger 2004b). The first is the distinction between varying objectives of health policy. This book develops and defends the use of a particular objective—health capability—for assessing justice and efficiency in health policy.

The second distinction is between health policy and other policies (e.g. housing or income policy), even though they are not independent. Thus, it is important to clarify, first what health policy is and is not, and second, the distinctiveness of other policies (e.g. income, housing, or employment policy) that also can affect health and health capability.

A third distinction is between supplementing and replacing domain-specific criteria in policy assessment. On the one hand, the assessment of other policy domains (e.g. employment policy) could be improved by supplementing traditional effectiveness criteria with indicators that take their effects on health into account. Alternatively, the other policy domains (e.g. economic policies) could be assessed by measuring *only* their impact on health. The first approach is more rational.

This book defines health policy to include public health, pharmaceuticals, health-related research (including biomedical and genetic research) and treatments, individual health care services, and outreach and community-based health services. It excludes policies, such as income, economic, tax, housing, or employment policies that touch on health but are not central. In addressing the social determinants of health within a theory of health and social justice, these policy domains should remain as they are; their effects on health should be taken into account, without redefining health policy or extending the traditional boundaries of health policy. Employment indicators, for example, cannot always serve as health indicators because unemployment does not pose the same health risk to a wealthy person who chooses not to work as to a person who has no other source of income. Thus, unemployment can be a precursor to depression, which can lead to suicide. However, employment carries its own risks. For instance, workers who work in environments that are highly stressful and offer them little control may develop depression, anxiety, high blood pressure, or a suppressed immune system, all of which raise the risk for illness and death. Studies have shown that workers in high-demand, low-control job situations experience greater depression, anxiety, and are at higher risk of developing and dying from cardiovascular disease than those not in such situations (Amick et al. 1995; Karasek and Theorell 1990). Thus, traditional employment statistics do not reveal the full situation. Unemployment, or employment *per se*, should not be identified with health in a linear way, instead, it is necessary to determine how employment status affects a particular person's health. The distinction between employment and health policy is important for maintaining the strength of both policy domains (e.g. employment policy is about employment and it should continue as a policy domain focused on improving employment prospects even after taking note of the effects of employment on health, while health policy should be focused on improving health). This distinction is important for maintaining the strengths of both policy domains.

It therefore makes sense to maintain the traditional criteria of a given policy domain (e.g. employment rates for employment policy, knowledge outcomes for education policy) and to *supplement* those indicators with measurements of that domain's effects on health, as when assessing the effects of employment status on a person's health. A final example is useful for illustrating the importance of the three distinctions above—the case of smoking, especially during pregnancy, among low-income uneducated women.

Traditional smoking cessation interventions face barriers when offered to low-income and underserved women because they may be unable to give necessary attention to smoking's role in a broader life context (Emmons 2000; Emmons et al. 2000; Floyd et al. 1993; Romano et al. 1991; Sexton and Hebel 1984; Windsor et al. 1985; Woodard and Edouard 1992). For these women, smoking cessation may not be a priority in light of other pressing life issues (such as unemployment, hunger, and housing). These women tend to have insufficient knowledge and beliefs regarding the harmful effects of smoking on the foetus. Programmes that have been successful in influencing smoking quit rates among this group have focused on socio-economic needs around basic life issues (e.g. unemployment, food, and housing) in addition to attempting to educate individuals about risks. These women may also be unaware of how cost-effective smoking cessation can be (Ruger et al. 2008; Ruger and Emmons 2008). Education is one of the strongest factors in prenatal and perinatal care. While these more multidimensional smoking cessation interventions may be helpful in improving quit rates during pregnancy, relapse is problematic, as is the threat of death and disease from related causes. These programmes are part of the answer, but they are not the only answer. Regardless of efforts to reduce smoking during pregnancy, the environment and behaviours of low-income women will still pose a risk to their own and their children's health. Smoking during pregnancy might be averted in these situations through a number of other changes. One aspect of the solution might involve increasing the individual's power to choose a healthy life through education and employment policies. Education and the prospects for earning a good income and entering an occupation that commands respect could possibly avert pregnancy altogether. Social and economic policies—a well-developed educational system with high literacy rates that endows men and women with analytical skills—can better the position of low-income and minority women in any society. In these cases, the success of education and employment programmes should be assessed in light of their eventual effects on health. Including health measures allows different employment approaches to be assessed in terms of health. A more adequate understanding of health requires examining the pathways through which it is influenced.

Ultimately an integrated approach to public policy is required (Ruger 2005a). The health capability paradigm reconceptualizes the social determinants of health from a causal, reductionist model of multilevel pathways of linear and hierarchical influence to a complex system of factors in which heterogeneity and endogeneity are central. The policy prescription is to assess the whole system with health capability at its core (Ruger in press).

Ethics of the social determinants of health come together at the individual level—the social determinants of health can be operating both exogenously and endogenously on health capabilities—indeed individual health capabilities may themselves be socially dependent. While this book does not entirely reject the 'separate spheres of justice' argument because it does require taking into account other social policies, it does take a more modified view, cautioning against taking all of human flourishing and its determinants as the focal space for evaluations of justice and health. This account relies heavily on the results of social scientific and epidemiological research to add to our understanding of priority areas. More epidemiological and social scientific research is necessary (House 2002; Krieger 2007). Without a full analysis of the multiple and leveled factors affecting any given person at the individual level, it is impossible to say with certainty or exactitude that some social determinants are more important than others at the supra-individual level.

4.5. Limitations and objections

4.5.1. Capability, not opportunity or utility

Although there has been no previous systematic analysis of the implications of the capability approach for health policy, health, or health care, prior to this work, some have inferred how various aspects of the approach might reveal themselves in particular health care contexts. These conjectures have created a need for both critical review and further clarification. While this attention raises the profile of the capability approach and highlights its potential relevance to public policy and social justice, existing objections betray a limited understanding of the approach and how it might be applied to health policy, health, and health care.

One criticism of the capability approach posits the model as just one of many versions of an equality of opportunity approach to health care, while claiming that it prescribes a 'broader role for health care' than other such approaches (Sabin and Daniels 1994, p. 10). For example, critics claim that the capability approach 'holds that the distribution of personal capabilities like confidence, resilience, and sociability in the natural lottery should not be taken as a given' (Sabin and Daniels 1994, p. 10) and that health care 'should strive to give people equal personal capabilities, or at least give priority to those whose diminished capability (whatever the cause) puts them at a relative disadvantage' (Sabin and Daniels 1994, p. 10). It is also suggested that 'the capability model makes no moral distinction between treatment of illness and enhancement of disadvantageous personal capabilities' (Sabin and Daniels 1994, p. 10). These authors prefer a normal function model derived from fair equality of opportunity, which they regard as less expansive than the capability model. The latter, they argue, 'cast[s] too broad a net and pose[s] severe problems for administration and cost' (Sabin and Daniels 1994, p. 11). Under their interpretation, the capability approach would justify alleviating disadvantages such as normal shyness and extreme shortness.

The capability approach has also been defined as one form of an equality of opportunity approach by its supposed genetic implications. In their work on genetics and justice, Buchanan et al. (2000) offer three models of the relationship between equal opportunity and health care goals:

(1) the Normal Function Model;
(2) the Equal Capabilities Model; and
(3) the Equal Opportunity for Welfare Model.

They argue that 'each can be read as a different gloss on the scope of our concerns about equality of opportunity' (Buchanan et al. 2000, p. 125). They add, 'If we think that concerns about equal opportunity should guide the design of a health care system, then each leads us to a different view of our obligations to assist others through health care services, including genetic interventions' (Buchanan et al. 2000, p. 125). While this chapter is not directly concerned with models (1) and (3) above, which seem to represent two different interpretations of an equality of opportunity approach to health care, it takes issue with the authors' assertion that the capability approach is an interpretation of a broader equality of opportunity account. This misunderstanding results in an inaccurate definition and classification of the capability approach and its implications.

Labelling the capability approach as an 'equal capabilities model' (Buchanan et al. 2000, p. 130) misses a central tenet of the approach. As noted elsewhere, the capability approach does not naively expect to achieve equal capabilities for all. Instead, it advocates giving everyone 'equal consideration in *some* space' (Sen 1992, p. 3) and evaluates inequality in terms of the freedom to achieve. Capability comparisons are also generally incomplete (Sen 1992, p. 7) and inequality can be measured in terms of shortfall inequality or attainment equality but rarely full equality. The principle of 'equal consideration for all may demand very unequal treatment in favour of the disadvantaged' (Sen 1992, p. 1). And reducing inequality in one domain may increase it in another.

A second point is that the capability concept differs from the concept of opportunity. Both Sabin and Daniels (1994) and Buchanan et al. (2000) classify the equal capabilities model as an interpretation of the equal opportunities model. Buchanan and colleagues note that 'Sen views this account as an explication of the idea of "positive freedom," but it is not implausible to view it as an account of equality of opportunity' (Buchanan et al. 2000, p. 131). They add that 'we have equality of opportunity when our capability sets are equal' (Buchanan et al. 2000, p. 131). Other objections posit that the capability approach is nothing more than another variety of resource-based or welfare-based theories (Dworkin 2000; Pogge 2002b; Roemer 1996). These statements miss the core idea of the capability approach: a demand that human diversity should be considered when policies are being evaluated. They also fail to recognize the difference between opportunity and capability. Sen has, in fact, addressed this difference:

'Equality of opportunities' does not amount to anything like equality of *overall* freedoms. This is so because of (1) the fundamental diversity of human beings, and (2) the existence and importance of various means (such as income or wealth) that do not fall within the purview of standardly defined 'equality of opportunities' (Sen 1992, p. 7).

Indeed, one can turn the debate around as Sen notes, 'a more adequate way of considering "real" equality of opportunities must be through equality of capabilities (or through the elimination of unambiguous inequalities in capabilities, since capability comparisons are typically incomplete)' (Sen 1992, p. 7). Moreover, although there may be difficulties in operationalizing or measuring functionings and capabilities, their distinctiveness for a theory of health and social justice in terms of what individuals are able to do and be are tantamount and the health capability paradigm's emphasis on health capabilities as health functioning and health agency addresses valid concerns about arbitrariness and subjectivity in evaluation. Health capabilities, for example, are distinct from health utilities or happiness and unlike utilitarianism, utilities are not the sole focal variable for evaluating justice. Welfare in terms of subjective psychological states of happiness, pleasure, or utility, can thus be distinguished from what individuals are able to do or be.

A third and related problem lies in Sabin and Daniels's claim that the capability approach 'would use health care to help people become *equal* competitors, free from disadvantageous lack of capabilities regardless of etiology' (Sabin and Daniels 1994, p. 10). In their view, it would support the financing and provision of, for example, fluoxetine, so as to give 'the introvert the social skills of a salesman' (Kramer 1993, p. xv; Sabin and Daniels 1994, p. 10). On the contrary, the health capability paradigm presented here would hold that the central goal of health policy and thus health care is to maintain and improve health through its objective of reducing inequalities in the central health capabilities. None of the arguments in the capability approach more broadly, nor the health capability paradigm more specifically, equates personal traits, such as shyness, with health. As argued in Chapter 8, the meaning of medical necessity put forth by the account is consistent with this view.

A fourth problem appears in the claim by Buchanan and colleagues that what they call the 'equal capabilities model' cannot be translated into an 'account of the goals of health care' (Buchanan et al. 2000, p. 131). They note that:

if we could simply translate this claim[7] about equality of opportunity into an account of the goals of health care—which we shall argue we cannot—then those goals would be dramatically expanded from the limits set by the normal functioning rationale discussed earlier (Buchanan et al. 2000, p. 131).

They add that,

health care would now have as its task the goal of reconstructing people in ways that make their capabilities more equal. With this expansion, there would simply be no point in drawing a line between treatments and enhancements. Society would be just as obliged to enhance the capabilities . . . as to keep people functioning as close to normally as possible (Buchanan et al. 2000, p. 131–2).

Contrary to these claims, as we shall see in the following chapters, the health capability paradigm would not dramatically expand the goals of health care beyond health capabilities and thus health, nor would health care have the task of enhancing capabilities to make people more equal. The distinction between central and non-central health capabilities, though not the same as that between treatment and enhancement, helps set priorities for societal obligations.

A fifth point involves efficiency. While previous explanations of the capability approach have not been very specific about 'what justice requires us to do' (Buchanan et al. 2000, p. 132) to promote efficiency, the health capability paradigm does offer a systematic framework for addressing the competing claims of equality and efficiency that the just health care model or normal functioning model does not. Buchanan and colleagues make the widely accepted claim that 'a theory of justice requires integrating concerns for equality with concerns for liberty and efficiency.' They add that 'Sen does not discuss how this reconciliation of justice and efficiency would take place in a theory of justice' (Buchanan et al. 2000, p. 132). And they contrast Sen's way of dealing with this tension with that of Rawls, stating that 'Rawls . . . does attempt a particular reconciliation' by taking 'some natural distribution of talents and skills as a baseline' and then mitigating the effects of 'basic, residual inequality by requiring that inequalities in primary social goods like wealth and income be constrained so that they work to the advantage of those with the worst prospects in life' (Buchanan et al. 2000, p. 132). However, quite to the contrary, in addition to Sen's discussions, which place a high value on efficiency concerns (Sen 1999), the health capability paradigm presented here provides a strong framework for grappling with the tension between equality and efficiency through a stepwise, cost-minimization and cost-effectiveness strategy that employs analytical tools from inequality assessment and economic analysis. The fair equality of opportunity account has no such solution to efficiency problems. Again, the heath capability paradigm states that efficiency in health policy requires providing the highest attainable quality but with the fewest resources possible. This solution is discussed further in Chapter 8.

A sixth point involves statements by Buchanan and colleagues that Sen's 'approach to ranking differences in capabilities' ultimately leads to '"incommensurability" in the sense that these sets are ranked differently by people with different conceptions of what is good in life' (Buchanan et al. 2000, p. 133). They add that 'because of this, our commitment to pursuing equality of capabilities is seriously limited, since for a substantial range of capabilities, there is no common basis for determining what increases the equality of those sets' (Buchanan et al. 2000, pp. 133–4).

While the general point regarding incommensurability is indeed problematic for any theory that involves interpersonal comparison in any space (including a theory of equality of opportunity that is further specified than the one offered by the authors), the critique misses central tenets of both the broader capability approach and the health capability paradigm. A first tenet is the emphasis in social evaluation on 'reasoned "consensus" on weights, or at least on a range of weights' and hence public discussion (Sen 1999, pp. 78–9). A second tenet is the emphasis on 'partial ranking'[8] and 'incompleteness' in evaluation (Sen 1999, p. 81–4). A third is the previously noted difference between 'total comparison', involving the ranking of all vectors, and '"distinguished capability comparison," involving the comparison of some particular capability chosen as the focus, without looking for completeness of coverage' (Sen 1999, p. 82). A fourth tenet involves, in the case of the health capability paradigm, the distinction between central and non-central health capabilities and also the ability to separate out a core set of capabilities. Individual and collective rational decisions usually have to be made among incommensurate alternatives. The health capability paradigm has grappled with this issue by supporting the idea of higher-order values, but it does not endorse lexical ordering that protects certain values against *all* trade-offs. Practically, it develops a distinction between central and non-central health capabilities. The main objective of health policy, and thus health care, is to reduce inequalities in central health capabilities—to prevent, ameliorate, and treat premature death and preventable morbidity that impedes individuals from reaching the optimal human ability for health. By contrast, neither Buchanan and colleagues nor Sabin and Daniels, despite their criticisms, provide a satisfactory analysis of how the incommensurability problem in health care should be handled.

At the end of their critique, Buchanan and colleagues conclude that, while they see the 'equal capabilities model' as more closely associated with the more expansive 'brute luck view' of equal opportunity, which calls for a complete levelling of the playing field in terms of opportunities,[9] they also see some convergence among 'the equal capabilities model' and the 'normal functioning model'. Unfortunately, they fall short of providing systematic analysis or rationale for this conclusion and much of their argumentation supports the divergence, rather than convergence, between capability and opportunity.

Briefly, there are also more recent attempts to equate or suggest the compatibility between capability and utility. Specifically, these efforts purport that traditional utility measures such as QALYs or DALYs (discussed in Chapter 1) can quantitatively represent capability for health or medical evaluation (Anand 2005; Birch and Gafni 2003; Cookson 2005). These efforts incorrectly equate utilities with capabilities—QALYs have their theoretical foundations in the welfare economic emphasis on individual preferences, desires, or satisfaction fulfilment, whereas capabilities are theoretically grounded in capability theory which focuses on what individuals are able to do and be.

4.5.2. Other critiques and objections

Before moving on, let me note some of the more general criticisms of the Aristotelian and capability perspectives. Like other philosophical perspectives, these views have limitations and have been the object of several types of objections. One of the most common criticisms of the capability approach is that it cannot be operationalized because it fails to provide a complete list of valuable functionings and a definitive account of the good life (Cohen 1993; Gasper 1997a; 1997b; Qizilbash 1996a; 1996 b; Roemer 1994; 1996; Scanlon 1993; Sugden 1993; Williams 1987; Ysander 1993) or to define the elements of life that seem to have validity for *all* human beings.[10]

These critics seem to attribute the absence of such a list to lack of agreement. The capability approach falls 'short of providing an adequate foundation for a new paradigm of development' (Qizilbash 1996a, p. 1209), some claim. They argue that Nussbaum's Aristotelian account of human flourishing is more robust than Sen's capability approach because Nussbaum offers a unique list of capabilities (Qizilbash 1996a, p. 1214). However, they do not entirely espouse Nussbaum's view either. Thus, they argue, somewhat inconsistently, that Aristotle's unique view of the good life is too singular and that it may be impossible for any external source to validate such a view. They also assert that, while it may be possible to form a consensus around Nussbaum's list of capabilities, that alone is not enough to operationalize the approach (Qizilbash 1996a, p. 1215). The same is said for the capability approach, because it does not allow us to assess whether one person's capability is better or worse than another's. Thus far, those who express these criticisms have not provided an acceptable alternative (Alkire and Black 1997; Crocker 1995; Gasper 1997a; 1997b; Qizilbash 1996a; 1996b).

A second and related line of criticism argues that the capability approach is incommensurable in that it 'fails to give a complete account of interpersonal comparisons' (Qizilbash 1996b, p. 147). The concern here, as noted previously, is that it may not be possible to compare one person's capability gain or loss with another's, or to compare gains and losses across different domains of capability (Beitz 1986; Nussbaum 1986; Qizilbash 1996a; Sen 1982). People have conflicting and incommensurable values and views of human capabilities. However, we have already seen that the problem of incommensurable human values is not unique to the capability approach or to Nussbaum's view but is problematic for any theory involving interpersonal comparisons in any space. This conundrum is part of the ongoing debate about whether any one scale can assess human values.[11] The use of functionings, however, in combination with a rational process for selecting, weighting, and evaluating the impact of policies on individuals' functionings, helps in part to address the concerns of interpersonal comparisons, because functionings are more objective than preferences or utilities.

A third set of criticisms focuses more precisely on the subjectivity of the capability approach, arguing that Sen has 'made his theory less of an *objective* one' by including happiness and self-respect as functionings in the theory (Roemer 1994, p. 556). They level the same criticism at other approaches as well (Roemer 1994). A distinction must be made, however, between subjective judgements of states of affairs (e.g. utility of preferences) and observing individuals' happiness. These critics do note the value of the capability approach in distinguishing itself from welfarist and resourcist accounts of justice, especially the approaches of Rawls (primary goods) and Dworkin (equality of resources).

A fourth area of criticism centres on the issue of responsibility. The critique favours a view of egalitarianism that treats people according to whether they are responsible for their state of well-being (Roemer 1994). 'Ethically cogent egalitarianism recommends equalizing outcomes for people insofar as those outcomes flow from causes for which the person cannot be held responsible, but allowing differences in outcome insofar as they flow from causes for which the person should be deemed responsible' (Roemer 1994, p. 556). The capability approach certainly does hold people partly responsible for the life they choose to lead—the set of valuable functionings they ultimately choose—but it says less about responsibility for their state of well-being. Generally speaking, the health capability paradigm presented here does not differentiate among people *solely* in terms of responsibility for a given health state. That said, if the effectiveness of certain measures varies by the causality of a given health condition, such factors are taken into account. Moreover, responsibility is a central feature of the health capability paradigm (Chapter 6).

A fifth set of criticisms focuses on three main drawbacks of the capability approach as applied to the ethics of economic development:

(a) the need to incorporate 'in capability thinking greater attention to human capacity for self-extension and self-transformation';

(b) the need to build on 'experiences of grass-roots, local group action to develop collective capabilities'; and

(c) the need to better understand 'the ideal of limitless material opulence, in its own right and also build the case for releasing resources for capability development on a global scale' (Gasper and Cameron 2000, p. 986).

All three concerns stem from the belief that terms like capability and freedom are too ambiguous and vague[12] to deal with the real deprivation and powerlessness that people around the world experience. These critics argue that the capability approach must be broadened ('to cover opulence not only poverty'), deepened (to enrich its conceptions of persons and capabilities), and extended to more adequately include the human, social, and political aspects of human development (Cameron 2000; Carmen 2000; Gasper and Cameron 2000, p. 988; Giri 2000). A related concern is that the approach is not relevant for both rich and poor countries because it is concerned primarily with 'development in terms of liberation from, or removal of, the most extreme forms of deprivation' (Qizilbash 1996b, p. 158). However, the analysis presented in this book demonstrates the appropriateness of the health capability paradigm more specifically for *both* higher- and lower-income countries. It is possible to provide a basis for a consensual view of health in the midst of pluralism (containing aspects of health that are essential for anyone) *and* still allow for some aspects of health to vary with differing conceptions of the good life. In the health capability paradigm, it is not necessary to address the issue of a broader substantive account of well-being or quality of life. Thus, one need not make a 'total comparison' and compare *all* vectors of capability. Moreover, it is well recognized that deprivation exists even in the wealthiest of societies (Sen 1992; 1999).

No theory or perspective is without its objections and limitations. However, both the more general capability approach and the more specific health capability paradigm promise new insights in the field of social ethics. The chapters that follow address the more specific issues that arise when the health capability paradigm is applied to policy analysis.

4.6. Principles of the health capability paradigm

The health capability paradigm integrates elements of alternative conceptions (e.g. consequentialism and autonomy) in an effort to address unresolved disagreement about the right or the good. Consequently, it favours justice and health policies that, while not necessarily perfect or ideal, are 'mutually acceptable to people whose preferences diverge' (Scanlon 1975, p. 668).

To promote the good life, the health capability paradigm values avoiding disease and premature death and emphasizes prevention and treatment, favouring those below the maximum average over those above it. It also emphasizes individual health agency and supports efforts to improve health for individuals so that they have the mental and physical ability required for agency. Moreover, it values cost-minimization analysis and a restricted use of cost-effectiveness analysis (CEA) as discussed in Chapter 8. Restricting the use of CEA to within group comparisons obviates the need to compare and thus weight interventions across disease states, which ultimately leads to interpersonal comparison problems (as with the use of league tables) and discrimination against those with severe disabilities. Additionally, the approach emphasizes shared governance at the policy, health policy, and individual levels. This rational, evidence-based deliberative process involves individuals and physician-experts.

To reiterate then, the following principles undergird the health capability paradigm:

(1) Health is justified as the objective of health policy both indirectly from the Aristotelian philosophical foundation of human flourishing and directly from Aristotle's conception that health is the end of medicine.[13]

(2) Health care and other resources are not considered ends. Their value is primarily instrumental,[14] as a means to the end of good health.

(3) Justice in health policy should be assessed in terms of health capabilities (which include health functioning and health agency), rather than health achievements alone, and equality in health policy should be measured in terms of shortfall equality—a comparison of the 'shortfalls' of actual achievement from the optimal average achievements.

(4) Justice in health policy requires allocating differential resources and circumstances to different people in order to advance shortfall equality—to attempt to obtain similar levels of shortfalls in actual achievement from optimal average achievements—for all. Differential resources and circumstances are required to achieve this objective due to the *heterogeneity* in internal and external human characteristics.

(5) In terms of prioritization among health capabilities, some health capabilities are more central than others. These are the capability to

avoid premature death and the capability to avoid escapable morbidity (disease, dysfunction, deformity, malnutrition, disability, etc.), all deviations from good functioning. These health capabilities should be taken as prior to other health capabilities. The selection and valuation of all other health capabilities (non-central capabilities) should be left open to be selected and weighted through a public discussion and public process of a joint scientific and deliberative approach or to be addressed through the free market mechanisms. There is a certain amount of agreement on the tremendous importance of types of fundamental, central health capabilities and associated health needs. They are wholly consistent with what medicine and health policy prioritize at a practical level. They do not necessarily require full epistemological understanding, or a fully theorized agreement about this prioritization.

(6) The selection and weighting of health capabilities can be based on an iterative process of dominance partial ordering. A complete ordering of health capabilities is not demanded. Instead, justice requires ensuring certain fundamental and crucially important capabilities and functionings—the central health capabilities—to certain levels before addressing the inequalities in the non-central health capabilities. Thus, the theory provides a complete and determinant prioritization on the partial ordering of central health capabilities above non-central health capabilities as a substantive moral constraint on health-related resources.

(7) The selection and weighting of the non-central health capabilities shall be done at a subsequent stage—sequentially and iteratively— to expand the focal ethical space for evaluating health policy through a public process of extending partial orderings. Tweaking a complete ordering with perfect precision is not required. The market can also help prioritize non-central capabilities.

(8) In terms of health policy evaluation, health capabilities are measured by using observable data on health functionings to get a partial view of health capabilities (freedoms) and to get a sense of humans' ability for health. Health capabilities map onto the definition and operationalization of health and can be defined narrowly or broadly ranging from the most fundamental capabilities—avoiding premature death and escapable morbidity (disease, dysfunction, deformity, malnutrition, disability, etc.)—to

more complex functionings, such as the capability to take part in the life of the community and to engage in various forms of social interaction. For the practical purposes of health policy evaluation in this paradigm, the specifications of health capabilities, health functionings, and health needs follow the conceptualization of health noted above.

(9) The set of health functioning indicators of central health capabilities include, for example, life expectancy, mortality (at all ages), prevalence of disease, disability, dysfunction, deformity, malnutrition, and genetic mapping. These indicators are rooted in the empiricism of both health care and public health and are thus consistent with the scientific definition of health. We must look to science, education, research, and practice for guidance in specifying these indicators. Health agency is discussed in Chapter 6 and elsewhere (Ruger in press).

(10) Inequalities in functionings shed light on inequalities in respective capabilities and provide a basis for assessing health capability inequalities.

(11) Equality in health policy should be measured in terms of shortfall equality and not just attainment equality (equality in health outcomes). Justice in health policy requires allocating resources and circumstances to reduce shortfall inequalities (as opposed to attainment equality) in health capabilities. The theory supports the use of shortfall equality rather than attainment equality because the latter requires equal absolute levels of achievement (equal health outcomes), which are impossible to achieve, while the former targets the equal use of respective potentials— attempting to reduce the shortfall from an optimal average level or target of health outcomes. Implementing this goal requires establishing goals and guaranteeing health related goods and services to reduce the shortfall from an optimal average or specified level of health functioning.

(12) Choice, severity, and temporal considerations are important for assessing the moral significance of health capability inequalities. Inequalities in health capabilities are thus unjust if they represent a shortfall from the optimal standard and can be prevented, avoided, or ameliorated. The larger the shortfall (greater severity) the more unjust such inequalities are (greater moral weight and urgency). Moreover, individual choice must be evaluated in terms of shortfall

inequalities in health capabilities as well—in individual health agency—to more precisely understand whether health inequalities exist as a matter of constrained or unconstrained effective (option) freedom (choice). Acceptance of the *current* inability to diagnose, treat, or prevent certain health inequalities does not by that very nature render those health inequalities just (not unjust) since the moral relevance of claiming such health inequalities unjust can have significant influence on the development of medical technologies and alternative treatments (e.g. through health-related research) that will at some future point render such health inequalities preventable and treatable. Moreover, health inequalities caused by diseases with a genetic orientation require our moral attention consistent with these principles and through interventions (genetic or otherwise) to reduce shortfall inequalities in the health capabilities of current and future generations.

(13) Efficiency in health policy requires obtaining this objective with the highest attainable quality, but with the fewest resources possible. Thus, in the health capability paradigm, the demands of efficiency in health policy require that the government promote shortfall equality in health capabilities, beginning with the promotion of shortfall equality in central health capabilities, as efficiently as possible, using as few resources as possible. This implies that cost-minimization should guide resource allocation.

(14) In terms of how much priority should be given to achieving a given threshold level of health capabilities, justice requires the explicit aim of reducing shortfall inequalities in central health capabilities above non-central health capabilities up to the point at which all individuals have reached the given standard defined by the optimal average. Demands of redistribution are, however, pursued only up to the point at which another person's central health capabilities below the threshold would be threatened. No individual should be required to sacrifice her central health capabilities for the sake of another; sacrifices should come from outside the realm of central health capabilities. Applying principles of efficiency to this equity goal allows priority to go to all those below the threshold, including the worst off with greater moral urgency, but requires the minimization of the costs of achieving this objective. The threshold level for evaluating shortfall equality

is an optimal or maximal absolute average level, not a decent minimum, absolute minimum or basic minimum. Moreover, while group differences are important for policy and public health purposes, assessing individual disadvantage is the most morally relevant criterion of justice.

The chapters that follow will further elucidate and apply these principles.

Notes

1. The broader concept of needs is difficult to fully determine without ambiguity. For some clarification, the definition of need characterized by Beauchamp and Childress as a material principle of justice is useful (Beauchamp and Childress 1994, pp. 329–30). In their work, Beauchamp and Childress note that a person needs something when its absence affects the person detrimentally. Fundamental needs are differentiated from non-fundamental needs. Fundamental needs are roughly equivalent to basic needs. Through their link to health capabilities, health needs—particularly the most fundamental or basic needs—are justified, specified, and further refined into a basis for justice and resource allocation in health policy.
2. See Ruger (in press) for conceptual model, profile, and index of health capability.
3. Some might argue that any effort to come up with a universal notion of the good is perfectionism. Such efforts also cause concern for cultural reasons. Arneson (2000; 2006), for example, argues that the capability approach is a perfectionist theory of the good. The inclination here is to agree with Nussbaum who defends a more moderate form of perfectionism and Sen who defends positionally objective values as universally shared.
4. Indeed, this concern has been noted as a reason for *not* making health a primary good in social evaluation. (See Daniels 1985, pp. 7–8; Rawls 1971, p. 62).
5. Applying cost-effectiveness analysis in this case obviates concerns over two controversial issues—(1) distribution and (2) non-separateness of persons—when the technique is applied in invoking utilitarian frameworks. For instance, when the technique was employed in the Oregon experiment, several life-saving services (e.g. organ transplantation) that were very costly were ranked below lower cost services such as treatment for thumb sucking or tooth capping. Under the current theory, isolating the evidence of premature mortality for all persons as a central health capability requires that no person be allowed to die prematurely for the sake of advancement of another's non-central health capabilities.
6. The Commission on Social Determinants of Health (CSDH) found continued dramatic shortfalls in health associated with socio-economic status (CSDH 2008).

7. Meaning the 'equal capabilities model'.

8. There is a critical view of the capability approach that, while not altogether eschewing partial ordering, does suggest that Sen provide more guidance on what that partial ordering might constitute and what would and would not qualify in the list of functions. (For more on this view, see Roemer (1994)). This pertains to the general capability approach. This view differs from others (see, for example, Qizilbash 1996a; 1996b) who do not recognize the value of partial ordering.

9. In general, throughout their book, Buchanan et al. (2000) synonymously use the concepts of capability and opportunity, despite their distinctive meaning and different justificatory structure. Indeed, Martha Nussbaum remarks on this in her review of the book, stating, 'I wish the authors had spent more time pondering the "capabilities approach" to questions of basic social justice.' She adds, 'the logic of their concerns leads them to use the language of capabilities, and yet they do not ponder the implications of this other theoretical approach' (Nussbaum 2000a, p. 42).

10. Others claim that the capability approach is extremely vague—indeed, one scholar has deemed that Sen's account suffers from 'a severe expositional obscurity' (Cohen 1993 quoted in Sterba 1994, pp. 198–9).

11. It should be noted that critiques of Sen's incommensurability problems fail to adequately propose alternatives that deal sufficiently with the issue of trade-offs between values. See, for example Qizilbash's (1996b) concession of this. They also fail to provide accounts of well-being that are considerably less vague (Qizilbash 1996a; 1996b; 1997; 1998).

12. Scholars like Cohen (1993) and Pettit (1995) have argued that terms like capability and freedom are equivocal and unclear in this theory. Sen (1993b) responds with his belief that the incompleteness of the approach is a strength and not a weakness.

13. Health capabilities are seen as a 'distinguished capability comparison' (Sen 1999, p. 82).

14. While there are those who will argue that health care is both intrinsically and instrumentally valuable, the position taken here is that health care is primarily instrumentally valuable—as a means to broader goals of health and well-being.

5

Grounding the Right to Health

The health capability paradigm offers a philosophical justification for a right to health.[1] It makes a case for the right to health as a meaningful and operational right and discusses the degree to which this right is necessarily 'justiciable' and enforceable as prescribed in international law; and it explicates societal obligations, both state and non-state, for progressive realization of this right. Furthermore, the paradigm recognizes, critically, that sustaining the effort to realize a right to health requires individual and societal commitments to *public moral norms*. In other words, the right to health involves an ethical demand for equity in health. This ethical demand will probably involve legal instruments for enforcement, but more importantly will require individuals, states, and non-state actors to internalize public ethical norms to implement and achieve compliance with a right to health in international human rights policy and law.

This work, therefore, has something in common with studies in international law compliance that focus on 'transnational legal processes' for internalizing norms (Chayes and Chayes 1993; Chayes et al. 1968; Finnemore and Sikkink 1998; Henkin 1979; Keck and Sikkink 1998; Koh 1996; 1999). What is different, however, is the focus on a particular type of norm—a public moral norm—as the basis of individual and societal commitments to a right to health, and on internalizing this public moral norm at both the collective and individual levels. The regulation of self and society requires not just legal instruments, but individuals and groups with internalized public moral norms—as part of their own internal value systems—informing the choices they make for themselves and their society to ensure all people the capability to be healthy. Such internalization in turn leads to the greater efficacy of, and greater compliance with, domestic policy and legal instruments, which are at least as important as international instruments (and institutions) for progressive realization of a right to health. Achieving this overarching goal is more likely to occur when individuals within a given society take ownership of the public moral norm as a guiding principle for their individual and collective efforts, as evidenced by their domestic social, political, and economic activity. Willingness to pay taxes for others' health insurance is such a public moral norm. Chapter 9 argues for internalizing this norm to achieve domestic health care reform on universal health insurance (Ruger 2007b).

One would be hard pressed to find a more controversial or nebulous human right than the 'right to health'—a right that stems primarily (although not exclusively) from Article 12 of the International Covenant on Economic, Social, and Cultural Rights (ICESCR) and requires governments to recognize 'the right of everyone to the enjoyment of the highest attainable standard of physical and mental health' (ICESCR 1966). While activists, non-governmental organizations, and scholars have made significant progress in promoting a human rights approach to health and the field of health and human rights more generally (Annas 2003; Cook and Dickens 2002a; 2002b; Cook et al. 2003; Farmer 2003; Gruskin and Dickens 2006; Gruskin and Tarantola 2001; Mann et al. 1994), the question of a philosophical and conceptual foundation—a theory—for the right to health has fallen through the cracks at the interdisciplinary intersection of medical ethics, international relations, international human rights law, health policy, health law, and public health law.

International human rights law scholars working in public health and health policy have typically focused on government's binding legal obligations to promote and protect both public health and human rights (Annas 2003; Chaoulli v. Quebec 2005; Mann 1996). They have drawn on human rights to address public health issues, especially the HIV/AIDS pandemic (Fidler 2004, p. 99; Mann 1999, p. 216). Although scholars in this field have 'developed a sophisticated understanding of civil and political rights', they 'have failed systematically to examine the meaning and enforcement of social and economic rights' (Gostin 2001, p. 29). Many have concerns about economic and social rights more generally (Cranston 1983; Cross 2001, p. 857; Ignatieff 2001; Jamar 1994; Leary 1994, p. 24; O'Neill 1996), although there are those who favour economic and social rights (Holmes and Sunstein 1999; Michelman 1999, pp. 181–199). And while General Comment No. 14, issued by the UN Committee on Economic, Social, and Cultural Rights (UNCESCR), provides the most reliable report on the right to health—defining the goal of this right as 'the highest attainable standard of mental and physical health'—it too, by necessity and purpose, lacks a systematic philosophical grounding for the right to health.

The few international relations scholars and practitioners who do focus on health issues have provided primarily three dominant arguments for international health cooperation: national and security interests; domestic and global economic development; and international human rights (Fidler 2004; Kickbusch 2003, p. 192; Walt and Buse 2006). Human rights approaches have filled a 'moral gap' in the international global health discourse left primarily by economic and geopolitical governance frameworks. But the human rights strategy has been only moderately effective, for example, in efforts to control and mitigate the HIV/AIDS epidemic (Fidler 2004), and to implement the constitution of the WHO. Furthermore, international relations as an academic discipline has not provided a theory of a right to health based in moral and political philosophy.

One of the most important scholarly realms bearing on the grounding of a right to health is medical ethics, bioethics, and public health ethics. Existing frameworks in medical ethics, even those that include health assessment, have typically justified health care as a special social good. They have paid less attention, however, to universal concerns of social justice with respect to health itself (Ruger 1997; 1998; 2003b). This bias, more recently addressed, stemmed from the assumption that health is not an appropriate focal variable for assessing social justice or human rights, whereas utilities, community values, liberties, opportunities, resources, and primary goods are. Daniels emphasized that 'a right claim to equal *health* is best construed as a demand for equality of access or entitlement to health *services*' (Daniels 1985, p. 7). Kristen Hessler and Allen Buchanan reiterate this view, stating that a '*right to health care* implies, on its face, a right to certain services; by contrast, a *right to health* seems to imply a right to be healthy, which is an impossible standard' (Hessler and Buchanan 2002, p. 85). The focus on health care suggests that the major inequity in domestic and international health is differential access to care, not differences in health (Brock 2000; Evans et al. 2001, p. 4). This emphasis has left scholars silent on the philosophical foundations underlying a right to health. Public health ethics has focused less on positive rights, such as a right to health, and more on a utilitarian framework of health and human rights (Kass 2001).

In addition, to the extent that the fields of health law and public health law address human rights at all, they do so by emphasizing civil and political rights, or by focusing on legal instruments (laws, regulations, court decisions) (Annas 2003; T. Ruger 2004) that affect the health care (Bloche 2002, p. 919; Hall et al. 2003) and public health systems (Gostin

2002). In the United States, in particular, health law has generally focused on two main categories. One includes laws regulating government-run programmes like Medicaid, Medicare, and the Veterans Administration and Federal Employees programmes. The other encompasses laws regulating private sector health insurance (e.g. managed care organizations) and provider groups (including pharmaceutical companies). Although public health law practitioners have worked diligently to advance a human rights approach to public health, this work has taken place primarily at a policy and court case level, leaving philosophical issues unaddressed.

Finally, traditional health policy analysis has often focused more on the *means* to health—questions of the organization, financing, and delivery of medical care—than on a right to health *per se*, in both developing and developed countries (Ginzberg 1991; Skocpol 1996; Starr 1982; World Bank 1993). In traditional health policy, for example, the focus even on health as an objective has had to compete with other priorities, such as:

(1) financing and organizing medical insurance (Altman and Ostby 1991; Davis and Rowland 1991; Health Security Act 1993; Luft 1978; Starr 1982);

(2) organizing and delivering medical care services (Enthoven 1988);

(3) physician supply and payment and the quality of medical care (Brook et al. 1990; Davies and Cleary 2005; Ginsburg and Lee 1991; Reinhardt 1991); and

(4) financing, distributing, and regulating pharmaceuticals (Danzon and Kim, 2002).

Health economics as a discipline has also devoted far more attention to the economics of medical care than to the economics of health as such. In the field of health economics, a limited number of scholars have focused on the economics of health *per se*, studying health as a function of medical care, age, income, education, sex, race, marital status, environmental factors, and individual behaviours such as smoking, exercise, diet, and alcohol consumption (Auster et al. 1969; Berger and Leigh 1989; Deaton and Paxson 1998; Farrell and Fuchs 1982; Fuchs 1993; Grossman 1972; Kenkel 1991). While it is important to deal with these health policy issues as means, the ultimate end is health and human flourishing.

Nevertheless, interest in health *per se* has resurfaced in policy debates. The beginnings of this resurgence are clear in the RAND Health Insurance

Experiment (Newhouse et al. 1993) in which social scientists studied, among other things, the consequences of health financing arrangements on people's health. This experiment fostered a movement to conceptualize and measure health for medical outcomes assessment. Its goal has been assessing the effects of medical care on health, especially health-related quality of life (Bergner et al. 1976; Brook et al. 1984; Bush 1984; Davies and Ware 1981; Kaplan and Anderson 1988; Patrick and Erickson 1993; Rosser and Kind 1978; Stewart and Ware 1992; Stewart et al. 1988; Tarlov et al. 1989). These efforts reclaimed a concern for health in health care, but this movement has worked primarily at a *practical* level, leaving philosophical questions about health unaddressed.

5.1. Scope and content of a right to health

One of the greatest obstacles to operationalizing a right to health is determining its scope and content. 'A right to health that is too broadly defined lacks clear content and is less likely to have a meaningful effect' (Gostin 2001, p. 29). For example, the WHO definition of health—'a state of complete physical, mental, and social well-being, and not merely the absence of disease or infirmity' (Constitution of the WHO, 1946)—is so broad as to constitute an unreasonable standard for human rights, policy, and law. It is certainly difficult to implement and adjudicate. But defining a human right to health is necessary for delineating obligations of state and non-state actors, including individuals, and to identify violations and guidelines for enforcement.

Chapter 4 elucidated a conception of health that is useful as a guiding consensus in implementing the right to health. This chapter now turns to presenting the ethical and social claims on others—state, non-state actors, groups, and individuals—that might be embodied in domestic policy and law. It especially asserts the need for all individuals to internalize the public moral norm of health equity, and to understand the obligations each of us has to help realize the right to health for every individual in every society in the global community. For positive rights, such as the right to health, this internalization process must entail a commitment to financial claims (e.g. tax contribution) to fulfil the right (e.g. through universal health insurance coverage). Internalizing the norm on an individual basis ought to ultimately lead to public policies, legislation, and agreed upon laws to guarantee a right to health.

5.2. Duties and obligations in domestic and international policy and law: ethical commitments and public moral norms

Actualizing a right to health involves both legal and non-legal instruments. The health capability paradigm proposes an *ethical commitment* to the right to health. This commitment sees the right to health as the basis and inspiration for new and specific legislation. It also sees it as an ethical claim, in this case on all individuals, especially the wealthier, to redistribute some of their resources to help meet the health needs of others, those who are unable to afford care. Under a health capability paradigm, this obligation involves an interest in the significant capabilities and freedoms of others, operationalized in terms of health needs, health functionings, health agency, and health capabilities, not preferences, desires, or utilities.

Because fulfilment of a right to health requires social organization for redistribution of resources and related legislation and regulation, this paradigm rests on an ethical commitment on the part of all individuals — those most fortunate and those in need—to the end goal of providing all people the capability to be healthy. Without this ethical commitment, redistributing resources from the wealthy to those less fortunate and from the well to the sick will not be possible, because the effort to do so must be voluntary, not coercive. As such, individuals must internalize the public moral norm that health is worthy of social recognition, investment, and regulation to the point of successfully operationalizing such a right. The ethical significance of the right to health provides strong grounding for individual and state action to respect, protect, and fulfil it through institutional change. The obligation and duties fall on all individuals, regardless of their specific relationship to any other particular individual, but the allocation of specific responsibility for respecting, protecting, and fulfilling the right to health depends on the respective roles of institutions and individuals at different levels of society (global, national, sub-national) as discussed elsewhere (Ruger 2006b). The specific allocation of responsibility for effective action may rest on personal and institutional relationships, but there is also a more practical turn to allocate duties based on functional effectiveness in respecting, protecting, and fulfilling a right to health as discussed elsewhere (Ruger 2006b).

From an ethical point of view, individuals and, by extension, states must address threats to human rights. Immanuel Kant's category of duties known as 'imperfect obligations' to human rights analysis may be applied as the basis for this obligation. In this analysis, human rights yield both perfect and imperfect obligations (Sen 2004, pp. 340–42). In the health domain, determining the extent and scope of these claims, our perfect and imperfect obligations to respect, protect, and fulfil an individual's right to health, requires a framework of normative reasoning. Such reasoning involves dialogue about the ethical dimensions of health and health policy and about the need for collective action through public financing, regulation, and in some cases, provision of services. It also requires regulation and oversight of the health system, and it calls for establishing social norms of inclusive diversity to create the conditions in which each individual may achieve her potential in health. In short, such realization is more likely to occur when individuals within a given society take ownership of the public moral norm as a guiding principle for their individual and collective efforts, as evidenced by their *domestic* social, political, and economic activity. Blunt legal instruments cannot fully embody this framework. Legal instruments will ultimately require interpretation in any case. This argues for a particular type of normative reasoning about justice and health policy, leaving the discussion of legal instruments and the role of the courts vis-à-vis legislation and policy to other works.

5.3. Positive and negative rights: a constitutional right to medical self-defence

The final section of this chapter addresses a growing controversy in the rights literature that pertains to health (including abortion rights), that will help elucidate the difference between the health capability paradigm's approach to rights and health (a more positive notion) and the long-standing and more traditional approach (a more negative notion of freedom from interference). The issue of a right to medical self-defence arose in a recent essay by Eugene Volokh (2007) and a discussion of this view in contrast to that expressed in this book helps to illustrate the distinctions.

Volokh argues for a constitutional right to 'medical self-defence' for two purposes: first, to allow terminally ill patients to purchase, at their own expense, drugs that have not completed the US Food and Drug Administration's (FDA) approval process and, second, to allow all individuals access to transplanted organs for which there are current bans on payment. His claim, in essence, is that we should allow markets for experimental drugs and human organs and that prohibition of such markets is unconstitutional. He grounds this 'constitutional right' to 'medical self-defence' in the common law justification of lethal self-defence, and sees this principle as analogously justifying abortion jurisprudence and therefore a relevant justificatory claim for other domains of health care. Taking the controversial Abigail Alliance case as his point of departure (Abigail Alliance for Better Access to Developmental Drugs v. Von Eschenbach 2007), Volokh's reasoning adroitly connects the dots in a web of libertarian thought that takes, as its basis, negative rights of freedom from interference. More specifically, he uses the concepts of ordered liberty and justice to make his claim.

Some have already claimed that this line of argument is not sufficiently justified on either common law or constitutional grounds (Snead 2007). The health capability paradigm, on the other hand, questions the philosophical and theoretical justification of Volokh's position, asserting that a right to health care does not need to be, indeed cannot be, framed in an absolute libertarian framework of wholly individualistic rights against the state. Rather, the health capability paradigm grounds a right to health in the more positive conceptualization of freedom, of human flourishing, arguing for treating the right to health as an ethical demand for equity in health. Unlike the legalistic (and theoretically ungrounded) guarantee of a 'right to medical self-defence', a right to health under a health capability paradigm argues that the regulation of self and society necessitates not just justiciable and enforceable legal rights or instruments, but also individuals and the collective imbued with public moral norms that inform the choices they make for themselves and their society to ensure all people the capability to be healthy.

This understanding provides a framework for reforming the state, where necessary, to ensure its effectiveness in creating the collective goods required for progressive realization of a right to health. The state is obligated to generate public goods, through scientific evaluation, that are required for consumption by individual agents to effectuate a right to health. Aristotle's notion of combining ethical and technical rationality informs this process. The FDA and other state-supported entities have not only a legislative mandate but also a moral duty to draw on society's collective scientific resources in providing the most rigorous and scientifically grounded evidence base so *all individuals* have the capability to be healthy. Efforts to undermine and delegitimize this role rob all individuals (present and future) of the necessary conditions for their optimal health functioning and health agency.

One of the main reasons Volokh's libertarian argument is unconvincing is that the nature of health and health care does not lend itself well to libertarian doctrinal thinking. Libertarian theories of justice, as advocated

125

by Robert Nozick (1974) and others, would deny altogether any political obligation to provide medical care or health insurance to all. Libertarianism takes the principle of liberty as absolute and does not give health or health care special standing.

The long history of so-called negative rights, for example Nozick's (1974) libertarian emphasis in a Lockean tradition, focuses on rights as side-constraints. This envisions a minimalist state with narrow functions of ensuring non-interference and sees such measures as coercive and unimportant from a moral view-point. Redistributing resources for health and health care would infringe on individual liberties. Thus, consequentialist health concerns, such as delimiting the special status of terminally ill patients or patients requiring organ donation, are not part of the libertarian theoretical framework. The libertarian approach in rights scholarship pertaining to health generally endorses the fulfilment of negative rights (civil and political rights), but fails to endorse the fulfilment of positive rights (Evans 2002, pp. 197, 199–203). This perspective rejects social, economic, and cultural rights.

Proponents of a libertarian framework argue that a market mechanism is the ideal way to distribute health care and health. This approach generally stems from an overarching philosophy in which individual liberties and autonomy are the predominant societal values, and the government's role is to protect individual rights—especially property rights. This framework does not support a right to health care because efforts to guarantee such a right could infringe on individual liberties (by requiring people to pay taxes, even for regulation or medical research). Autonomous individuals may freely choose to purchase or forgo health care or health insurance. Thus, a strict libertarian or market-based approach would allow the more affluent and those with strong preferences for certain goods and services to receive more and better health care, regardless of need or capability.

Part I has discussed concerns with the libertarian and free-market perspectives, especially that the conditions for efficient market allocation based on supply and demand do not exist in either the health care or the health insurance markets, including the pharmaceutical market and any organ market that would be legalized.

As discussed above, in opposition to the libertarian or free-market view, the health capability paradigm argues for a right to health grounded in the Aristotelian principle of human flourishing, offering a philosophical justification for a right to health and asserting an ethical demand for equity in health. Sustaining the effort to realize a right to health requires individual and societal commitments to public moral norms. This ethical demand may involve legal instruments for enforcement, but more likely will require individuals, states, and non-state actors to internalize public ethical norms to enhance implementation and compliance with a right to health in national and international policy and law. The regulation of self and society requires not just legal instruments, but also individuals and groups with internalized public moral norms—as part of their own internal value systems—that inform the choices they make for themselves and their society to ensure capabilities for all people to be healthy. Such internalization in turn leads to the greater efficacy of, and greater compliance with, domestic policy and legal instruments, which are altogether as important as international instruments and institutions for progressive realization of a right to health. Such realization is more likely to occur when individuals within a given society take ownership of the public moral norm as a guiding principle for their individual and collective efforts, as evidenced by their domestic social, political, and economic activity.

In contrast to the very narrow right to health care—the right to be free from government interference in choosing health care—the health capability vision of a right to health and health care is grounded in the principle of *health equity*. Volokh's right to 'medical self-defence', if adopted, would likely lead to substantial inequities in health care. For example, the rich could pay for new organs and transplantation, and testing drugs and devices would be limited to the lower and middle classes, since the rich would buy experimental drugs rather than risk being randomized to a placebo in a double-blind clinical trial.

The state's goal and purpose under a right to health theory grounded in human flourishing thus differs from those informed by libertarian perspectives. The health capability paradigm does not necessarily view the state as the culprit in suppressing individuals' rights. Rather, it views the state and its entities (e.g. the FDA and the NIH) as having not only a legislative mandate, but also a moral duty to provide the rigorous and scientifically grounded evidence base necessary for good health. Efforts to undermine and delegitimize this role and responsibility rob all individuals today and in the future of the necessary conditions for their optimal health functioning and health agency. Unencumbered access to experimental drugs outside of society's efforts to draw on its collective scientific resources could, for example, hinder the success of the clinical trial system designed to provide valid and reliable scientific data for clinical decision-making. Even efforts to collect data on patients who might otherwise have access to experimental drugs outside the context of a clinical trial in fact undermine the scientific integrity of this information. This is because such patients are not randomly assigned and thus pose questions about adverse selection and confounding by other variables. The randomized control trial is still the gold standard in pharmaceutical research.

Continuing with this critique of strict and even modified libertarian and market-based approaches to health care and health, the health capability paradigm recognizes the need for the creation and dissemination of public goods to bring the right to health within reach for all individuals. Furthermore, it recognizes the need to create and disseminate public goods at the collective level, transcending any one individual or interest group. Generating and disseminating scientific research on the efficacy of pharmaceuticals is, after all, a problem of the 'commons', as delineated in Garrett Hardin's (1968) classic article on the tragedy of the commons. From this perspective, individual decisions based on property rights are not terribly relevant because resource use, medical knowledge, and scientific evidence cannot be consumed exclusively by a single individual or interest group. The primary solution to the problem of the commons in this realm is the creation and dissemination of collective public goods and the regulation of positive and negative externalities resulting from the scientific process (e.g. clinical trials). Without efforts at the collective level, individuals themselves would not have the capacity, in financial or human resources, to invest in the creation and development of scientific evidence and medical knowledge. Pharmaceutical research and development is a critical public good and standards are essential for its use at the societal level. Promoting this public good requires financial and human resources mobilized through institutions like the FDA and the NIH.

While the state has the legislative and moral claim to advance the collective good and protect the lives of all persons through entities like the FDA and the NIH, this claim does not mean that individuals' autonomy should not be respected. And, while the FDA is unlikely to revert to allowing terminally ill patients access to experimental drugs (due to prior episodes where many such drugs turned out to be more harmful than beneficial), it would not be out of the question to modify the process to allow greater input from individuals through better deliberation and participation. Indeed, feedback from patients and doctors to the scientific process enables further progress to be made and errors reduced. Moreover, the system by which individuals become aware of prospects for clinical trial enrolment for investigative drugs must be reformed to enable greater access and enhance individuals' health agency. At the moment, the system is both complex and overwhelming and not equally accessible to all patients. Efforts to help terminally ill patients develop their health agency and help them navigate the process would expand both the number and sickness level of patients in the system. Financial incentives and government reimbursements could help in subsidizing the costs for those unable to pay, as would improvement in geographic access and disallowing exploitative pricing to vulnerable patients (Falit and Gross 2008). Marrying scientific evidence with such deliberations is very much in the spirit of the health capability paradigm (discussed in Chapter 8).

Rather than creating a negative right of medical self-defence to address this problem, this theory operationalizes a right to health through the justification of medically necessary and medically appropriate health care. Not all health care is medically necessary or medically appropriate. A lot of what health care has to offer is only marginally effective; it might extend life for just a few weeks or months or have a very low probability (less than 5–10 per cent) of success. This is particularly true with today's advanced medical technology, including experimental drugs and transplant operations.

Thus, experimental drugs that have not passed Phase II and Phase III of the FDA drug approval process and have not been proven efficacious or effective would not be deemed medically necessary or medically appropriate. While experimental drugs may offer hope, the odds are that they will not be deemed efficacious and even fewer will be deemed medically necessary and medically appropriate (only 10 per cent of potential drugs make it to the human trial stage and an even smaller fraction of those tested make it through the final approval process to go to market) (Conway 2003). Moreover, without further scientific evidence and public access to data on drug safety (Kesselheim and Mello 2007), it is unknown whether such drugs may cause more harm than good to patients.

Guaranteeing constitutional 'rights to medical self-defence', by allowing terminally ill patients to buy experimental drugs that have not completed the FDA approval process, would run counter to the health capability paradigm. In it, drugs not yet proven efficacious would not be available for purchase, nor would they be made available through government-sponsored programmes such as Medicare and Medicaid. Rather than determining policy according to individual rights against state interference, this paradigm would seek to bolster the scientific process and apply standards of safety, efficacy, medical necessity, and medical appropriateness to the assessment of an experimental drug. Concerns that the FDA process is too slow and cumbersome to churn out potentially life-saving experimental drugs in a timely manner are legitimate and deserve our attention, but they are best addressed by reform of the FDA process itself, not bypassing or undercutting that process for certain privileged social groups.

Similarly, the health capability paradigm would take a different approach to the problem of organ scarcity. Rather than frame the problem as state suppression of individual rights, this view would frame it in supply and demand terms that would guard against body part commodification and exploitation of the poor and vulnerable by the wealthy and well-connected. Rather than open this very serious individual health and public health problem to potential exploitation of some groups (and potentially threatening their agency) by others, the health capability paradigm would address this problem through application of scientific principles and policy prescriptions. For example, in the application of scientific principles, investments in promising lines of research known as regenerative medicine, artificial and biohybrid organs and tissues, and stem and adult cell therapy, offer hope for enabling those in need of organ and tissue transplantation to use their own body and lab-developed tissue and organs, not those of others, as a source of transplant elements. On the policy side, investments would be supported in efforts to encourage voluntary organ and tissue donation through living wills, advance directives, driver's licences, presumed consent, public education, and counselling. The aim of these interventions would be reducing the gap between public preferences and organ donation (roughly 95 per cent of Americans support organ donation but only 53 per cent are consented donors) (Gallup Organization 2005, pp. 5, 9). These options show increasing success and warrant support. Such policy measures aim to increase the supply of organs while obviating the potential to cause harm to others.

In conclusion, a right to health care need not, indeed cannot, be framed in an absolute libertarian framework of wholly individualistic rights against the state. Rather, the health capability paradigm proposes an alternative theoretical framework grounding a right to health in the more positive conceptualization of freedom, human flourishing.

Note

1. Nussbaum (1997) and Sen (2004) provide excellent discussions of capabilities and human rights, though neither directly discusses the right to health in their work.

Part III

Domestic Health Policy Applications

6

A Health Capability Account
of Equal Access

The theory presented here evaluates the impact of health care on individuals' health capability (Ruger 1998; 2004a). It assesses health capability by examining health functioning and health needs (Ruger 1998; 2004a), health agency (Ruger 1998; 2007a), and health norms (Ruger 2004c; 2005b; 2007a).

6.1. Rethinking equal access: agency, quality, and norms

In 2003, health ministers from Europe, South America, and Oceania established The International Forum on Common Access to Health Care Services as an evidence-sharing network to promote equitable health care access in all countries. In 2005, the Global Health Council convened health care providers, community organizers, policymakers, and researchers at 'Health Systems: Putting Pieces Together', a conference to discuss health from a systems perspective. In the USA, Institute of Medicine reports in 1999 and 2001 found disparities in health care quality and recommended broad health system reforms (IOM 1999; 2001; Kohn et al. 2000). Together these reports have established health care access and quality as two of the most important issues in health policy in all societies today.

However, little agreement exists on what equal access and quality mean for health system development (Oliver and Mossialos 2004, p. 656). At the philosophical level there has been little effort to understand why disparities in health care quality *per se* (as the direct object of ethical inquiry) are so morally troubling. While work in medical ethics has investigated equal access, these efforts have focused narrowly on the health care distribution required to remove disease-caused barriers to opportunity. The equality of opportunity view stems from an inadequate understanding of the ends and means of justice. It ignores society's role in fostering the freedom to be healthy. This focus neglects the key concepts of health agency and health norms, both of which influence individuals' capability for health.

This book proposes rethinking equal access in terms of an alternative ethical aim: to ensure the social conditions in which all individuals have the capability to be healthy. This alternative view of equality allows us to examine injustices besides inequitable distribution of health care resources. While other accounts focus on guaranteeing equal access to decent minimum health care, this approach requires effective access so that all have the ability to achieve health functionings and health agency. Effective access rests on assessing health care quality, health agency, and health norms. This perspective explains why inequities in health care quality concern us and why society should reduce them; it examines the quality of health care resources and whether they support health functioning. It also examines the extent to which society supports individuals' health agency so people can convert health care resources into health functioning; and it probes the nature of health norms, which influence individuals as they strive for health functioning, governing behaviours and choices. These principles (agency, quality, and norms) provide core elements of an alternative view of equal access.

6.1.1. Defining equal access and a right to health care

Most of the literature on health care access focuses on principles of justice, though some arguments appeal to charity, compassion, beneficence, and benevolence toward the sick.[1] Efforts to secure equitable health care access typically invoke a 'right to health care', that is, a right to either a decent minimum of care or equal access to health care. However, scholars disagree on whether the government should guarantee such a right (Baumrin 2002; Beauchamp and Childress 1994; Hessler and Buchanan 2002), the scope of a health care right, and the meaning of 'access to health care'. Appeals to health care rights are often referred to in the medical ethics literature, but are understood within the comprehensive ethical theories that justify them. Theories of justice touching on rights claims to health care include utilitarianism, which supports rights only if (and to the extent that) such claims contribute to the maximization of utility. A right to health care could be justified under communitarianism if the right best expressed the values of the community. A libertarian philosophy would likely not support a right to health care because the funds necessary to do so would infringe upon individual liberties of taxpayers.

Access to health care is defined at one end of the spectrum as a negative right (no one should be prevented from obtaining care) that does not require the government to guarantee equal care for everyone. The other end argues for government-guaranteed equal access to health care for all. In the middle is the right to a decent minimum or adequate level of care, typically a government-as-last-resort approach. A 'decent minimum' of care in contrast to optimal or high-quality care has been called 'minimally decent care', 'basic health services' (Enthoven 1980; Walzer 1983), 'basic health care' (Hiatt 1987), or 'essential health care' (Gibbard 1982).

Even these more limited guarantees of equal access require further definition. Most of them attempt to specify lists of basic medical services that help define adequate health care. These lists vary from acute care and epidemic disease control to chronic care, reconstructive services, dental care, and nutrition. Inevitably, critics claim that such lists are too indeterminate and expansive to guide decision-making about service provision. Critics fear that a detailed list might become a carte blanche for unlimited care and believe that services cannot define an adequate level or decent minimum of care (Emanuel 1991; Hessler and Buchanan 2002; President's Commission for the Study of Ethical Problems in Medicine and Biomedical and Behavioral Research 1983).

Some suggest that financial incentives, such as copayments and deductibles, should accompany lists to limit care. However, critics charge this approach with adopting a 'monetary criterion' for adequate care as opposed to a publicly determined selection of care (Emanuel 1991). Unless an adequate minimum includes a philosophical justification for providing or withholding specific types of care, lists seem arbitrary. A better approach would base conditions and related goods and services on general criteria to which reasonable people would agree through a legitimate decision-making procedure. Concerns about more expansive views of equal access, which would possibly employ the standard of 'optimum' care, have also arisen, arguing that this standard cannot be 'justified in a socially funded policy' (Beauchamp and Childress 1994, p. 356). Beauchamp and Childress (1994, p. 356) assert that the decent minimum standard holds 'the potential for compromise among libertarians, utilitarians, communitarians, and egalitarians, because it incorporates some moral concerns stressed by each of these theories.' Concern for equal access to health care has spawned many ethical frameworks to address this problem.

6.1.2. Equal opportunity and equal resources

The most prominent family of egalitarian theories that pertain to equal access stems from the 'equality of opportunity' and 'equality of resources' views (Van Parijs 1991) derived partly from John Rawls's theory of justice as put forth primarily in *A Theory of Justice* (Rawls 1971). A number of theorists, including Richard Arneson (1989; 1990), Gerald Cohen (1989), Ronald Dworkin (1981a; 1981b), Thomas Nagel (1991), Eric Rakowski (1991), John Roemer (1996), and Thomas Scanlon (1975), espouse this general framework. Many have applied variations of this view to health care, although with different implications. For example, the 'Formal Equality of Opportunity' or 'careers open to talents' view states that equal opportunity requires society to eliminate legal barriers for individuals with similar talents and abilities so that careers are open to those persons. Justice therefore requires the elimination of barriers that limit careers by racial, ethnic, gender, class, sexual orientation, or religious discrimination. Another approach, the level playing field conception of equal opportunity, takes society's obligation a step further, requiring efforts to eliminate the effects of 'bad luck' in life's social lottery. Many egalitarian theorists espouse some form of this view, whether called luck egalitarianism or equality of fortune (Rakowski 1991).

One variant of this view distinguishes 'brute luck' from 'option luck'. In this approach, argued by Thomas Scanlon (1975) and others, justice requires compensation to victims of brute luck or misfortunes not within their control, as opposed to victims of option luck or misfortunes brought about by their choices, for which society owes no obligation. Further distinction exists between those who support remedies for brute luck from the 'social lottery' of life, the social structural view, and those who go further to support such remedies along with those misfortunes from the 'natural lottery' of life. Ronald Dworkin (1981a; 1981b) argues that justice requires redistribution of resources in efforts to compensate individuals for inequalities in natural attributes. From a brute luck perspective, inequalities in natural assets that limit opportunities, including diseases, require remedy under justice. Resource egalitarians within the brute luck school argue for distributing resources equally among all persons, compensating for inequalities in natural assets through the distribution of social assets (Dworkin 1981a; 1981b; Roemer 1996). There is a further distinction between those who argue society's compensation rests on equal opportunity of welfare (Arneson 1989; 1990) or satisfaction of individual preferences and equal access to advantage (Cohen 1989) and those who base compensation on equality of resources (Dworkin 1981a; 1981b; Rakowski 1991; Van Parijs 1991).

Each argument has obvious flaws. Some individuals inevitably have unsatiated tastes or preferences. Equality of resources will not help individuals who involuntarily need more resources than others.

The option luck argument absolves society from compensating individuals for 'deserved' misfortune. In this view, individuals who rock climb, cause automobile accidents, or abuse drugs do not merit society's health care protection, since their medical conditions result from their own decisions or behaviours (Arneson 1990; Rakowski 1991). Arneson (1989), however, asserts that it is not fair always to hold people responsible for outcomes; society owes options of health and disability insurance to all. Dworkin (1981a; 1981b) argues that the sheer scope of this obligation would necessarily limit insurance to what individuals would choose *ex ante*, behind a 'veil of ignorance' about what type of health or disability they might have. Ultimately, this type of choice is biased against individuals with rare conditions, which most people might not insure against or treat.

In sum, the equality of opportunity views focus on removing barriers to fair competition for what Rawls (1971) calls offices and positions in society. This view's historical roots lie in Rawls's argument for careers open to talents through enhancing access to opportunity. It argues that society should ensure individuals the 'characteristics necessary to be a "normal competitor" for desirable social positions' (Buchanan et al. 2000, p. 74). In the context of equal health care access, society must intervene to address diseases because disease 'can prevent an individual from being a normal competitor'. Furthermore, 'equal opportunity has to do with ensuring fair competition for those who are able to compete *and* with preventing or curing disease that hinders people from developing the abilities that would allow them to compete' (Buchanan et al. 2000, p. 74).

Drawing on Rawls's theory, Daniels (1985; 2008) provides a philosophical justification for equal health care access. He argues that equal access enhances opportunities. Thus, Rawls's fair equality of opportunity criterion justifies health care required to maintain, restore, or compensate for the loss of normal human functioning that impacts individuals' opportunities. Such care includes preventive services, treatment, rehabilitation, nursing, and social services. The right to health care rests on health care's power to promote equal opportunity.

Though a sensible approach, critics argue that it 'fails to provide an adequate way of identifying basic medical services that should be guaranteed by society as a matter of justice', has 'no principled limit on the demand for medical services', and must include a process such as hypo-thetical choice or democratic procedures 'for balancing such demands' (Emanuel 1991, pp. 123–4). We have seen how hypothetical choice behind a 'veil of ignorance' skews health care decisions. Daniels originally pro-posed a quantitative scheme for measuring the curtailment of life plans and specifying medical services to offset these diminishments. Assess-ments defied quantification, however, because to deny medical care to certain groups is to 'enhance the opportunities of others in society' (Ema-nuel 1991, p. 134). For example, kidney dialysis 'ameliorates a disease which restricts a smaller range of life plans to fewer people than do other medical services' (Emanuel 1991, p. 134). Subsequently, this approach was revised by supplementing the list with a fair process for determining how to ration scarce medical resources. Individuals are entitled to coverage decisions made through fair processes, rather than to the same sets of health care. Even so, critics found this process too indeterminate and passive (Emanuel 2002, p. 954). Dworkin (1981a; 1981b) proposed that important opportunities should be defined as what is valued by most people or the average person. However, there is no such thing as the average person's view of the most important opportunities, and ranking opportunities violates the liberal ideal of neutrality that is central to the hypothetical choice procedure. As one critic notes, 'the hypothetical choice procedure leaves the liberal legislator without a standard of assess-ment by which to weigh the various opportunities to be secured by each scheme of health care services and thus without a way to justify selecting one health scheme over another. Indeed, without such a standard there really seem to be no grounds for deliberation' (Emanuel 1991, p. 145). This philosophical debate highlights problems with using opportunities and fair procedures as justification for equal health care access.

Applying Rawls's theory to equal access raises further concerns. Empha-sizing societal responsibility for distribution of primary goods such as health care focuses on means rather than ends. From a capability perspec-tive, resources (the means for a flourishing life) do not have intrinsic value. They are good only insofar as they promote human functioning. Thus, Rawlsian egalitarianism focuses too narrowly on the distribution of goods.

Another objection concerns human diversity. The Rawlsian account does not consider, as Nussbaum points out, that 'human beings have variable needs for resources, and any adequate definition of the better off and worse off must reflect that fact' (Nussbaum 1992, p. 233). Sen observes that 'two persons holding the same bundle of primary goods can have very different freedoms to pursue their respective conceptions of the good' (Sen

1992, p. 8). A disability could force one to divert resources from other purposes, for instance. Furthermore, the impact of these resources on health varies considerably by health care quality.

It is necessary to assess the impact of resources on health to understand their instrumental effectiveness and to allocate them equitably and efficiently. As Nussbaum (1992, p. 233) notes, Rawls's theory, 'by defining being well-off in terms of possessions alone, fails to go deep enough in imagining the impediments to functioning that are actually present in many human lives'. The family of Rawlsian approaches prioritizes equality of opportunity, and none gives health a morally privileged place (Ruger 1998; 2004a).

Accordingly, the Fair Equality of Opportunity (FEO) account endorses the provision of equal access to 'adequate care' or health care that is the product of fair decisions. FEO purports that people under a 'veil of ignorance' would choose adequate care allocations to achieve an age-relative normal opportunity range at each stage of life (Daniels 1985). Later FEO stipulates that health care allocations be based on fair procedures satisfying conditions of 'accountability for reasonableness' (Daniels 2008; Daniels and Sabin 2002). The FEO account is silent on health care quality disparities that might arise from such applications and on securing conditions of health agency and health norms.

Would health deprivations diminish simply through ensuring possession of primary goods, without attention to quality, the health agency necessary to convert them into health functioning, and health norms affecting individuals' ability to be healthy? Here follows an argument to the contrary, and thus a critique of the Rawlsian approach and the family of equality of opportunity views derived from it. This critique highlights the distinction between the Rawlsian 'resource-orientation' and the capability approach's 'results-orientation' in public policy. 'If the object is to concentrate on the individual's real opportunity to pursue her objectives (as Rawls explicitly recommends)', Sen notes, 'then account would have to be taken not only of the primary goods the persons respectively hold, but also of the relevant personal characteristics that govern the *conversion* of primary goods into the person's ability to promote her ends' (Sen 1999, p. 74). When applied to health care, the Rawlsian approach cannot accommodate the needs of different health conditions and populations. For example, since 'adequate care for all' fails to consider differences in health care quality, health agency, and health norms, an equal opportunity account falls short of enabling all individuals, disabled or not, to live flourishing lives that they value. Furthermore, coverage decisions made by fair procedures fail to ensure equity by denying individuals' entitlements to similar sets of health care goods and services under similar circumstances. The next section expands on these issues.

6.1.3. Rethinking equal access: a health capability perspective

Rather than justify a right to health care, a health capability account of equal access assesses the impact of health care on individuals' capability to function (Ruger 1998; 2003b; 2004a; 2004b). It gives special moral importance to, and evaluates the justness of, health care services by their effectiveness in enhancing health capability (Ruger 1998; 2003b; 2004a; 2004b). It gauges these freedoms by assessing individuals' health needs (Ruger 1998; 2004a; 2006d), health agency (Ruger 1998; 2003b; 2004a; 2004c; 2007a), and the health norms of their environment (Ruger 2004c; 2005b), among other important criteria. This line of reasoning contrasts with the idea that health care is special because of its impact on fair equality of opportunity. It also contrasts with notions that 'equality of fortune' or 'equality of resources or assets' should guide principles for distributive justice that generally imply that justice requires compensating individuals for misfortune.

The distinction is rooted in the different foci of these theories. Capability describes what individuals are able to do and be, offering a realistic sense of their freedom to pursue the lives they value. Thus, society should avert or ameliorate loss in physical or mental functioning even if opportunities of employment, careers, talents, or education remain possible. From this perspective, ability to function-rather than employment, careers open to talents, or educational opportunities-should be the criterion for assessing policy (Ruger 1998; 2004a; 2004b). The remainder of this chapter demonstrates how this approach reflects a more accurate conception of equal access, one informed by a better understanding of the requirements of justice when proportionality is at stake. It also reflects a deeper understanding of the essential individual and social elements of health functioning; the quality of resources; individuals' ability to pursue valuable health goals; and societal norms about health that govern the environment in which individuals navigate choices for a healthier life.

Equal Results

Although in many respects consequentialist in nature, this account of equal access does not guarantee equal results or equal outcomes among recipients. It does not, for example, guarantee the right to be healthy, the impossible task of equal health outcomes, or equal amounts of health care. Rather, it evaluates equality in health capabilities by the principle of 'shortfall equality', which compares shortfalls of achievement from the optimal average or from one's own potential in health (Ruger 1998; 2004a; 2006a). Under this paradigm, society creates conditions under which individuals and groups have the ability to deal with living circumstances and obtain optimal health functioning levels. Threshold levels of health serve as a guide. Rather than guarantee equal or good health, this approach focuses on societies' obligation to enable conditions under which individuals and groups can realize threshold levels of health, reducing the gap between health achievement and health potential (Ruger 1998; 2004a; 2006a).

This account of equal access also requires society to ensure social conditions, goods, and services in proportion to individuals' and groups' health needs, as determined by the requirements each individual or group has to achieve their potential in health. These requirements will differ by individual and group and thus will not necessarily constitute equal amounts. This principle of proportionality builds on Aristotle's principle of just distribution (proportional justice) and his assertion that like cases should be treated similarly and unlike cases differently in proportion to their difference (Irwin 1999, pp. 71–2). Under the health capability paradigm, cases are considered alike if they have the same health needs and unlike if they have different health needs. This principle implies that society should strive to prevent, ameliorate, or eradicate deprivations in individual freedoms for health functioning, even though equal outcomes cannot be guaranteed. In this way, the health capability paradigm focuses on reducing the current gaps among different individuals' health functionings and among their varying capabilities to achieve a given level of health functioning (Ruger 1998; 2004a; 2006a). These capabilities rest, in turn, on health agency and health norms.

Equal Amounts of Care

This account of equal access is needs-based, although it goes further by requiring that health care goods and services be necessary and appropriate and that patients and their physicians assess medical necessity and medical appropriateness (Ruger 2004a; 2006d). Following the principle of proportional distribution, the account supports the allocation of resources to those with greater medical needs, to certain limits, and subject to medical necessity and medical appropriateness criteria (Ruger

2006d). It justifies unequal amounts of care for patients with different conditions, to bring them as close as their circumstances permit to their potential ability to function. Under this account, it is fair to allocate more health care resources to individuals with special needs to restore their functioning to a given level as much as possible—complementary to the way the Americans with Disabilities Act requires building access expenditures on behalf of disabled persons. However, other individuals with similar needs must receive the same level of care. These formulations generally imply that the government should work to bring each individual as close to a target level of health functioning as their circumstances permit, but that these efforts should not reduce the functioning of others below the optimal average (Ruger 2006d).

A potential problem arises when people require different amounts of health care to meet the same health need, as when cases differ in severity or in their ability to convert resources into improved health. For example, one infant born with a heart condition called patent ductus arteriosus (PDA) might require surgery to correct the defect and restore cardiovascular and pulmonary function, whereas another might not (HealthAtoZ; Friedman et al. 1976). Although both infants would have an opening between the aortic arch and pulmonary artery (Lohr 1999), the location and size of the defect might differ considerably (Children's Hospital & Regional Medical Center: Heart Center 2006). One infant's PDA might close naturally, as happens in roughly 90 per cent of cases, whereas the other infant's might not. The equal access principle would require differential provision of health resources to two infants with the same original medical condition to achieve the same desired health achievement. Under this approach, individuals merit the resources they need to reach a medically determined level of health functioning (Ruger 1998; 2006d).

This paradigm is consistent with Aristotle's principle of vertical and horizontal equity. Vertical equity requires that individuals with different needs receive different amounts and levels of services. For example, tuberculosis, pneumonia, or asthma patients require different courses of treatment to achieve a similar end-point of normal pulmonary functioning. Horizontal equity requires equal treatment for individuals with equal needs. Horizontal inequity occurs when individuals with equal needs receive different care based, for example, on the ability to pay or quality.

Although this account offers principles to guide health services delivery, it does not specify which goods and services should be provided or to what level. Limited resources ultimately limit the provision of beneficial health care. Moreover, health care can be beneficial without being necessary or appropriate. Mammography might be beneficial, but it is not necessary or appropriate for certain patients, such as asymptomatic women under thirty years without a family history of breast cancer. Unlimited spending on beneficial medical care could significantly reduce society's ability to provide other social goods (Callahan 1976; President's Commission for the Study of Ethical Problems in Medicine and Biomedical and Behavioral Research 1983; Scitovsky and Capron 1986).

To determine which health care goods and services should be guaranteed and to what level, a decision-making framework must supplement this equal access account (Ruger 1998; 2006d). This framework combines procedural and substantive principles and integrates clinical and economic considerations (Ruger 2006d). Such a framework (outlined in Chapter 8) helps define a comprehensive package of health benefits to which all should have equal access, and it can prioritize different types of health care to optimize all individuals' health with a given level of resources. This approach differs from efforts to identify fair procedures based on conditions that satisfy 'accountability for reasonableness'. Under that approach, justice does not require that all persons be entitled to the same set of health care services, and cases with the same medical appropriateness might receive different health care according to individual health plans. Different health plans would be allowed different coverage specifications. Under that view, as long as each health plan follows procedures for coverage decisions that satisfy the conditions of accountability for reasonableness, then differential access to health care is considered fair and ethical. Under the health capability paradigm, by contrast, health care entitlements rest on medical necessity and medical appropriateness as determined by physicians and patients. Individuals would be entitled to the same set of goods and services, rather than health care coverage determined through fair processes.

6.1.4. Justification for high-quality care

Under this account of equal access, differences in health care quality are morally troubling and unjust. The argument for a decent minimum or adequate level of health care is typically phrased 'a government obligation to meet the basic health needs of all citizens, at least an obligation to function as a last resort' (Beauchamp and Childress 1994, p. 356). The net result is generally two tiers of health care, one involving 'enforced social coverage for basic and catastrophic health needs' (Beauchamp and Childress 1994, p. 356) and the other permitting 'voluntary private coverage for other health needs and desires' (Beauchamp and Childress 1994, p. 356). However, it is difficult to operationalize, and regional, temporal, and socio-economic variations can result in suboptimal care.

Why should disparities in health care quality concern us? How can we justify efforts to reduce them? Quite simply, unequal access can reduce individuals' capability to function. Thus, the health capability paradigm evaluates the justness of health care services according to their effectiveness in preventing, ameliorating, or eradicating, deprivations in individual health functioning. It assesses quality of care by its effectiveness in preventing or reducing functional impairment caused, for example, by disease or injury. Differences in health care quality are therefore unjust because lower-quality care undermines individuals' capability for health functioning. For example, giving the wrong type of blood during organ transplantation is morally troubling, not because it reduces a patient's opportunities for employment or education, or provides less than a decent minimum of care, but because it diminishes the patient's ability to function, even to survive.

This reasoning applies to all variations in health care quality that can lead to complications, disease, dysfunction, deformity, disability, and premature death. Two people with the same health condition experience different health functionings if one has access to high-quality health care and the other does not. Medical evidence demonstrates, for instance, that children with asthma need daily drug therapy to prevent airway swelling, but many do not receive that standard of care (Agency for Healthcare Research and Quality 2000a). Although tight control of blood sugar levels in type 1 diabetes reduces the risk of kidney disease by two thirds and halves the risk of eye disease (Agency for Healthcare Research and Quality 2000b), 40 per cent of Americans with type 1 diabetes do not receive routine glucose monitoring. Quality differences can be a life or death proposition, for example, in cardiac care, when prompt percutaneous coronary intervention is necessary for patients with ST-segment elevation myocardial infarction (STEMI) (Bradley et al. 2005).

Another limitation of the adequate-care standard relates to rare conditions. Applying an *ex ante* 'veil of ignorance' criterion for health care compensation, like some approaches do, could discriminate against individuals with rare and severe disabilities. Consider Maple Syrup Urine Disease (MSUD). MSUD is a rare condition in which infants cannot metabolize certain amino acids. Early detection is critical for survival and prevents significant impairment, yet diagnosis and evaluation require highly trained health professionals with evidence-based knowledge and resources. These professionals provide low-protein formula, which prevents neurological and physical impairment, mental retardation, and death (Fallik 2002a; 2002b; Morton et al. 2002). Without access to this high-quality care, the odds of survival and full functioning drop significantly. A hypothetical choice process would not necessarily provide this care because MSUD is so rare and little known.

Developing countries present even more dramatic quality disparities. Exposure to substandard or dangerous fake drug formulations, for example, can be common. A study in Nigeria found that half of drugs from pharmacies had drug concentrations 'outside upper and lower pharmacopoeial limits' and that 'some of the antimalarial preparations had less than 25% active ingredient' (Po 2001, p. 1904). A study in some Asian countries found that a third of samples of tablets labelled 'artesunate' contained no drug (Po 2001). A lack of human resources—doctors, nurses, researchers— in the world's poorest countries hinders the delivery of quality health care (Chen et al. 2004). Under a health capability paradigm, such inferior care is morally troubling because it reduces individuals' functioning ability.

To err is human, and no perfect health care system exists. Still, equal access to high-quality evidence-based care is a worthy health system goal. Reaching this goal requires continuous effort to standardize medicine, reduce medical errors, and move toward a gold standard of care (IOM 1999; 2001; Kohn et al. 2000). A health capability account of equal access calls all societies to shoulder this responsibility and strive for high-quality care.

At least two objections to the high-quality standard for equal access surface. The first argues that it gives more priority to equality than efficiency. It rises from a reasonable fear that the prohibitive cost of a high-quality standard will undermine even adequate care for all. However, holding health systems accountable only to low standards often results in suboptimal care, which wastes more resources than it saves. For example, paying for substandard drugs does little to improve health, while wasting funds that could instead provide drugs with proven effectiveness. The long-term costs of failing to treat disease early with effective medicines might well exceed the initial expense of providing high-quality medicines.

The second objection claims that high-quality universal care might be politically or administratively unfeasible. It is essential that we educate the public and elected representatives to gain widespread commitment to this obligation. Such efforts have begun to bear fruit in the UK, where a National Policy Forum Consultation Document on the British National Health Service emphasized the importance of health care quality (Socialist Health Association 2005).

The same high-quality physical and mental health care, public health, and social services must be provided to all individuals with the same type and level of health need as long as those services are available to anyone. Equal access includes preventative measures, and that in turn anticipates grappling with the potentially preventative effects of public health and genetic initiatives, to which this equal access principle applies. Preventative measures directly address deprivations in health capabilities and are essential to this approach. The health capability paradigm goes well beyond a 'decent minimum' (Beauchamp and Childress 1994; Daniels 1985) and notions of 'equal quality' and 'equal opportunity for care' (Gutmann 1981) in its ethical argument for equal access.

6.1.5. Health agency

Adherence to this quality principle should reduce barriers to effective, efficient, and timely health care. In addition to geographic, cultural, sociolinguistic, or economic obstacles to equal access, additional barriers might appear on the demand side of health care—limitations individuals themselves face in converting public health interventions and health care into health functioning. Even if society guarantees equal access to high-quality health care, individuals must exercise their health agency to make use of these resources and translate them into maximal levels of health functioning. Health agency entails a more specific form of human agency that relates particularly to one's health and constitutes individuals' and groups' ability to pursue valuable health goals and to play an effective role in bringing about health. Health agency thus also embodies a conception of the good—of optimal health functioning—as a valuable goal. Part of developing health agency involves developing this value through self-scrutiny, self-actualization, and recognition that good health is the right choice. In other words, the idea of enhancing health agency, as defined here, is inconsistent with a notion of aiding someone to continue or maintain an addiction to drugs. The reason is that the conception of the good embodied in health agency, here defined, is positionally objective (noted in Chapter 4.1). As a matter of justice, then, it favours positionally objective values of health as opposed to superficial individual preferences or desires. And as a practical matter of public policy, when individuals' preferences for poor health states (e.g. continued drug addiction) weaken their own health capabilities, this theory supports measures to develop individuals' health agency and their health functioning, recognizing their need to ultimately (in the long run) self-realise and voluntarily embrace this widely shared conception of optimal and potential health.

More specifically, health agency includes not only health knowledge but also effective decision-making about health, self-management and self-regulation skills, and the ability to control personal and professional situations to pursue health, among other important qualities. Under this account, society must foster basic conditions of health agency so individuals can make informed judgements and take effective action to convert health resources into health functioning. The focus of justice is thus on both health (health achievements or functionings) and health agency since the achievement of health will in many respects *depend* on the development of health agency.

Nearly all aspects of health require health agency to achieve health functioning. Consider chronic diseases such as diabetes, cardiovascular disease, and AIDS, and acute conditions such as pregnancy, malaria, and TB; for all, adherence to guidelines and treatment is critical. To manage their disease, for instance, diabetics must have health knowledge. They must know what diabetes is, its causes, current science about glucose, and how to control blood sugar with insulin, medication, diet, and exercise. Meal planning, vital to a diabetic's functioning, requires decision-making ability about nutrition and carbohydrates and basic mathematical skills to balance insulin with blood sugar level readings. Diabetics must know about postprandial hyperglycemia (high blood glucose after meals) to avoid this condition or medicate when necessary. Individuals must have current scientific knowledge about diabetes-related complications, including damage to nerves, eyes, and kidneys, and understand how to prevent, treat, and manage such complications. They must know which health care professional to contact in case of an emergency and what medical and nutritional supplies must be at their disposal in such situations. Diabetes is a condition in which individuals' knowledge and ability to judge, make, and act on decisions can be a matter of life and death.

Effective management of other health conditions, such as Autism Spectrum Disorders, also requires basic conditions of health agency. Early diagnosis and treatment of pervasive developmental disorders critically enhance an autistic person's potential for physical, mental, and social functioning. This requires thorough diagnostic, developmental, and educational assessments in a multidisciplinary approach (National Institute of Mental Health 1999). Health professionals who conduct these evaluations must be highly skilled and their treatment recommendations scientifically based (Autism Program Quality Indicators 2001). Parents must be able to pursue health goals, detect problems, and obtain treatment for their children at an early stage to increase the probability of treatment success (National Institute of Mental Health 1999). Since the spectrum of autism disorders is so wide, and since treatments vary and are designed specifically for children's unique needs, parents must be knowledgeable about different treatment options and be able to visit and judge programmes both in the medical context, in schools, and in after-school settings. Parents need to integrate care across these social boundaries, requiring active management, sequencing, and negotiation skills. In many behavioural management programmes, communications and occupational therapies, at least one parent is involved as a treatment provider (National Institute of Mental Health 1999). Without the ability to obtain and process information, weigh costs and benefits, and act effectively on the array of treatment options, parents of autistic children could not effectively translate available resources into improved physical, mental, and social functioning. In these and many other cases, a child's health functioning will depend on his parent's health agency. Health agency must be a core element of any equal access theory and in a view of shared health governance, individuals, and society—as the collective of individuals—share responsibility to develop and effectuate health agency. In some cases, being healthy or the ability to be healthy will, however, depend on the attitudes and actions of non-custodians or society as a whole through the social structure, for example, when a public health programme funded and implemented by a state government provides clean water through a sanitation system. In other cases, the attitudes of others (health norms) have an effect on health (achievement and functioning) and the ability to be healthy.

6.1.6. Health norms

To ensure that everyone has the capability to be healthy, we must critically scrutinize health norms that bear on cultural and personal choice. Take the case of HIV and AIDS in Africa, where health norms invariably impact individuals' capability to prevent and treat this disease. One sub-Saharan African norm about HIV and AIDS asserts that raping a virgin will cure a man with AIDS (Meel 2003). This myth has increased the spread of AIDS and created a child rape epidemic. It has encouraged men to consider themselves innately superior to girls and women, entitled to dominate, inflict violence, and even death. This health norm relegates women to subordinate status.

Another sub-Saharan African health norm insists that HIV is not spread through sexual intercourse, despite scientific certainty to the contrary. The implications of this health norm for sexual behaviour are apparent. Yet another health norm about HIV and AIDS in sub-Saharan Africa demeans AIDS sufferers as inferior. Clearly these health norms diminish the capability to avoid HIV and receive treatment for AIDS, especially for women. No amount or quality of health care can prevent the spread of HIV resulting from these misperceptions.

The remedy for this injustice lies in correcting false and harmful health norms. Social marketing and social movements broadly can deliver accurate and science-based health information and impress it upon populations. They can also foster norms that honour the moral worth of all persons.

Norms about lifestyle factors known to influence health, for example, smoking, drinking, diet, drug use, driving while intoxicated, and seat belt use (Haines et al. 2003; Wolfson 2000), are cases in point. These health norms have proved to be strong predictors of individual behaviour, even if the norms are misperceived (Evans et al. 1995). In a study of adolescent views about drinking, individual perceptions of a 'drinking norm' (the amount of alcohol consumed by peers) most strongly predicted personal alcohol consumption, even compared to socio-economic and other demographic factors (Perkins et al. 2005). Misperceived norms can be a deadly problem, further demonstrating the importance of a norms-based approach to health promotion.

Consider again Autism Spectrum Disorders (ASD). While parents of autistic children must have access to high-quality care and effective health agency to aid their children, societal norms about ASD are also critical in order for children to achieve their functioning potential. Societal norms toward autistic children must be inclusive, ensuring dignity and granting equal moral worth for every child. Society must remove any social disadvantages that result from social exclusion. An equal opportunity account would focus on changing an autistic person through resources; a health capability paradigm would provide necessary and appropriate health care and social services, but would also seek to change norm-based inequalities that impact health and to ensure the conditions for parents' health agency on their children's behalf.

The health capability paradigm is an integrative model of disability, requiring respect for difference (and thus requiring evaluation for determining individuals' shortfalls in capabilities for health functioning) and appropriate accommodation of needs. It also respects sameness and requires universal treatment in terms of the equal moral worth of all persons. This integrative framework of disability falls midpoint along the spectrum from the medical model of disability (disability is located in the person and impairment equals disability), which appears more closely aligned with an equal opportunity view, and the social model of disability (disability is located in society and society creates disability). In the health capability paradigm, human diversity is embraced as a fact of life and is not seen as an abnormality.

Health norms affect individuals' ability to be healthy in other ways. A number of studies have documented the extent to which individuals hold misperceptions about health norms and the degree to which these misperceptions affect behaviour (Berkowitz 2005; Borsari and Carey 2003; Perkins 2003a). The AIDS–virgin and adolescent drinking case studies provide examples of pervasive myths and of the positive effects of reducing such misperceptions. Such studies demonstrate how critical health norms are, to the social order, to human behaviour (Campbell 1964; Durkheim 1951) and, ultimately, to health. In order to achieve a societal level of good health by reducing shortfall health inequalities, it is thus necessary to invest in development and exercise of health achievements, health agency, and positive health norms. A just social structure will aim to provide the conditions for individuals' health capabilities so that they may achieve optimal health functionings. These health norms are morally significant for a theory of justice and health and must be remedied through a norms-based approach to public health and health policy.

6.2. High-quality care and a two-tiered system

Equal access to high-quality care and a two-tiered system are mutually exclusive concepts. Unfortunately, universal access to high-quality health care is not always available, even in wealthy countries like the United States, where health care quality differentials are widespread. For example, the National Committee for Quality Assurance found that 50 per cent of diabetics enrolled in managed care plans in New England received annual eye exams compared with only 33 per cent in plans in the South Central US region (National Committee of Quality Assurance 1997). Another study across three US states found that in some locales twice as many diabetics get routine care (glycosylated haemoglobin measurement, eye exams, and total cholesterol measurement) as in others (Weiner et al. 1995).

In every society, various factors impede access to high-quality health care, including:

(1) economic barriers (lack of insurance, underinsurance, out-of-pocket payments, poverty);

(2) supply and distributional barriers (goods and services are inappropriate, not available or of sufficient quality, or not geographically accessible);

(3) sociocultural and ethnic barriers (misunderstandings between providers and clients of different backgrounds) (Center for Health Economics Research for the Robert Wood Johnson Foundation 1993); and

(4) ignorance, misinformation, and misapprehension.

In many societies, eliminating financial barriers to care solves many access problems, although other impediments to access persist.

Geographic impediments are particularly problematic. Patients in remote rural areas, for example, are more likely to receive lower quality care than those in more urban, populated areas. One study found that HIV-infected patients living in US rural areas were less likely to be taking anti-HIV drug cocktails and receiving medication to prevent *Pneumocystis carinii* pneumonia than those living in urban areas. Rural HIV patients were also more likely to have doctors significantly less experienced in dealing with HIV (Cohn et al. 2001). One study of heart bypass surgery in the US found that privately insured HMO patients in California received higher quality coronary artery bypass graft surgery than non-HMO patients in the same region, but there was no significant difference between the quality of care for the two groups in Florida (Escarce et al. 1999).

Similarly, sociocultural barriers to access can result in misunderstandings (in some cases, hostility) between providers and patients, maltreatment or lack of treatment, and wasted resources. Ethnic and sociolinguistic barriers to care have been problematic in the United States. One study that controlled for differences in health insurance and socioeconomic status found that the Hispanic children of non-English speakers experienced difficulty in accessing health care (Weinick and Krauss 2000). In a 2001 Robert Wood Johnson Foundation survey on language barriers and access to care, 19 per cent of Latinos reported that language problems kept them from seeking medical care (Robert Wood Johnson Foundation 2001). A different study found that Asians and Pacific Islanders on the west coast had less access to health care than any other ethnic group, including African Americans, Hispanics, Native Americans, and Caucasians. Asians and Pacific Islanders had the worst overall scores for access to treatment when needed, as measured in length of waiting time before seeing a specialist or service approval, with a few exceptions (Snyder et al. 2000, p. 203). The many measures that could reduce or even eliminate such impediments include outreach, transportation, translation, interpretive services, health information, communication campaigns in multiple languages, and simply respecting human dignity. Health communication strategies that are socially, linguistically, and culturally appropriate are especially effective in reducing gaps in health education and knowledge regarding treatment options.

Shortages of high-quality health goods and services, including health personnel, equipment, medicines, and facilities, erect significant supply-side barriers to access. Some countries have addressed these issues, although more effort is needed. For example, the United States Public Health Service Commissioned Corps has provided scholarships and loan repayments to health professionals who practice in underserved communities in the United States. In the United Kingdom, physicians earn roughly 70 per cent more to provide health services in underserved communities. Another problem is the mismatch between health resources and the health needs of the population.

Some of the most important impediments to equal access are economic. Different payment methodologies and financial arrangements within the health sector can affect both health care quality and access. In the US, health insurance status influences both access to services and the quality of care received. Health insurance coverage also bears on individual health. Research has repeatedly shown that people without health insurance use less health care than insured individuals (Swartz 1989). One national US study found that uninsured adults were two to four times more likely to have access problems than the insured. These access failures included not filling a prescription, not seeing a specialist when needed, skipping a medical test, treatment, or follow-up, or not seeing a doctor when sick (Duchon et al. 2001).

Uninsured patients are also up to four times more likely than insured patients to require both hospitalization and emergency hospital care. When hospitalized, those without health insurance receive less care and are more likely to die during their stay than patients who are insured (Blendon 1988; Hadley et al. 1991; Swartz 1994).

In spite of the higher percentage of GDP expenditure on health, the United States does not compare favourably to other industrialized countries in terms of equal access to high-quality care. For example, a study of ten OECD countries (United States, United Kingdom, Switzerland, Spain, Portugal, Netherlands, Italy, Ireland, France, and Denmark) found inequalities in health care delivery that favoured the rich, especially in Spain, the United States, and the United Kingdom (Van Doorslaer et al. 1993).

6.3. Responsibility and health: voluntary risk compared with involuntary risk

Another matter that must be addressed in a theory of health and social justice is how to handle the issue of voluntary versus involuntary risk—risks individuals could mitigate or eliminate by behavioural decisions compared to those over which they have no control. Should a principle of equal access to high-quality health care differ by the voluntary or involuntary nature of risk?

At first glance it appears that some people are not voluntarily risk averse to health consequences, for example, smokers who continue to smoke although they know the dangers. Some theorists argue that people who knowingly take risks with their health should pay additional sums of money or be solely responsible for their health insurance and health care and fend for themselves with the consequences of such risky behaviour. Such a system, these theorists believe, would:

(1) help raise additional financing for services caused by bad health habits, and
(2) help mitigate the moral hazards of such situations by giving people incentives to change their habits (Rakowski 1991).

Moreover, society is not obligated to address or pay the costs of the consequences of such behaviour. However, there are significant holes in this theory. First, there is some evidence that certain bad health habits, such as smoking and heavy drinking, actually contribute more financially, to society, than they cost. For example, society saves money when smokers fail to collect social security payments because they die prematurely (Manning et al. 1989). Early death from smoking could also avoid long-term care costs incurred by older patients. Second, many poor health habits, such as tobacco use, are highly addictive or heavily influenced by social factors, and it is not clear that they are solely voluntary. Third, even if these voluntary behaviours were responsible for significant additional health care costs, financial disincentives in the form of higher health insurance premiums might not change those behaviours.[2]

Discussions by Gerald Dworkin (1981) and Elliott Sober (2000) are instructive here. On the question of financial liability, Dworkin argues that three conditions must be met before individuals should be held financially responsible for health risks. First, society must be able to understand the respective causal determinants of voluntary versus involuntary contributors to health risks. Second, it must determine the difference between involuntary and voluntary behaviour. Third, society must be able to differentiate between genetic and non-genetic predisposition to disease.

Sober's analysis focuses on interactions between biological and environmental factors. Like Dworkin, he notes that several conditions must be met in order to determine causation. He also observes that illness typically results from the interaction between genes and environmental factors, such as lifestyle and diet. For example, the relative contributions of alcohol abuse, genes, and environmental factors to the onset and severity of chronic pancreatitis are difficult to disentangle. It is also difficult to understand why some who do not abuse alcohol develop pancreatitis whereas others who drink heavily escape it. Moreover, sociocultural factors, such as poverty, also associate with poor health habits: disadvantaged people are less equipped to bear the potential costs of mitigating the risks of such habits. They are also less able to pay for the resulting health effects. For all of these reasons, it is unjust to always blame individuals for their health problems, but rather a focus on developing health agency is essential for achieving optimal health outcomes. In this sense, this view differs, for example, from that of Pogge (2002a), who would grant less moral weight to guaranteeing medical treatment for a 'self-caused' medical condition. He notes:

whether it is unjust for social institutions not to entitle indigent persons to treatment for a certain lung disease—and, if so, how unjust this is—may be greatly affected by whether this disease is contracted through legally authorised pollution by others...or self-caused through smoking in full awareness of its risks (Pogge 2004, p. 157).

In the health capability paradigm, individuals are responsible for the choices they make, but the ethos is focused less on determining blame to diminish societal compensation, leaving people to their own devices, and more on societal and individual efforts to create the conditions for individuals to make good choices. On a view of shared health governance, responsibility is shared among different individual and social structures, but with the individual at the centre. While in an ideal world, it would be useful to try to perfectly attribute bad choices to individual and social causes, assigning proportional causality is likely to be unfeasible with the current state of the behavioural and social sciences. Drawing a clear line between voluntary and involuntary actions, especially where individuals' health agency is socially conditioned, is difficult, at best. This account is responsibility-sensitive. Responsibility here is thus seen as a continuum from individual to social responsibility in which most cases lie somewhere along that continuum. Loss (e.g. death), or severe deprivation (e.g. significant loss in pulmonary function or mobility) in the domain of central health capabilities is too high a cost to make people pay for the results of behaviour that may be caused by the interaction between individual responsibility and social factors. Thus, under a health capability paradigm, in contrast to the various theories discussed in this chapter, ranging from brute luck and option luck to equal resource and equal opportunity views, society should err on the side of greater social responsibility while at the same time supporting the development of individual responsibility and choice in the context of complex background social conditions. Both a short term and long term goal is developing prudent behaviour through health agency and preparing each individual to think like a social planner in the sense of better understanding how his individual choices will affect the costs and opportunities of others and society as a whole.

6.4. Paternalism, libertarian paternalism, and free will

A final issue in this chapter that is central to an equal access account is the appeal of policy and programmatic measures at the practical level in public health and health policy that embody degrees of coercion and free will. On the more coercive end of the spectrum are sanctions, laws, regulations, and mandates, such as seat belt laws, required immunizations in schools, smoking prohibition, illicit drug laws, and water purification. Such programmes typically fall within the scope of national and sub-national public health programmes, although there are efforts to extend the authority of international organizations such as the WHO to oversee nation states as well (e.g. disease surveillance). The tension is between the libertarian who would like complete or nearly complete autonomy to dominate public policy development and the paternalist who would like the collective enterprise of the state to take actions on behalf of individuals to improve well-being.

The health capability paradigm presented here would be consistent with policies all along this spectrum. That said, the theory does offer an alternate view on the issues, that especially takes a long term and counter factual perspective on states of affairs and policy prescriptions that balance health agency and health functioning to improve health capability at various points in time. For example, this approach would support a public health programme to provide safe water through a government-run water sanitation system even though any given individual covered by the programme may not have been directly involved in its development (although as noted in Chapter 8, individuals could provide input in designing effective programmes). While this programme is autonomy limiting in many respects, the programme improves any given individual's central health capabilities by enabling him to live free from water-borne diseases. At the same time, the theory would support a public health campaign that enhances health knowledge and skills and thus builds health agency to also reduce the risk of water borne diseases. An example is a campaign to build an individual's health agency as it relates to the management of a water well. This scenario would enable people to opt out of the government provided sanitation system, have water wells on their property, but provide them with the necessary skills and help them apply these skills to keep the well water safe for consumption. There are other examples that could demonstrate how a health capability paradigm can fit with different interventions and programmes along this spectrum.[3]

It is worth noting, however, before leaving this subject, a tension between the currently highly visible subfield of libertarian paternalism within the broader field of behavioural economics and the emphasis placed here on health agency. Libertarian paternalistic policies and programmes range widely from health care (especially health insurance choice) to financing retirement (e.g. 401k options and portfolio choice). Grounded in behavioural economics, libertarian paternalism is based on empirical evidence demonstrating that individuals, for a number of reasons (cognitive difficulties processing and weighing trade-offs among pros and cons, will power, memory, attention, etc.) do not make 'rational' decisions in line with what neoclassical economic theory would predict (Thaler and Sunstein 2003). As such, policies and programmes designed under the rubric of libertarian paternalism attempt to use this empirical evidence to 'nudge' or help individuals make 'rational' choices that are in their self-interest. These programmes lie somewhere in-between the paternalistic (coercive) and the autonomous.

The idea is that altering people's choices (e.g. default rules, framing effects, commitment contracts, and starting points), for example, through opt-in organ donation, HIV/AIDS screening, health plan enrolment, or return medical visit scheduling programmes (Loewenstein et al. 2007) to increase the odds that they will make the 'right' choice is a valid policy approach (for both private and public institutions) because it is both directive towards a particular outcome, but also preserves a role for choice. While these programmes may be useful short-term measures, their long-term impact is in question. For example, contingency management, an effort to create financial incentives to treat drug addiction, has been found to produce significant short-term effects that diminish over time (Olmstead et al. 2007). The paradigm developed here espouses both short-term policies designed to improve individuals' choices and behaviour toward better health functioning *and* longer term investment in individuals' health agency. Then people might both make healthier choices in the short and long run for themselves *and* participate collectively in developing public policies to improve the health functioning and health agency of others (the population at large) and future selves (future generations) over the long run. Investments in health agency (non-coercive policies that promote autonomy), however, could be more effective over time because they would lead to changes in both individual behaviour (in the short and long term) and social structures (through collective action among individuals equipped with more developed health agency) that in combination create the conditions to enable individuals to be healthy. It is at this stage of the game that individuals ultimately and voluntarily embrace the role of government and public policy and willingly give up some of their autonomy for the government to provide services and support its core functions (through coercion or degrees of coercion as in libertarian paternalism) of redistribution, oversight, regulation, tax and finance, mandates, and provision.

Notes

1. See Beauchamp and Childress (1994) for an overview of equal access arguments. On the obligation of beneficence to provide health care, see Buchanan (1984). On libertarian arguments endorsing a free-market for health care, see Engelhardt (1986). For discussions of equal access, see Daniels (1985), Gutmann (1981), and Menzel (1990).

2. For an illuminating critique of luck and other forms of egalitarianism see Elizabeth Anderson (1999) and for a more detailed discussion of personal and social responsibility specifically in the health care context see Wikler (2004).
3. For a discussion of the perspective that mandatory treatment can be justified on grounds of autonomy see Caplan (2006).

7

A Health Capability Account of Equitable and Efficient Health Financing and Insurance

Universal health insurance coverage is fundamental to the health capability paradigm.

One of the primary economic barriers to high-quality health care is lack of health insurance. Moreover, resource allocation in this paradigm rests on medical necessity and medical appropriateness, not ability to pay. The costs of health care can also affect health directly by reducing demand for necessary care or increasing consumption of unnecessary care. And finally, the uncertainty of health need, the catastrophic costs of medical care, individuals' risk averse nature, and the need to redistribute resources from well to ill and rich to poor place *risk pooling* at the centre of health care financing.

The health capability paradigm requires that health system financing, organization, and delivery ensure access to medically necessary and medically appropriate care and protect individuals from health-related financial burdens that could substantially erode their freedom to flourish.

This means that health policy should provide *continuous* universal health insurance so that gaps in coverage do not handicap health functioning and health agency. This arrangement should include all individuals at all times, regardless of changes in income, employment, marital or health status.

This account argues for financing health care according to ability to pay (adjusting contributions to health care costs by income level) and delivering it according to medical necessity and medical appropriateness (see Chapter 8). Thus, society distributes health care resources according to individuals' health capability (health functioning and health agency), not according to their ethnicity, how much money they have, where they live, whether they are married, or what they do for a living.

An equitable health system requires financial protection of all individuals, especially the poor and most disadvantaged, against the monetary burdens associated with health risks. Pooling risks and collecting prepayments unrelated to health status or use secures this protection. Thus, provision of health care rests on community-rating (where health insurance premiums are the same across individuals) as opposed to experience-rating, with premiums based on previous health care expenditures or pre-existing health conditions, and not on an individual's health status.

Maximizing the quantity of resources available for health care improves the ability to meet individuals' health needs. At the same time, health care financing must be efficient in any country adopting universal coverage because limited resources must be used wisely, and wasted resources undermine important health goals. To achieve both administrative and technical efficiency (Mills and Ranson 2001), systems should minimize the costs of collecting and distributing revenue and guard carefully against corruption and fraud (below). The US and numerous developing countries do not provide universal health insurance coverage to their populations.

Academic approaches to health insurance (Pauly et al. 2006) have typically adopted a neoclassical economic perspective, assuming that individuals make rational decisions to maximize their preferred outcomes, and businesses (including insurance companies) make rational decisions to maximize profits. In that particular approach, individuals who are risk averse will purchase health insurance to reduce variation in the costs of health care between healthy and sick periods (Cutler and Zeckhauser 2000). In empirical studies, however, individuals do not always make rational choices. They also find it difficult to assess their health risks and to know how much insurance they need (Cutler and Zeckhauser 2004).

By contrast, medical ethics has focused on the issue of equal access to health care, but provided little in the way of philosophical justification for risk management through health insurance *per se*. Nor has the field shown how the practice whereby many at-risk individuals pay premiums to cover one individual's expensive health outcome (risk-pooling) is ethically desirable, except insofar as it ensures equal access to health care and equal funding to purchase it for all contributors.

This book offers an alternative moral framework for analysing health insurance: that universal health insurance is essential for human flourishing. In this theory, the central ethical aims of universal health insurance coverage are to make and keep people healthy, to develop their health functioning and health agency, and to enhance their security by promoting health and protecting them from both ill health and its economic consequences, issues not adequately considered to date. Universal health insurance coverage requires redistribution through taxation, and so individuals in societies providing this entitlement must voluntarily embrace sharing these costs. This redistribution is another ethical aim of universal health insurance unaddressed by other frameworks; as such it must be analysed in the context of mainstream economic theory of health insurance.

7.1. Theory of demand for health insurance

In neoclassical welfare economic theory, individuals make choices to maximize their preferences over time. The goal of society is to maximize social welfare, or aggregate preferences. It assumes that individuals make rational choices based on cost-benefit calculations under varying conditions (Culyer and Newhouse 2000).

This approach asserts that the free market is the best way to allocate resources, as it values efficiency over equity. Individuals averse to risk are predicted to choose insurance against large risks, leaving smaller risks uncovered, thereby improving their overall welfare (Arrow 1963, p. 961). As we have seen, however, empirical studies show that individuals find such choices difficult (Cutler and Zeckhauser 2004).

Health insurance markets are also not entirely free. Insurance companies have an information advantage, which they can use to 'cherry-pick' (Newhouse 1984) both the kinds of consumers they insure and the kinds of coverage they offer them, to increase profits. In consequence, more comprehensive coverage tends to be confined to wealthier individuals, reducing the pooling of risk across the population. Conversely, poorer individuals often fail to choose coverage that meets their health needs (Cutler and Reber 1998).

7.2. Behavioural economics and prospect theory

In health insurance markets, as in other areas of economics, people do not perfectly forecast their preferences or desires under different conditions, nor can they always estimate the consequences of changes in their circumstances (Gilbert et al. 2002). They also have relatively little knowledge about individual health insurance plans when choosing between them (Kaiser Family Foundation 2000). Neoclassical theory predicts that consumers will insure against catastrophic medical events and cover lower-cost services themselves; in reality consumers typically choose policies with low deductibles and copayments. Economists explain this divergence as a matter of 'regret': individuals choose plans with no deductibles to avoid making trade-offs between medical care and money, trade-offs they might 'regret' after the fact (Thaler 1980).

Prospect theory (Kahneman and Tversky 1979) offers a different explanation for this behaviour. In empirical research, given equal cash amounts of loss and gain, consumers place a higher value on the amount lost than on the same amount gained. This strong aversion to loss might lead consumers to buy low-deductible policies to eliminate barriers to health care. Such efforts to minimize regret, loss, and anxiety reflect a concern for overall well-being, rather than the preference maximization efforts described by the neoclassical model.

7.3. Medical ethics and equal access to health care

In medical ethics, several principles support a right to health care and equal access to it, as discussed in Chapter 6. Approaches ranging from egalitarian to communitarian have been used to justify equal access to health care or health coverage. However, they have not provided an adequate analysis of health insurance in relation to risks, their consequences and management. Consequently, medical ethics does not adequately consider loss aversion, regret, anxiety, forecasting, discounting, and redistribution, all of which are important issues for a theory of health insurance.

Mainstream economic theory, while often inconsistent with practice, recognizes these human characteristics, and can provide many helpful insights, both into people's behaviour and their underlying motives. Using it, we turn now to an alternative framework for understanding health insurance issues and rationalizing universal health insurance to resolve them.

7.4. Welfare economics and the capability approach

As an alternative to the neoclassical economic model, the capability approach evaluates an individual's well-being and social welfare in terms of functionings and capabilities (Sen 1992).

From this perspective, the major premise of neoclassical economics, that welfare rests on an individual's willingness to pay for a commodity (e.g.

health insurance), is flawed. Rather than focusing on the individual's pursuit of maximum satisfaction, with priority given to satisfying individual and aggregate preferences, the capability approach gives moral significance to human capability and human flourishing. Welfare economics, moreover, depends on the standard rational actor model. The capability approach does not make those assumptions: in the real world, individuals do not invariably make rational choices.

The health capability paradigm focuses on individuals' exposure to risk and their ability to manage it adequately, rather than their preferences regarding it. When individuals lack access to the means of reducing or mitigating risks, they become insecure. Vulnerability and insecurity diminish well-being and inhibit human flourishing.

7.5. Vulnerability and insecurity

Vulnerability and insecurity in health are an inescapable fact of life. Because the risk of ill health is uncertain in frequency, timing, and magnitude, it is difficult to insure against at the individual level. Most measures of risk give equal weight to both upward and downward variation in factors such as income, but downward changes both affect and concern most people far more than upward changes do.

Lack of health care access increases risk exposure: failing to meet health needs when they occur can expose individuals to even greater risk of illness or injury later on. Illness itself brings vulnerabilities: a potential further decline in health, lost income due to absence from work and medical expenses, and lost opportunities at work or school. The irreversibility of worst-case scenarios—severe disability or death—heightens individuals' insecurity and vulnerability.

Without health insurance, individuals and households must self-insure, use informal risk-sharing arrangements, diversify assets, draw on savings, sell assets, borrow, or go into debt to cover needed services, all of which offer moderate to little effective income smoothing over time. In many cases, individuals who lack health insurance must go without necessary medical care.

7.6. Moral foundations of health insurance

In this new paradigm, the moral foundations of health insurance build on the concept of human flourishing. If health policy is to promote human flourishing, its goal should be to enable individuals to function best, given their circumstances, and thus reduce the vulnerability and insecurity associated with ill health (Ruger 2006a). It is not enough simply to provide resources to individuals (for example, cash payouts or direct medical services) (Ruger 2007a). Justice requires that individuals and households have a measure of protection against the vulnerabilities resulting from ill health (Ruger 2006a), and if used appropriately, insurance offers this protection.

From this view, protective security (Sen 1999, p. 38) through health insurance is a necessary safety net that shields individuals from physical and mental harm and preventable death. This is valuable both in itself and also in providing the other opportunities that result from good health. Because protective security supports a person's overall health and capabilities beyond health, the way society finances health care has equity implications above and beyond health services delivery and health capability inequalities. Public policies relating to health and health care should thus promote protective security.

In this approach, universal health insurance is critical to protect individuals from deprivations caused by illness or injury, as well as changes in material circumstances, such as exorbitant health care debt. Society must protect people from financial insecurity resulting from 'changes in the economic or other circumstances or from uncorrected mistakes of policy' (Sen 1999, pp. 52–3) such as an economic downturn and rising unemployment. Protecting health, for example, and preventing bankruptcy and financial debt are therefore major goals of public policy.

On this view of health and social justice, universal health insurance is therefore morally justified because it ensures some of the conditions for human flourishing, by reducing, mitigating, and coping with the risks of ill health and the resulting financial insecurity. Major illness and/or disability cause significant economic costs both in income losses and medical expenses. Lack of insurance, underinsurance, self-insurance, informal insurance, and discontinuous insurance not only provide insufficient protection, but are also barriers to receiving high-quality (Hadley et al. 1991; Swartz 1989), medically necessary and appropriate health care (Ruger 2006d) and obtaining access to new technologies (Glied and Little 2003). In the United States, socio-economic and health insurance status relate to emergency department (ED) utilization such that, in particular, those without health insurance have significantly more ED visits and those visits occur for seemingly non-urgent medical problems as compared to their insured counterparts (Ruger et al. 2004). Uninsurance and underinsurance disproportionately influence underserved populations.

Health care costs can also affect health directly by suppressing demand for necessary medical services. Direct out-of-pocket payments (co-payments, user fees, user charges, waiting periods, and deductibles) can discriminate against the sick and impede use of necessary health care. Attempts to exempt poorer individuals from user fees in public facilities and to use ability to pay sliding scales for user fees have had limited success (Bennett et al. 1998). Copayments, deductibles, user fees, and other costs of health care thus create inequities and raise important moral concerns. Financial disincentives that discourage patients from using necessary health services leave people behind economic barriers and therefore fail to promote health capabilities (Ruger 2007c). Studies of small copayments are necessary to assess their effect on the demand for needed health care and their ability to prevent unlimited demand for care.

Health insurance can reduce risk by providing preventative health care (immunizations, prenatal and maternity care, infant care, cancer screening, nutritional services, regular wellness exams, and physical exams), as well as covering health care costs in times of illness or injury. Given a sufficiently large pool, insurance effectively pools risk across time and across individuals such that the financial risks of illness can be predicted and premiums (including actuarially fair premiums plus administrative costs) can be estimated with good reliability. For all these reasons, formal, institutional, and guaranteed health insurance is not only critical but also the rational choice in a just society.

An equitable health system requires protection of all individuals, especially the poor and most disadvantaged, from the monetary burdens associated with health risks. Experience-rated insurance premiums, which penalize those who have used more health care, violate this principle of provision. They can cause sicker individuals to avoid seeking care, by making them pay more than healthier individuals. In contrast, community-rated premiums require everyone to pay the same rate, regardless of health status. The equity implications of financing and of access are inseparable.

If universal health insurance is not to exacerbate other inequities, such as income, the population should share the health insurance tax burden justly, so that insurance premiums do not impoverish the poor or sick. Financing systems can be regressive (contributions consume a progressively smaller proportion of income as income rises), neutral (all income groups pay the same percentage of their income), or progressive (premiums represent a rising percentage of income as income rises). Health insurance financing needs to be progressive to improve health and overall

165

capabilities, because the high cost of health care requires expanded support from those able to pay. Risk pooling and wealth redistribution are essential for equitable and efficient health care financing.

The justification for progressive financing and community rating is bolstered by the close relationship between income and reduced capability. A sick person who cannot earn a decent income or pay for needed health care has compounded disadvantages. Illness not only diminishes his earning power but also increases demands on his income, for medication, prosthetic devices, surgery, professional care, and other medical expenses—just to achieve a basic level of functioning.

Universal health insurance boosts the economic security of both individuals and communities. Good health can expand people's productivity and incomes, allowing them to support a more prosperous overall economy, which can then afford more and better health care and other social services. By contrast, uninsured health care costs can force a person into poverty, and aggregated over many individuals, these consequences can undermine the economy at large. Health security and economic security are thus interrelated, and promotion of human flourishing requires attention to both. Health policy must ensure universal health insurance to enhance human capabilities and promote individuals' ability to flourish, and it must do so efficiently. Health insurance helps create opportunities for both good health and economic security; these interrelated freedoms support the individual's overall capability and thus build stronger communities.

7.7. Gains in well-being from risk pooling and health insurance

A critical benefit of equitable and efficient health system financing is the extent of gains in well-being that can accrue from risk pooling. Health risks and the financial costs associated with them are difficult to predict, and even predictable ones are difficult for individuals to plan for and cover financially. Efforts to predict future health care use patterns and costs have found that between 50 per cent and 85 per cent of individual health care use is unpredictable, even given a complete set of predictive variables, including disease profiles, functional status, and prior utilization patterns in addition to age, income, education, race, and gender (Newhouse et al. 1993).

In collective arrangements for funding health care, such as health insurance, individual risk is reduced by pooling a large number of people. The larger the risk pool, the more precisely insurers can predict the probability of financial loss due to illness; therefore, insurers can plan for and spread risk. Even though health insurance that is experience-rated can be seen as efficient and actually fair in markets with high degrees of risk segmentation, such models do not fully achieve the gains in well-being that can accrue from risk pooling that is community-rated.

7.8. Empirical evidence on the equity of health financing models

Health financing mechanisms differ in their effects on equity and efficiency. With the exception of the United States, nearly all higher-income market-oriented economies have institutionalized universal health care coverage for their populations. However, the equity of financing these schemes differs by country. In a study of ten OECD countries (United States, United Kingdom, Switzerland, Spain, Portugal, Netherlands, Italy, Ireland, France, and Denmark), researchers analysed the percentage of funding from four general types of health care financing: taxation, social insurance, private insurance, and out-of-pocket payments (Van Doorslaer et al. 1993). Using this information to assess the overall progressivity of a country's financing system, they found that countries that publicly finance the majority of their health care expenditures with either tax-financed systems (Denmark, Ireland, Portugal, and the United Kingdom) or social insurance funds (France, the Netherlands, and Spain) and that raise most of their funds through progressive taxation were typically more progressive. Percentages of funding from direct taxes were: Denmark, 49 per cent; United Kingdom, 38 per cent; Ireland, 29 per cent, and Portugal, 20 per cent. General revenue taxation was found to be a progressive means of raising funds, although the degree of equity depended on the progressivity and mix of taxes in a given system. Denmark's relatively high percentage of indirect taxes (36 per cent) made it slightly less progressive overall than the other three countries. Italy, with 42 per cent of tax-based funding, 38 per cent of social insurance-based funding, and 20 per cent of out-of-pocket payments, was slightly less progressive overall than Denmark and the next two countries, the Netherlands and Spain, due in part to its relatively high percentage of out-of-pocket expenditures (Van Doorslaer et al. 1993).

The study also found that social insurance is a more regressive method of raising health care revenue when contributions are capped, as happens with US Medicare payments, where marginal rates of contribution decline as income increases. France, the Netherlands, and Spain have a high proportion of health care financing through social insurance: 76 per cent, 66 per cent, and 62 per cent respectively. Each country also uses a low percentage of total taxes for funding: 2 per cent, 7 per cent, and 14 per cent, respectively. One progressive aspect of social insurance schemes is that they typically exempt certain groups, such as the elderly and very poor, from payments.

The study found private insurance and out-of-pocket payments more regressive than social insurance because the former are not necessarily based on earnings. Out-of-pocket payments are even more regressive because they are not generally income-adjusted and because the poor typically have greater rates of illness than the more affluent. A study in South Korea found those in the lowest socio-economic groups (and those with the most severe chronic conditions) disproportionately shouldered out-of-pocket payments (Ruger and Kim 2007). Among OECD countries, the United States and Switzerland have the highest percentages of payments from private sources, at 56 per cent and 60 per cent, respectively. Switzerland has a slightly higher percentage of payments from direct taxes (32 per cent) and a slightly lower percentage of out-of-pocket payments (19 per cent) than the United States, which gets 23 per cent of funding from direct taxes and roughly 30 per cent from out-of-pocket expenditures.

When out-of-pocket expenditures, low levels of prepayment, and regressively financed prepayments coexist, the poor suffer the most because their share of prepayments *and* their out-of-pocket expenditures are disproportionately high. In societies in which health systems fail to protect everyone, some families and individuals will slide into poverty and/or chronic illness because they must purchase necessary health care without assistance or forgo medical care they cannot afford.

7.9. Market failures, public goods, and the role of the public sector

Health care financing, delivery, and organization can involve either private (profit and non-profit) or public entities or a mix of the two. In the health capability paradigm, society must compare the advantages and disadvantages of the free market with those of the government and other political and social institutions. This view differs from strictly capitalist or socialist constructs (Benatar et al. 2005; Pogge 2002a; Ruger 2005c). Like the case of information technology, where the public sector created the Internet as a military communication tool and the free market increased productivity and made the technology accessible to consumers, roles for both public and private sectors are appropriate in health care, where numerous market failures have created a rationale for public sector involvement.

Contagion and epidemics are among the most common causes of health care market failure. When social benefits accruing from a given activity exceed individual benefits, insufficient investment or consumption by individuals results. Immunization and treatment for communicable diseases are two examples. In these cases, public financing and public-based delivery are likely to be necessary to achieve socially desirable ends. Public goods—those whose benefits should extend to everyone and whose consumption by one person does not preclude consumption by another—also require public financing, because private markets typically will not produce goods they cannot sell exclusively to one person. Such goods include clean air and water, sanitation systems, medical research and knowledge, environmental health, epidemiology, health information, communication, and promotion activities. There are also mixed goods that benefit specific individuals but have societal benefits as well. Rehabilitation services, for example, improve patients' physical functioning but also enhance economic progress through better labour productivity. In all these areas, private enterprise typically falls short.

Another market failure in health care is information asymmetry, in which health providers or insurers have significantly more information about a patient's condition than the patient does or vice versa. Although providers typically make decisions that are in their patients' best interests, self-interest sometimes plays a role. In recent years especially, economic incentives offered by managed care companies have undercut physicians' abilities to act on their patients' behalf. And even if the interests of patients and doctors are perfectly aligned, asymmetric information denies patients the ability to make decisions entirely independently. Indeed, information symmetry might never be possible, because doctors have many years of medical training and patients do not. Paying for a medical consultation is hardly equivalent to the purchase of other marketable products such as clothing, cars, or furniture.

The uncertain nature of health care (Arrow 1963)—the unpredictability of illness, and the impact and cost of treatment—makes risk-reduction measures such as health insurance appealing. However, it is also true that insurance market failures, credit shortages, and information insufficiencies can undermine the economic benefits insurance should provide.

Finally, market failures, such as adverse selection and moral hazard, inhibit the efficient functioning of private health insurance markets. Moral hazards occur when individuals who are insured, and therefore do not pay the full cost of medical care, have less financial incentive to avoid either poor health behaviours or high-cost services. Insulating people from the true costs of medical care through insurance might actually increase risky behaviour and the probability of an insurance-covered health event. An obvious counterargument is that the risk of ill health itself is the most important deterrent to risky behaviour. Efforts to mitigate the effects of moral hazard have included economic measures that sensitize patients to the real costs of medical care. However, they have had limited success.

Adverse selection can also create market failures. In both private and social insurance systems, adverse selection means sicker than average individuals self-select into insurance plans that offer superior health benefits. This raises the average cost of premiums, causing healthier patients to leave the plan and obtain less expensive coverage elsewhere. Private insurers attempt to reduce adverse selection by excluding potentially costly pre-existing conditions, requiring medical exams, refusing high-risk individuals, and instituting waiting periods for insured care. A US study found that on average HMOs enrolled younger (and thus healthier) members than traditional fee-for-service (FFS) plans. The study also found a lower percentage of enrollees with chronic diseases such as cancer, diabetes, and cardiovascular disease among HMOs as compared to FFS plans (Taylor et al. 1995). These measures typically increase the profits of private insurers but undermine effective risk-pooling.

Moral hazard and adverse selection require public action such as regulation of private insurers and mandatory public insurance with risk pools that include healthy and sick, wealthy and poor contributors.

Every type of health system has its advantages and disadvantages in terms of efficiency and equity. The drawbacks of an entirely public health sector or an entirely private health sector suggest that mixed public-private systems might be optimal. Market failure types suggest a greater role for public financing and private provision through non-profit institutions. The health capability paradigm, with its emphasis on an integrated and multifaceted system, argues for a blended approach in which the free market and the government work to improve health capability (Ruger 2005a). To create and maintain equitable and efficient health systems, governments must offer significant direction, regulation, financing, and, in some cases, provision of care, working with a private sector that effectively provides goods and services. In virtually every area of the health sector, especially in generating medical knowledge, technologies, goods, and services, public-private collaboration and investment are critical.

8

Allocating Resources: A Joint Scientific and Deliberative Approach

We turn now to the question of determining priorities for competing needs when resources are scarce. We begin with the broader societal perspective, because fair decisions must balance spending on health with spending elsewhere. We then work inward to prioritize competing claims within the health budget and re-examine the health budget itself.

8.1. Reasoned consensus through scientific and deliberative processes

The paradigm proposed here involves a joint scientific and deliberative process, integrating substantive and procedural principles, as a framework for allocating resources. This public process combines the evidence-base of health care (medicine and health related research) and public health with input from individuals, physicians, and public health experts to assess the value of treatments, medications, and other health care and public health interventions. It is important to assess both the *necessity* and the *appropriateness* of a health intervention.

Although individuals have primary authority for health care decisions that affect them directly, physicians can help determine 'medical appropriateness' and 'medical necessity'. Thus, individuals employ their health agency, and physicians, by virtue of their medical expertise and allegiance to the Hippocratic Oath, seek their patients' best interest. In this framework, physicians share expert knowledge (e.g. benefits, risks, costs) with each other and with patients to achieve ethical rationality and practical reasonableness, balancing technical rationality with ethical rationality in collective choice.

This process emphasizes deliberatively derived public policy for human flourishing and reasoned consensus to evaluate arrangements for improving human functioning. Aristotle stressed the need for deliberative decision-making based on prudence and practical wisdom about how to ensure the good of human life (Irwin 1999, p. 89). Indeed, he argued that medicine was an appropriate object of deliberation, and he also recognized the need for both ethical and technical forms of reasoning (Irwin 1999, p. 35). A more expansive account of rationality incorporates both.

Such deliberations help guide the allocation of health resources and facilitate the development of health policy and health laws through a new conception, called here shared health governance. This view contrasts with notions that consumers alone, physicians alone, public health experts alone, strict algorithms, cost-benefit calculations, fair procedures, government officials or technocrats, shared decision-making within an informed consent model, or third parties such as insurers, should make health allocation decisions. While it endorses many of the principles of the shared decision-making approach to individual medical treatment decisions, it focuses differently on shared health governance, a paradigm in which individuals, providers, and institutions work together to empower individuals and create an environment enabling all to be healthy. It also contrasts with both a strictly technocratic approach and a purely procedural approach to collective choice. It differs from efforts to develop a decision-making process 'to set fair limits to health care' (Daniels 2008; Daniels and Sabin 2002, p. 2). It promotes consensus on substantive—especially scientific—principles of distribution. It also offers a method for achieving consensus (incompletely theorized agreements) that differs from aggregative tools such as a strict majority vote. It empowers individuals and underscores their responsibility through health agency; and its judgements place special importance on the results and scientific basis of health policies (effectiveness and costs).

Finally, it promotes public deliberation through a collaboration around problem solving among physicians, public health experts, and citizens. These formulations focus on reasoning—whether at higher levels of abstraction or lower levels of particulars—and on mutual respect among citizens and experts, but do not accept procedural criteria as sufficient for just outcomes. This framework thus integrates both consequentialist and proceduralist elements of justice.

This approach stresses that participatory decision-making is instrumentally important for forming values and setting priorities when policy choices are difficult (Sen 1999, p. 152). Participatory decision-making has a constructive role in health, because a critical understanding of health and social needs requires interactive discussion and exchange among participants at the individual and collective levels. This approach focuses particularly on the individual's health agency. Health agency is important for health policy because it gives members of the public their rightful role in collective choice, but it also holds a special place for individuals' responsibility both in terms of their own behaviour and in terms of decisions made on behalf of and that impact society. Participation and open dialogue are especially important for the health-politics nexus (Ruger 2005b; 2005d).

When policies and laws require even greater specification, further iterations of public discussions could be necessary to make difficult choices about which health services merit societal investment. Health policy cannot result from technical formulas. Rather, this paradigm proposes that policy should emerge from a stepwise process that reviews scientific evidence about the consequences of polices on health. If evidence is incomplete or inconsistent, recommendations should reflect the judgement of individuals and experts. The deliberative process should also update its recommendations continually to account for changes in medical knowledge, technology, and costs when determining what probability of success would make an intervention worthwhile. Ethical rules should adapt to new circumstances. Because these recommendations form the basis for defining a benefits package, making resource allocation decisions, and constructing general guidelines, the underlying reasoning should be explicit and public. An appeals mechanism for re-evaluating decisions should be instated.

Health policy must promote objectives as efficiently as possible. Therefore, some limits must apply when allocating resources and evaluating medical technologies, and allocation decisions must consider cost. For efficiency evaluation, cost-minimization analysis (CMA) is an invaluable tool for decision-making. Cost-effectiveness analysis (CEA) can also play a role by comparing the marginal benefits and marginal costs of two or more interventions for a single condition or population, such as AIDS patients. This approach contrasts with the utilitarian aggregation methodology, the use of utilities, and with methodologies to incorporate equity or deliberatively determined weights *into* CEA. Instead, it recommends the use of CMA and CEA in a stepwise manner in which economic considerations follow clinical input, not vice versa. It cautions against the sole use of techniques such as cost per life saved or cost per QALY gained when setting budget priorities among different public measures

174

in different policy domains (Tengs et al. 1995), or when analysing government regulations (Breyer 1993).

8.2. Frameworks for combining technical and ethical rationality for collective choice

The precise combination of technical and ethical rationalities will vary depending on the scope and nature of the social choice exercise. For example, broader decision-making at the national level requires participation by popularly elected representative groups (e.g. legislatures or councils) and entails trade-offs between health and other social policies, while decision-making about a benefits package focuses more on broad categories of health care and public health to meet individuals' health needs. In contrast, more specific treatment decisions engage patients and providers at the local and individual levels. This project's scope does not extend to specifying procedures for various circumstances; however, the following sections will emphasize certain substantive and procedural aspects of the paradigm and discuss how they are combined. This approach emphasizes including *both* clinical and economic analysis for evidence-based decision-making. These scientific components of a paradigm are outlined below. Deliberative components to the process build on existing literature, but move beyond that work by integrating deliberation with technical rationality and augmenting it with incomplete theorization and partial ordering in order to come to consensus amidst pluralism and wide disagreement.

8.3. Allocations within the broader social budget

In a broader resource allocation exercise and more general theory of distributive justice, health capabilities compete with other capabilities. The capability approach offers the entire capability set as the focal variable for decisions about macro resource allocation for a theory of social justice. Although a thorough analysis of partitioning is beyond this project's scope, it is important to note that macro-level decisions belong within the context of a political unit. Under this approach, the decision-making process would be an open, deliberative, and democratic process that divides the overall budget and legislation into allocations for the health sector as well as education, housing, culture, defence, and other functions.

Many examples of deliberative democratic processes are found in the world's democratic polities, but no one model is singled out for the current proposal. In the United States, the federal government devises this budget through an interactive process between the legislative and executive branches, but this process is typically extended and contentious; indeed, the government has been known to shut down on occasion because it could not agree on a budget. Reform efforts around specific legislation, universal coverage, for example, have foundered in part because of this process's shortcomings, so although beyond the scope of this book, reforms (e.g. campaign finance reforms) to the current democratic process could be necessary.

Empirical evidence on national budgets reveals that countries tend to devote more resources and increasing shares of their national income to the health sector as their income increases (World Bank 2000). Lower-income countries on average spend less per capita on health in terms of both percentage of Gross Domestic Product (GDP) and actual dollars (World Bank 2000, p. 92). In the late 1990s, for example, low-income countries spent an annual average of $21 per capita on health, compared with $116 for middle-income countries and $2,736 for high-income countries (World Bank). In the poorest countries, per capita health spending can be as low as $2 or $3, with most funds coming from private sources. In percentage of GDP, low-income countries spend roughly 4 per cent on health, middle-income countries spend 6 per cent, and high-income countries 10 per cent (World Bank). The public share of health expenditures, as a percentage of total health spending in 1999, was 62 per cent (or 7 per cent of GDP) in high-income countries, 52 per cent (or 4 per cent of GDP) in middle-income countries, and 27 per cent (or 2 per cent of GDP) in low-income countries. One study found that the public portion of health expenditures will increase by 2 per cent for every 1 per cent increase in per capita income in middle- and high-income countries and by 1 per cent for every 1 per cent increase in per capita income in lower-income countries (Schieber and Maeda 1997).

Health system efficiency determines the extent to which better health is achieved with a given level of resources. While it is critical to allocate more national resources to the health sector—a major theme of the World Health Organization's Macroeconomics and Health Commission—efficient allocation of these resources *within* the health system is critical as well. Efficient allocation avoids excessive administrative costs, unnecessary procedures, and allocative and technical inefficiencies. It effectively realizes the economic benefits of risk sharing. Efficient allocation also requires generating resources to finance health systems effectively and equitably (see Chapter 7). Thus, incentives or disincentives associated with taxation, financing, and insurance policies need close scrutiny (Ruger et al. 2001).

8.4. Allocating within the health policy budget: benefits package: types of goods and services guaranteed

A major ethical issue in health resource allocation involves determining a standard benefits package of goods and services guaranteed to all. Under this paradigm the following principles apply.

First, all covered goods and services must be of high quality (Chapter 6). This principle addresses the significant inequities that occur when individuals might have equal claim to particular goods and services but in practice receive care of significantly different quality. Second, a high quality allocation scheme guarantees equitable access to both prevention and treatment. Third, it guarantees equitably financed health insurance that covers this guaranteed benefits package (Chapter 7).

Fourth, under this paradigm, goods and services that are 'medically appropriate' (a term that encompasses medical necessity) to ensure central health capabilities would form the basis of a guaranteed benefits package. Society could then expand the package through reasoned consensus on an iterative basis if so desired. Thus, the government-guaranteed benefits package would cover appropriate and necessary care to prevent, diagnose, or treat illness, disease, injury, disability, or other health conditions associated with escapable morbidity or premature mortality. Fifth, in terms of content, this paradigm allows defining the benefits package more broadly through a public process and permits individuals to purchase additional health care on the free market. However, the government would regulate the emergence, development, and functioning of private health insurance and health care.

A major difference between this account and other views is the requirement that goods and services be 'medically appropriate' as well as medically necessary. They would have to be consistent with high quality standards of good health care and public health practice. They would exclude goods and services that are for the personal comfort, convenience, or custodial care of the patient, family, or provider. Adding medical appropriateness and established evidence-based clinical practice guidelines to the medical necessity standard introduces another level of prioritization grounded in scientifically based, publicly accepted methods of medicine, public health, and health-related research. This account gives authority back to physicians and patients, allowing them to make informed judgements about resource allocation on a category by category and case by case basis. Where medicine is more art than science, clinical judgement is critical to decision-making. However, evidence-based guidelines, appeal procedures, and conservative utilization reviews should inform the decision-making process continuously and help hold physicians accountable for their decisions. It is also important to have safeguards in place to counter, ameliorate, or suppress physician behaviour due, for example, to immediate financial gain (e.g. when compensation associates with a degree of utilization), or defensive medicine (e.g. to avoid personal malpractice lawsuits and thus higher insurance premiums).

Applying these additional standards to the prioritization process improves the prospect of acceptable outcomes that are both substantive and legitimized by a fair and evidence-based procedure. By contrast, attempts to agree on abstract moral principles alone are likely to fail. In practice, individuals often make health decisions quickly, and members of society frequently reach agreement on a particular course of action whether or not they agree on the underlying justification. Individuals are rarely able to completely theorize a decision when plural and ambiguous concepts and values are involved. This difficulty is exacerbated on a collective level; people rarely agree on all aspects and at all theoretical levels of a particular solution.

8.5. An evidence-based approach: medical appropriateness and clinical practice guidelines

Evidence-based health policy integrates the best available evidence with patient input to offer standardized health policy and public health to provide optimal care and public health programmes for individuals. Physicians, public health providers, individuals, scientists, and researchers should be involved in developing the standards. Not all health care is medically necessary and medically appropriate. A lot of what health care has to offer, particularly in the modern day of advanced medical technology, is only marginally effective. Moreover, while millions of people in the world have received high-quality health care, many others experience underuse, overuse, misuse, or inconsistent health care. Some have estimated that up to 30 per cent of all health care in the United States is wasted and could be reduced through greater efficiency in clinical practice (Brook and Lohr 1986). Although economic approaches have been implemented to address this problem, studies demonstrate that these non-clinical solutions *alter the distribution of both necessary and unnecessary medical care*, creating additional health problems.

Well-established, evidence-based clinical guidelines can be helpful because they systematically bring together experience and evidence on various conditions and provide recommendations for treatment. There are considerable data on clinical outcomes of health interventions. In the United States, the federal Agency for Healthcare Research and Quality (AHRQ), for example, tracks the research on clinical effectiveness and has created practice guidelines that offer standardized treatment protocols for certain conditions. Other organizations providing evidence-based best practice standards include the Joint Commission, the National Quality Forum, and the Centers for Disease Control and Prevention (CDC) (Mathews and Pronovost 2008).

The process of developing these guidelines is quite involved. A number of medical subspecialties have established evidence-based clinical guidelines from extensive meta-analysis of existing studies (US Department of Health and Human Services 2000). For example, guidelines for pre-eclampsia screening, vaginal birth after caesarean (VBAC), immunizations and chemoprophylaxis, and hundreds more have been established (National Guideline Clearinghouse, http://www.guideline.gov/). The American Medical Association and the American College of Cardiology have also endorsed the practice guidelines approach. Guideline architects search, review, and synthesize extensive amounts of literature to evaluate empirical evidence and significant outcomes. Peer and field reviewers subsequently evaluate the validity, reliability, and utility of the guidelines and solicit input from practitioners and patients. When evidence is incomplete or inconsistent, reviewers seek the professional judgement of an expert panel. Admittedly, these guideline recommendations might not be appropriate for all circumstances and specific co-morbidities, subpopulations, and geographic considerations should be taken into account (Boyd et al. 2005). Clinical guidelines must also be continuously tested and updated. A review of guidelines for obtaining histopathologic diagnosis on tonsillectomy and/or adenoidectomy specimens found new evidence suggesting that this diagnosis might not be necessary for every patient, particularly in the paediatric subgroup (Younis et al. 2001). Another study of the use of cervical spine X-rays in patients with blunt trauma found that physicians could reduce unnecessary X-rays by using five clinical criteria (Hoffman et al. 2000).

Furthermore, while effective in recommending evidence-based care, clinical guidelines alone cannot reduce differences in health care quality, nor can they evaluate medical technologies. They must be embedded in broader efforts involving physicians and patients in shared health governance through assessment of medically appropriate and medically necessary care. One component of such a model can be found in the RAND/UCLA appropriateness method, combining the evidence base of medicine and public health with input from physicians, public health experts, and individuals to assess the value of treatments, medications, and other health interventions. A version of the RAND/UCLA appropriateness method offers potential as one element of a shared health governance system.

The method involves a range of factors and nine stages:

(1) procedure selection;
(2) literature search;
(3) creation of indication lists;
(4) panel selection;
(5) rating;
(6) measurement scale development;
(7) data analysis of appropriateness;
(8) necessity assessment; and
(9) reliability and validity tests.

In the initial stages, the research team uses three selection criteria: the procedures must be frequently used; associated with significant morbidity and/or mortality; and found to consume considerable resources.

Some examples of procedures that meet these criteria include coronary angiography, coronary artery bypass surgery, coronary angioplasty, carotid endarterectomy, colonoscopy, upper gastrointestinal endoscopy, cataract surgery, hysterectomy, and cholecystectomy. Once the procedures are selected, the research team assembles a multispecialty panel and conducts a literature search to collect data on the efficacy, utilization, complications, cost, and stated indications for the procedure of interest. These data are used to develop a list of indications that categorize patients by symptoms, past medical history, and results of previous diagnostic tests. These clinical groupings become the basis for triaging patients who present symptoms. The multispecialty panel rates the indications' appropriateness on a scale from 9 (very appropriate) to 1 (very inappropriate). By definition, an indication is deemed medically appropriate if the expected medical benefit to the patient, in terms of life expectancy and health-related quality of life, exceeds the expected health risks. The procedure's cost is not incorporated in the appropriateness ranking (Brook 1994).

This method combines expert judgement with scientific evidence to develop procedures for measuring the appropriateness of health care. Patients have input after physicians assess an intervention's clinical effectiveness. Its purpose is to improve health status by reducing overuse and underuse of care. The method is transparent, scientific, and deliberative. It requires medical specialists to agree on medical guidelines, with patient input. Once courses of action are established, advanced medical information systems can help physicians, patients, insurers, and health planners improve medical decision-making at policy and delivery levels.

Since 1986, more than thirty studies in the United States have used the RAND/UCLA appropriateness method to rate the appropriateness of a number of clinical procedures. The resulting literature suggests that the percentage of inappropriate use across procedures ranges from 2 per cent to 75 per cent, while the percentage of appropriate care ranges from 35 per cent to 91 per cent, and the percentage of equivocal use ranges from 7 per cent to 32 per cent. For example, a study of carotid endarterectomy performed on 1,302 Medicare patients in three geographic areas of the United States found that roughly 35 per cent were appropriate, 32 per cent were equivocal, and 32 per cent were inappropriate. In other words, it was found that this procedure was unnecessarily used in one out of three cases (Winslow et al. 1988a; 1988b). A study of non-emergency, non-oncological hysterectomies performed in seven managed care organizations over a one-year period deemed roughly 16 per cent of the procedures inappropriate (Bernstein et al. 1993). A study of 1,338 patients undergoing isolated coronary artery bypass graft surgery in fifteen different New York State hospitals judged only 2 per cent inappropriate, nearly 91 per cent appropriate, and 7 per cent equivocal (Leape et al. 1993). Finally, a study of the appropriateness of tympanostomy tube surgery for recurrent acute otitis media and/or otitis media with effusion found that 41 per cent of 6,611 cases were appropriate while 32 per cent were equivocal and 27 per cent were inappropriate (Kleinman et al. 1994). This sample demonstrates that the percentage of inappropriate care varies by type of procedure, hospital, and other factors. Further analysis reveals variations by geographic location and health care volume. There has been less work on the costs and determinants of inappropriate care. One study that examined the overall magnitude of inappropriate use in US health care suggested that, for policy purposes, roughly 30 per cent of the procedures studied were inappropriate (Brook and Lohr 1986).

Studies of medical care appropriateness, combined with clinical practice guidelines, can provide some of the evidence base for assessing health interventions. Work examining rates of surgery in Canada, for instance, demonstrates the potential of population-based data *both* for developing clinical guidelines *and* for influencing physician practice (Black et al. 1999). Combining these efforts on a category by category basis, in an iterative fashion, reveals areas of improvement for processes integrating science-based methodologies, expert clinical judgement, and patient input. The medical appropriateness and medical necessity ratings, along with efforts to develop clinical guidelines combined with patient input, offer opportunities for reasoned consensus on categories of health interventions. Patient input is especially critical in this process as citizens, through deliberation, help guide providers and policymakers on the value especially of marginally effective technologies (where increases in longevity or the odds of survival are low). The National Institute for Health and Clinical Excellence (NICE) in the United Kingdom[1] is another example of a method useful to a system of shared health governance.[2]

Moreover, incomplete theorization allows individuals to decide, for example, to deny some interventions that might extend life by a few weeks or months, while at the same time guaranteeing interventions that extend life for years. Incomplete theorization allows for agreement where agreement is possible without requiring a full solution to the trade-off between small gains for many compared with large gains for a few or without a strict application of survival at all cost (life saving lexical priority) in all situations (differentiating between different stages of life and prospects for life extension). This process, encompassing reasoned consensus in conjunction with substantive values of health capabilities, can help assess the value of health care services and form deliberative decisions on guaranteed benefits for all. All effective health care cannot be included, but this process combines technical and ethical rationality to guide policy choice. Over time, these methods will evolve and become a more accepted part of health care.

At the individual level, however, clinicians must ultimately use their professional judgement, with input from their patients and with reference to guidelines, when recommending a course of treatment. Peer review of their behaviour will provide clinicians an incentive to act in accordance with established standards of medicine. For example, a US study evaluating computerized guidelines for prescribing the currently overprescribed and costly antibiotic vancomycin found that physicians who followed the vancomycin guidelines reduced their overall vancomycin use by 30 per cent compared with physicians who did not have access to the guidelines (Shojania et al. 1998). Researchers surmised that these modifications in physician behaviour would decrease costs and increase the appropriateness of medical care.

A common concern about 'medical necessity' judgements is that they are subject to bias, error, or uncertainty. It is clear from the literature that both the concept and operationalization of medical necessity vary. While some argue that this variation represents deeper differences about the goals of medicine, others believe that the concept is unclear at a more practical level (Elhauge 1994; Emanuel 1991; Hall and Anderson 1992), and still others attribute the divergence to insurance companies' efforts to reduce costs or control resources (Bergthold 1995). Despite these issues, in this paradigm, health resource allocation models are unworkable *unless they consider the necessity and appropriateness of health care*. Thus, we should work towards greater uniformity in clinical diagnosis and treatment. To address these concerns, the health capability paradigm proposes using medical appropriateness and evidence-based clinical practice guidelines along with the principle of medical necessity. These scientifically based, publicly accepted methods, combined with clinicians' judgement and patients' input, will help draw the line between what is and is not medically necessary.

8.6. Medical futility[3] and setting limits

Determining the appropriateness of medical care will also help limit treatment. It will help illuminate specific cases of medical futility, when withholding or withdrawing interventions might be most appropriate, because it attempts to determine when possible treatments are beyond social and medical obligations. While the issue of medical futility is implicit in concepts of medical appropriateness and necessity, it is worth emphasizing again here. Much has been written on the medical futility concept (Horton 1996; Ward 1997), in particular the potential cost savings in the United Kingdom of advance directives, Do Not Resuscitate orders, futile care withdrawal, and hospice care (Ward 1997), but in brief, a legitimate process for determining medical care appropriateness should help physicians, patients, and families determine when medical care is futile. For example, the Society of Critical Care Medicine Ethics Task Force (SCCMETF) has come to some consensus on dealing with treatment issues for critically ill patients. SCCMETF notes that terminally ill patients may be excluded from an Intensive Care Unit (ICU) when they have one of three conditions:

(1) severe irreversible brain damage;
(2) multiorgan failure;
(3) metastatic cancer unresponsive to chemotherapy or radiation therapy.

SCCMETF also permits the exclusion of patients who are in a persistent vegetative or permanently unconscious state. If patients or their families have previously specified that patients wish to avoid futile care, their wishes should be met (e.g. through advance directives, Do Not Resuscitate orders, futile care withdrawal, and hospice care orders) (American Thoracic Society 1991; Society of Critical Care Medicine Ethics Committee 1994).

Employing medical futility criteria, above and beyond medical appropriateness criteria, helps in avoiding the so-called 'bottomless pit' problem. Case-by-case analysis demonstrates that aid to the worse off gives way to aid for others because nothing can be done to further improve their health.

8.7. Universal benefits package

If we define a universal benefits package that includes goods and services that are medically necessary and medically appropriate for addressing central health capabilities, the goods and services provided would include public health, health care, and health-related social services. While this book does not aim to provide a specific list of goods and services, some examples of categories of health care subject to medical necessity and medical appropriateness assessments include:

- Medical goods and services provided by physicians and other health professionals (e.g. imaging, lab, X-ray, and other diagnostic tests; preventive care for both adults and children, including periodic physical exams and office visits; immunizations and flu shots; screenings; family planning and maternity care; therapeutic treatments, including physical medicine, occupational and speech therapy; rehabilitative therapies; hearing and vision services including testing, treatment, and supplies; orthopaedic and prosthetic devices; durable medical equipment; medical supplies; home health services; educational classes and programmes; surgical and anaesthetic goods and services provided by physicians and other health care professionals).

- Services provided by hospitals, ambulatory surgery centres, clinics, nursing care facilities, home health care agencies, and health posts.

- Services for medical emergencies and injuries; ambulance service.

- Parity with other benefits for mental health and substance abuse services provided by licensed psychiatrists, psychologists, clinical social workers, or psychiatric nurses; inpatient visits and intensive outpatient treatment; and diagnostic tests.

- Prescription drug benefits (e.g. drugs, vitamins and minerals, nutritional supplements, contraceptive drugs and devices[4]).

- Dental benefits (e.g. clinical oral evaluations, radiographs, tests and laboratory exams, preventive care and restorations, extractions).

Providers and patients should determine goods and services in particular cases.

A comparison of elements of a guaranteed benefits package under this paradigm with those advocated by other accounts highlights several important distinctions. First, libertarian and market-based approaches do not guarantee individuals any health care. Second, fair equality of opportunity accounts have been vague in determining a benefits package and could conceivably include health care subject to its impact on opportunity, offering a vague concept of adequate care and allowing fair procedures to determine differential coverage by insurance plans. The FEO account, for example, asserts that all health care should be an isolated social good of special moral importance due to its role in protecting equality of opportunity. By insulating health care from other social goods, it implies that all forms of health care (even care that might not be medically appropriate) should be isolated from trade-offs with other social goods (Daniels 1985). The FEO account also provides little guidance on efficiency or on the question of which goods and services are medically appropriate. The solution is to retreat to accountability for reasonableness. Emanuel (1991, p. 123) has criticized the FEO for advocating 'most of what modern medicine has to offer.' Third, approaches that rely on a 'prudential insurer' to choose a benefits package might or might not provide goods and services individuals need. Much of the demand for health care is unpredictable due to uncertainty of health needs. A health capability paradigm, on the other hand, would guarantee medically appropriate and necessary health care to reduce shortfall inequalities in individuals' central health capabilities; the process would eliminate the need for *ex ante* decisions about coverage. However, this account gives individuals the freedom to reject benefits or interventions and applies the cost-minimization principle (below) and CEA in specific situations to achieve given health objectives with the fewest resources.

This paradigm also differs from other perspectives in the way in which it regards specific categories of goods and services. For example, it might be more horizontally (although not necessarily more vertically) expansive than some views, because the benefits package might cover high-quality goods and services for some conditions that other approaches might leave uncovered. First, it would cover nutritional supplements, such as vitamins and minerals for individuals who are, or are at risk of being, malnourished because nutritional deficiencies undermine physical and cognitive capabilities. Prenatal iodine deficiency, for example, can cause permanent mental retardation, and chronic iodine deficiency can lead to mild mental impairment among school aged children and adults (Leslie and Jamison 1990). Micronutrient supplementation for children can alleviate childhood health problems and prevent diseases later in life (Bhargava 1994). Providing iodine and iron to micronutrient-deficient girls can help restore their cognitive functions to normal levels. Similarly, neurological and physical impairment, mental retardation, and death can be prevented by providing low-protein formula (excluding leucine, isoleucine, and valine) to infants with Maple Syrup Urine Disease, who are unable to metabolize certain amino acids (Maple Syrup Urine Disease Support Group; Morton et al. 2002).

Nutritional supplementation during pregnancy has benefits for fetal development. Dietary supplementation of folic acid (Vitamin B9) during the first trimester of pregnancy significantly reduces the incidence of spina bifida and other neural tube defects. Thus, folic acid and regular vitamin supplements for pregnant women should be included in the benefits package, as should vitamin supplements and safe drinking water for children.

Dental health benefits also distinguish this benefits package. Dental health is unduly influenced by some acute and chronic conditions. For example, children with hypohidrotic ectodermal dysplasia (HED) lose or totally lack teeth (Clarke et al. 1987), often requiring tooth replacement or false teeth to restore their oral functioning. However, US insurance companies often refuse to cover dental health. Under this approach, children and adults would be guaranteed dental health benefits and access to dentists to ensure their ability for oral functioning.

Third, the account would also cover mental health and substance abuse services, which would gain parity with other benefits. The main objective

186

would be to ensure individuals' capability for mental health functioning. The package would cover both episodic and chronic conditions if they were diagnosed by DSM-IV criteria and treated with scientifically accepted methods of care (American Association of Community Psychiatrists 2007). Principles of medical appropriateness and medical necessity would determine goods and services recommendations. For example, a patient presenting with acute depression would receive antidepressants and/or cognitive therapy, depending upon the extent and severity of the condition. Mental health functioning is also linked to health agency (Ruger 2007a).

Fourth, the account would cover family planning, and contraceptive and maternity-related goods and services. Some other approaches would exclude such care. These are just a few examples of elements of this account that would differ from other approaches.

This paradigm differs from previous interpretations of the capability approach. Sabin and Daniels, for example, argued that the capability model would advocate insurance coverage for all personal attributes, such as shyness or lack of confidence, resilience, and sociability, which put individuals at a relative disadvantage. Under their interpretation of the capability approach, the central purpose of health care is to 'use health care to help people become *equal* competitors, free from disadvantageous lack of capabilities regardless of etiology' (Sabin and Daniels 1994, p. 10). Thus, they argue, erroneously, that the capability approach fails to make a 'moral distinction between treatment of illness and enhancement of disadvantageous personal capabilities' (Sabin and Daniels 1994, p. 10). To the contrary, however, the health capability paradigm defines the central purpose of health care as addressing shortfall inequalities in *health capabilities*, rather than all personal traits, talents, skills, or capabilities unrelated to health.

8.8. Hard cases: the 'bottomless pit objection' and 'reasonable accommodation'

Critics have argued that some ethical theories give insufficient guidance about providing exorbitantly costly services to individuals with intractable illnesses or injuries (Buchanan 1984; Daniels 1981; Dworkin 1993). A particularly difficult problem is what some have called the 'bottomless pit objection' whereby one or a few individuals with seemingly infinite needs use significant resources without significantly improving health functioning.

Rawls's maximin or difference principle (Rawls 1971) and the FEO account have encountered particular criticism for these problems (Daniels 2001; Rai 1997; Sen 1992). Rawls himself does not apply this principle specifically to health care, but others who have point out that it could lead to the bottomless pit problem. Arrow (1973) offers criticism and notes that some health care procedures 'serve to keep people barely alive but with little satisfaction and . . . are yet so expensive as to reduce the rest of the population to poverty' (Arrow 1973, p. 251). Rai argues that Daniels's emphasis on priority for those diseases and disabilities that "involve a *greater* curtailment of an individual's share of the normal opportunity range" . . . could . . . give rise to the "bottomless pit" problem of patients whose health care costs are so high, and whose disabilities are so intractable, that promoting the normal opportunity range of these patients precludes spending to promote the normal opportunity range of all other individuals'(Rai 1997, p. 1024). The FEO account acknowledges the difficulties, noting the approach 'does not tell us which opportunities to protect when scarcity prevents us from equally protecting everyone's' (Daniels 1992, p. 42). Additionally, it concedes the 'approach provides little . . . [guidance on] hard . . . resource allocation decisions in which we must choose between services which remove serious impairments of opportunity for a few people and those which remove significant but less serious impairments from many' (Daniels 1981, p. 171), nor does accountability for reasonableness solve the problem.

On the other hand, consequentialist approaches that favour allocations producing the greatest net social benefit are criticized for discriminating against those most in need, especially the disabled, and for ignoring individuality.[5] These failings, liberal theorists argue, violate the Kantian principle of respect for individuals as moral agents who cannot be used solely to assist other individuals (Elhauge 1994). The health capability paradigm embraces this Kantian principle.

So how does society prioritize goods and services to the neediest but also set limits so as not to jeopardize a society's overall health achievements? Some advocate 'random selection', typically implemented by lottery, as a way to decide who gets which health resources (Beauchamp and Childress 1994). Kilner (1990) recognizes the potential use of 'modified random selection' to allocate scarce treatments among those who demonstrate a certain ability to benefit (thus excluding those who have not met that threshold). Orentlicher (1996) modifies the Kilner approach, arguing that this threshold should be used only when the difference between those who are likely to benefit and those who are not is 'large' and 'certain'.

The health capability paradigm addresses these competing claims in several stages. First, by prioritizing central health capabilities above non-central ones and leaving open the selection and valuation of the latter, the account explicitly prioritizes health services associated with core dimensions of health and limits others. Second, by using medical necessity, medical appropriateness, and evidence-based clinical guidelines as criteria, the account further prioritizes those health goods and services deemed medically appropriate over inappropriate or futile ones. Third, within the medically appropriate care associated with central health capabilities, the account prioritizes those goods and services that reduce shortfall inequalities in central health capabilities over those that do not (Ruger 1998; 2006a). Fourth, in medically appropriate health care that reduces these shortfall inequalities, the account applies the low-level principle of 'reasonable accommodation' and the related 'reasonable adjustments' to illuminate our obligations.[6] This principle emerged when the United States government had to interpret the scope of its obligations to individuals with disabilities under the Rehabilitation Act (1994) (29 U.S.C. §§ 701–797(b)) and the Americans with Disabilities Act (ADA) (1994) (42 U.S.C. §§ 12101–12213). The Acts require programmes to make 'reasonable accommodations' or 'modifications' so that disabled persons can meet the programs' 'essential eligibility requirements' (29 U.S.C. § 795 (1994); 42 U.S.C. §§ 12111–12113 (1994)). In general, 'reasonable accommodations or modifications' are those that are not 'fundamental' or will not cause 'undue hardship' to the programme in question. The Rehabilitation Act and the ADA stop short of requiring accommodations that could cause 'undue hardship', determined by the particular accommodation's nature and cost, and the financial and organizational capacity of the institution in question (42 U.S.C. § 12111(10) (1994)). In the UK, the Disability Discrimination Acts of 1995 and 2005 require 'reasonable adjustments' to remove barriers from disabled individuals' participation.

This paradigm considers absolute harm in terms of patients' capability for functioning, not a strict cost-benefit analysis. Several commentators have criticized the application of a rigid cost-benefit analysis to interventions on disabled individuals' behalf, on the grounds that such an allocative principle would discriminate against the disabled, who might receive less benefit relative to costs than non-disabled individuals. 'Primary reliance on measures of outcome such as increases in length of life... will disfavor persons with disabilities', Orentlicher points out. 'We should not prefer one patient over another just because the first patient will realize more benefit from the care' (Orentlicher 2000, p. 241).

The health capability paradigm acknowledges this critique and cautions against directly weighing cost considerations against the precise benefit of an intervention (for example, through CBA). It endorses directing resources to those who experience shortfall inequalities in the central health capabilities in proportion to their deprivations and the use of medical care necessity and appropriateness (and medical futility) as a standard for evaluating health care interventions. In operationalizing these normative principles and allocating health resources across society as a whole, however, considering the absolute costs of certain treatment protocols and their effects on total health system resources is appropriate (Chapter 8) and must be evaluated in the context of a model of shared health governance between individuals, physicians, and institutions that govern health.

Both the ADA statute itself and the Equal Employment Opportunity Commission (EEOC) regulations endorse an approach of considering absolute costs of accommodation as a relevant factor while *not* engaging in a direct cost-benefit analysis. The ADA defines undue hardship as 'an action requiring significant difficulty or expense' (42 U.S.C. § 12111 (10) (1994)). The EEOC regulations assess hardship by considering the 'nature and net cost' of the accommodation and the impact on the 'overall financial resources' of the organization involved (Code of Federal Regulations 2004) (29 C.F.R. § 1630.2). But the EEOC guidelines explain that 'neither the statute [the ADA] nor the legislative history supports a cost-benefit analysis to determine . . . undue hardship' (Equal Employment Opportunity Commission 2002, No. 45).

Even economically minded federal jurists are hesitant to apply strict cost-benefit analysis to the question of undue hardship in particular cases. In Vande Zande v. Wisconsin Department of Administration, Judge Richard Posner states that the costs of accommodation are important for determining reasonableness and undue hardship, but that 'it would not follow' from this 'that the costs and benefits . . . always have to be quantified, or even that an accommodation would have to be deemed unreasonable if the cost exceeded the benefit however slightly' (Vande Zande v. Wisconsin Department of Administration 1995, p. 542). Elsewhere in the opinion, however, Posner seems more predisposed to cost-benefit analysis, stating that an accommodation causes undue hardship, and thus is not 'reasonable', only if an institution must 'expend enormous sums in order to bring about a trivial improvement in the life of a disabled employee', or where 'the costs are excessive in relation either to . . . the employer's financial survival or health' (Vande Zande v. Wisconsin Department of Administration 1995, pp. 542–3).

Extending this argument to the question of intractable conditions and health resource allocation, two factors would be relevant in defining the social obligation. The first is medical appropriateness and medical futility; the second is the point beyond which the allocation sacrifices, unduly reduces, or otherwise impacts the central health capabilities of others. Ultimately, the obligation to address intractable needs does not extend beyond the point where others might suffer harm to their central health capabilities. At the societal level, resource allocation should focus on all deprivations in health capabilities below the agreed upon threshold level of health functioning. Combining the 'reasonable accommodation' standard with 'medical appropriateness' and 'medical necessity' principles could help society clarify its obligations. Existing case law could reveal the reasoning behind and the application of such a standard. Eventually, however, a body of case law and policy case studies in health resource allocation could develop to guide decision-making in this area.[7]

Fifth, as to advance directives and Do Not Resuscitate orders, the paradigm endorses efforts to ensure that end-of-life treatment complies with patients' values. Such compliance should be encouraged because it respects patient autonomy and also holds the potential to reduce costs and medically futile care (Emanuel 1996). Studies have shown that patients' end-of-life treatment preferences are often ignored (Ditto et al. 2001, p. 421); the wishes of patients in advance directives are often misinterpreted by surrogate decision makers and physicians. However, studies found that hospital-based physicians made more overtreatment errors than primary care physicians, without the use of advance directives, in efforts to do anything possible to preserve life (Coppola et al. 2001, p. 431). An analysis of hospice care found that increased use of advance directives could potentially save between 25 per cent and 40 per cent of health care costs during the last month of life, and between 10 per cent and 17 per cent of health care costs during the last six months of life (Emanuel 1996).

Sixth, this paradigm applies 'cost minimization' analysis and, in certain micro-level comparisons, cost-effectiveness analysis in order to promote shortfall equality in individuals' capabilities for health with the fewest resources possible. Cost-minimization studies assume a given objective and search for the least expensive way to achieve it. At the micro-level, cost-effectiveness compares the incremental health benefits and incremental costs of two or more interventions.

8.9. Joint clinical and economic solutions: incorporating efficiency

Meeting the dual social obligations of equality and efficiency in health resource allocation will require both clinical and economic solutions (see Table 8.1), but clinical and medical input must drive the process. This paradigm ensures that physician judgement (at the bedside and *a priori* through clinical guidelines and medical appropriateness assessments) and patient input are the primary determinants of care. Yet, successful implementation of effective clinical protocols requires economic incentives. Empirical evidence suggests that economic tools can influence the behaviour of patients, physicians, and planners.

Several measures have been implemented to encourage cost consciousness and improve efficiency. In the United States, for example, high and rising health care costs have produced various economic incentives on both the supply and demand sides to reduce health care use and expenditures. On the demand side, instruments such as copayment schemes and health insurance deductibles require patients to pay either a percentage or a fixed portion of the price of a given medical procedure or health premium. The economic rationale behind copays and deductibles is that they sensitize consumers to the price of health care and thus serve as a deterrent to consumption. Some free-market proponents would completely alter the incentive structure in the health care marketplace. To increase the cost consciousness of consumers, some have proposed making families, rather than employers, responsible for purchasing health insurance through mandates and tax credits (Butler and Haislmaier 1989). Enthoven and Kronick suggest that employees should pay the difference between what their employers pay, for example, 80 per cent of the cost of the average premium, and their choice of plan. This would maintain the current employer-related health insurance system while attempting to increase consumers' cost consciousness (Enthoven and Kronick 1989, pp. 94–101).

On the supply side, price, budgetary, and salary incentives (prospective and capitated payment schemes, global budgets, competition, and utilization and management review systems) are all efforts to reduce utilization costs. In the United Kingdom, National Health Service reforms in the 1990s proposed increasing competition through 'internal markets'. A review of these reforms concluded there was 'little evidence from the UK or elsewhere that competition in health care produces efficiency or improvements in resource allocation' (Maynard and Bloor 1998, p. 423). Another method of

Table 8.1. Changing Provider and Consumer Behaviour to Improve Efficiency

	Pros	Cons	Comment
(1) Economic and Administrative Solutions (e.g. copays, deductibles, capitation, global budgets)	(i) Reduce overall health care utilization	(i) Reduce both necessary and unnecessary care (ii) Can produce unnecessary and adverse health outcomes, especially among the medically indigent (iii) Might not reduce overall costs	
(2) Clinical Approaches	(i) Reduce inappropriate care and increase appropriate care (ii) Maintain and improve health outcomes, enhancing productivity and economic growth	(i) No immediate attention to costs (ii) Might not reduce costs (iii) Require change in the medical profession (education and practice)	(i) Require physician acceptance and cooperation (ii) Require medical education and professional peer review reforms (iii) Require advanced information systems
(3) Joint Economic and Clinical Approach	(i) Decreases inappropriate care, reduces misuse, overuse, underuse, and variations in care, and increases appropriate care (ii) Improves equity and efficiency in health (iii) Decreases costs and improves health care quality	(i) Requires change in the medical profession (ii) Difficult to implement	(i) Creates economic incentives for providers and planners (including insurers) to improve performance and quality of health care, motivates patients towards productive care (ii) Applies efficiency evaluation (CMA, CEA) of clinical objectives

rationing health care goods and services is the utilization review, in which health insurance companies, including managed care companies, employ panels of experts to review physicians' treatment decisions. The rationale for this process is rarely made explicit, but some work suggests that decisions are made on the basis of cost. In theory, these incentives force physicians and hospitals to internalize costs and to provide only the most cost-effective care. In some cases, they actually shift the financial risk of health expenditures from health insurers to health providers.

The increased use of payment mechanisms such as Diagnostic-Related Groups and health financing and delivery institutions such as managed care organizations (HMOs) have resulted from these efforts. Managed care organizations aim to control costs through pre-approval requirements, copayments, and negotiated fees with providers and to cut back on marginal value services through use review, pre-certification, and profiling. In the United States in 2000, the HMO penetration rate (including both traditional HMOs and point of service plans) was roughly 30 per cent, with 20 states having an HMO penetration rate of 30 per cent or more. In addition, 30 of 50 states gave financial incentives to providers for withholding covered health care in 2000 (Kaiser Family Foundation 2001). However, it is unclear whether these measures have actually reduced expenditures or maintained or improved effectiveness. For example, it has been argued that DRGs have shifted costs from one system to another instead of achieving real savings (Callahan 1990).

Both supply- and demand-side approaches to cost containment have advantages and disadvantages, which can be assessed by whether they reduce health care expenditures, maintain and improve health, and are medically feasible. One of the perceived benefits of both approaches is a reduction in health care utilization. In a randomly controlled health insurance experiment, for example, researchers found that increasing copayments on health insurance reduced demand for health care services by as much as 40 per cent (Newhouse et al. 1993). But the same study found that copayments did not differentiate between appropriate and inappropriate care (Lohr et al. 1986).

Cross-cultural comparisons of national health systems also help illuminate the effectiveness of capitation and global budgeting in reducing health care utilization. The UK has lower usage rates of various diagnostic and treatment options than the US. A classic study found that rates of coronary artery bypass surgery were less than one-fifth as prevalent in the United Kingdom as they were in the United States (Aaron and Schwartz 1984).

While such strategies might reduce the volume of health care provided, they are devoid of clinical input and therefore often reduce both inappropriate and appropriate care. Thus, they can have deleterious health consequences and can be inequitable, particularly by increasing patient cost-sharing and 'cream skimming' (Menzel 1987). They especially affect the poor and medically indigent, who often have the greatest health care needs and respond most sensitively to economic incentives to reduce consumption (Mechanic 1989). Therefore, attempts to reduce shortfall inequalities in individuals' capabilities for health with the fewest resources possible will require *a joint clinical and economic solution*—that is, one that combines careful financial stewardship with competent medical judgment.

Under the health capability paradigm, economic solutions should *follow* and *complement* clinical progress, not vice versa. As the evidence of the magnitude and determinants of inappropriate care accumulates, economists and health policy analysts can create policy instruments to move physicians, patients, and planners towards productive care. Particular attention should go to motivating and training physicians by rewarding appropriate care and penalizing inappropriate care with financial and/or non-financial incentives. This paradigm applies an iterative approach, first addressing equity by using clinical input to analyse deficits in individuals' ability for health functioning below a given threshold. It then addresses efficiency, using measures of medical care appropriateness, cost-minimization, and, in specific cases, cost-effectiveness analysis.

Cost-minimization analysis is an appropriate tool when the case for intervention has been established (Robinson 1993, p. 726–8), and it is increasingly becoming a mainstay of efficiency analysis in public health and medicine. In obstetrics and gynaecology, for example (Gardner 1998), researchers compared the costs of three alternative hysterectomy methods—abdominal hysterectomy (AH), vaginal hysterectomy (VH), and laparoscopically assisted vaginal hysterectomy (LAVH)—which have been judged equally effective (Dorsey et al. 1996). However, the study found that LAVH (at $6,116) was more costly than either AH (at $5,084) or VH (at $4,221) (Dorsey et al. 1996, p. 476). A study of pregnancy management beyond 41 weeks also compared the costs of three strategies: expectant management (EM), immediate induction of labour using prostaglandin gel (PGE$_2$), and elective induction (EI). All three strategies were determined to be acceptable approaches to prolonged pregnancy, but the PGE$_2$ treatment (at $3,312) was approximately 33 per cent more costly than EM and EI, which were equivalent in cost (Gardner 1998, p. 298).

Cost-minimization studies have also been applied to cancer therapy. Multiple studies compared the costs of peripheral blood progenitor cell (PBPC) transplantation with those for autologous bone marrow transplantation (ABMT) in patients with Hodgkin's or non-Hodgkin's lymphoma (Schmitz et al. 1996; Smith et al. 1997). While studies found both treatments roughly similar in effectiveness (Hartmann et al. 1997, p. 600, 606; Schmitz et al. 1996, p. 356), two studies found that ABMT cost roughly $13,600 more than the PBPC in terms of overall service rates (Smith et al. 1997, pp. 8–9). In another cost-minimization study of cancer therapy, researchers in the United Kingdom compared the combination chemotherapy known as CHOP (cyclophosphamide, doxorubicin, vincristine, prednisolone), fludarabine, and rituximab for treating relapsed indolent B-cell non-Hodgkin's lymphoma (Sweetenham et al. 1999, pp. 47–8). Similar clinical outcomes resulted from all three treatments. However, the per patient cost associated with fludarabine (£10,022) was considerably higher than that of either CHOP (£7,210) or rituximab (£6,080) (Sweetenham et al. 1999, p. 53).

Analysts have also applied cost-minimization to ambulatory anaesthesia. One study compared four protocols: methohexital-desflurane, methohexital-sevoflurane, propofol-desflurane, and propofol-sevoflurane (Sun et al. 1999). Results showed that when the outcome was induction of anaesthesia, methohexital costs less than propofol (Sun et al. 1999, pp. 314–15). Another study compared two rehabilitation programmes for stroke patients—early hospital discharge and home-based rehabilitation versus conventional in-hospital rehabilitation and community care (C. Anderson et al. 2000). The average cost per patient was lower for early hospital discharge and home-based rehabilitation, although the difference in cost was not statistically significant (C. Anderson et al. 2000, p. 1035). The study did incorporate indirect costs incurred by home-based caregivers and found that among the home-based rehabilitation group, caregivers had worse mental health (C. Anderson et al. 2000, pp. 1033–34).

Cost-minimization analysis has also highlighted potential cost savings in pharmaceuticals. A study of the use of prescription drugs by US Medicare patients estimated that increasing the use of generic medications would save Medicare's 40 million beneficiaries roughly $14 billion in 2003 and more than $250 billion over a ten-year period (Ritter et al. 2001). The study concluded that the biggest savings would be achieved by prescribing generic medications for conditions for which treatments are the most costly, such as ulcers and arthritis (Thomas et al. 2001, p. 272). Increased use of generic drugs would save an individual Medicare patient 16 per cent or roughly $270 (Ritter et al. 2001, p. 1). The elderly, who consume about three times as many prescriptions as younger Anderson et al persons, incurred an 18.5 per cent increase in drug costs between 1997 and 2000, while younger enrolees only experienced a 16 per cent increase (Thomas et al. 2001, p. 268). Given this significant differential, using generics could substantially reduce the cost of a Medicare prescription drug benefit (Ritter et al. 2001, p. 13).

More recently, cost-minimization studies have been conducted cross-nationally. For example, in a study of antiepileptic drugs for newly diagnosed epilepsy in 12 European countries, researchers found that while all four frequently prescribed antiepileptic drugs—lamotrigine (LTG), carbamazepine (CBZ), phenytoin (PHT), and valproate (VPA)—were equally able to prevent seizures, LTG was two to three times more expensive than the other three drugs in each country (Heaney et al. 2000). An earlier UK-based cost-minimization study also concluded that LTG costs more than the three other drugs and found no overall financial saving when differing side effects rates, tolerability, and other direct medical costs were accounted for (Heaney et al. 1998).

Lastly, cost-minimization has been used in studies pertaining to the treatment of HIV. A pilot study by the National Institute of Allergy and Infectious Diseases (NIAID) found that cycling antiretroviral treatment rather than administering a continuous dose might be as effective, have fewer side effects, and be significantly less expensive (Dybul et al. 2001; National Institute of Allergy and Infectious Diseases 2001).

Cost-effectiveness analysis (CEA) can be particularly useful in comparing interventions for a single population, such as AIDS patients, by weighing the marginal benefits and marginal costs of two alternative interventions. For example, evaluating the cost-effectiveness of combination antiretroviral therapy for HIV infection (Freedberg et al. 2001), or of preventing AIDS-related opportunistic infections (Freedberg et al. 1998), or simulation modelling of lifetime costs and life expectancy to inform clinical guidelines for the treatment of HIV-related *Pneumocystis carinii* pneumonia (PCP) (Goldie et al. 2002) can help identify the additional costs society must pay for the additional benefits of each intervention. This brief summary demonstrates the enormous potential of cost-minimization and cost-effectiveness studies for reducing costs and inefficiencies in health policy while avoiding some of the objectionable problems associated with other economic methodologies.

The health capability paradigm differs from other efforts to address the efficiency-equity trade-off. Menzel (1990), for example, asserts that individual consent to cost-effectiveness analysis should be used as a rationing option. Rakowski (1991), however, argues for using hypothetical choice constructs, such as the 'veil of ignorance', when allocating resources because hypothetical consent to rules of distributive justice is similar to actual consent. As to QALYs, Williams in particular has argued that they can 'accommodate a wide variety of health dimensions and sources of valuation', as well as 'the differential weighting of benefits according to who gets them, so they do not commit their users to any particular notion of distributive justice' (Williams 1996, p. 1795). However, Menzel believes that the QALY model requires considerable work to address moral concerns (Kaplan and Merson 2002; Menzel 1995).

The health capability paradigm, on the other hand, employs an iterative approach and various methodological techniques for assessing the competing claims of equality and efficiency. Nord has found that individuals tend to emphasize 'equality in value of life and in entitlement to treatment rather than level of health after treatment' (Nord 1993b, p. 37). Thus, people are reluctant to deny treatment to individuals based on benefit maximization (Nord et al. 1995, p. 1435). Nord (1994) and others propose an approach called 'cost-value analysis', which uses equity weights to incorporate concerns for both severity and potential health in QALY calculations. Neither the benefit maximization approach, which values saving life and improving/extending life equally, nor the strict lexical prioritization of life-saving and life-extending over all other health benefits are workable solutions to this problem. For example, the Oregon Health Services Commission (HSC) abandoned the cost-utility methodology and ranking of condition/treatment pairs, which had favoured relatively minor and inexpensive interventions over more expensive interventions that saved lives (US Congress Office of Technology Assessment 1992, pp. 6–7). The Oregonian public found it unacceptable (Hadorn 1991, p. 2220). The HSC commissioners then ranked 17 categories of medical interventions according to community health care values (Hadorn 1991, p. 2220; US Congress Office of Technology Assessment 1992, pp. 7–9; Tengs et al. 1996), without including costs. The HSC ranking criteria involved the category's perceived value to the individual and to society and the necessity of the types of interventions in a given category. This approach gave the highest ranking to interventions that would save lives and permit a full recovery (Hadorn 1991, p. 2221; US Congress Office of Technology Assessment 1992, p. 8). Maternity and newborn services ranked second, saving lives without a full recovery ranked third, and interventions for fatal or non-fatal conditions that have little effect on quality of life ranked last (Hadorn 1991, p. 2221; US Congress Office of Technology Assessment 1992, p. 8). The HSC commissioners then modified the rankings slightly by introducing costs, although they continued to give priority to life-saving treatments, despite exorbitant costs in many cases (US Congress Office of Technology Assessment 1992, pp. 7–9).

Although the HSC's approach to revising its rankings is consistent with the health capability paradigm, it differs in many ways. The health capability paradigm proposes that physicians and patients should play a larger role in determining medical appropriateness *and* in using evidence-based input to assess the net effectiveness of health interventions. The problem with lexical prioritization of life-saving or life-prolonging interventions is that it is *inflexible* when assessing the net benefits and costs of specific interventions on a case-by-base basis.

8.10. Resource allocation and age: reaching the highest average life expectancy

The question of how to distribute resources along the longevity spectrum is relevant to a theory of health resource allocation. Average life expectancy at birth has increased over the last several decades, the worldwide average in 2006 was 68, up from 61 in 1980 (World Bank Key Development Data and Statistics). However, this average masks large differences in life expectancy among different groups. Higher-income countries, for example, have an average life expectancy at birth of 78 years, and only 10 per cent of women and 20 per cent of men die before age 65. In middle-income countries, the life expectancy is 69 and 22 per cent of women and 39 per cent of men die before age 65. In low-income countries, average life expectancy is 63 years, and 31 per cent of women and 36 per cent of men die before age 65 (World Bank 2000, pp. 106–108). And within these broader income categories, there is considerable variation in life expectancy at birth: Burkina Faso (47), Guinea Bissau (47), Malawi (50), Sierra Leone (40), and Uganda (50) had average life expectancies at birth between 40 and 50 in 2006, while the United States (78), United Kingdom (79), Spain (81), Singapore (80), Italy (81), Israel (81), Japan (83), New Zealand (80), and Australia (82) had life expectancies in the high 70s to low 80s in the same year (WHO Statistical Information System 2006).

The capability to avoid premature death holds a central place in the health capability paradigm. While it is reasonable to regard premature death as a relative concept—death that occurs before average life expectancy at birth *in a given society*—this paradigm posits that the concept has more universal appeal, as argued earlier, because a life expectancy that can be achieved in one society should, in theory, be achievable in any other, unless genetic differences prevail. Therefore, the proposal here is that any society should aim to reach the maximum average life expectancy known.[8] While this interpretation of premature death may be viewed by some as expansive, it also provides the basis for prioritizing health goods and services to individuals below the average life expectancy rather than to those above that level. Thus, providing health goods and services to those below this high threshold would confer more life years of better quality than providing the same resources to those above the maximum average known.[9] Moreover, addressing illness early in life increases life expectancy overall, which lifts the maximum over time.

A number of scholars and accounts of medical ethics support age-based rationing. Some emphasize the need to prioritize addressing illness early in life over addressing it later in life, especially for those who have already reached their 'natural life span' (Callahan 1990; Daniels 1985; Menzel 1990) and that we should prioritize the probability of achieving a normal life span over increasing the probability of living longer than a normal life span (Daniels 1988). Callahan (1990), for example, argues for rationing health care after the point at which a person reaches his or her 'natural life span'—say their early 80s—by providing mostly palliative rather than life-extending care. Daniels (1988) argues that hypothetical choosers under the Rawlsian 'veil of ignorance' would choose to ration care for people beyond the normal life span in order to maximize the possibility of reaching that life span. Others argue that we can only achieve justice in health care if we give priority to treating illnesses that occur early in life, instead of those that occur later (Rakowski 1991; 1993). Menzel (1990) states that people in the prime of life should take priority, while Kamm has generally supported age-based rationing.

The view taken here is that it is difficult to employ an *ex ante* rationing principle such as 'age-based rationing'. Instead, this paradigm endorses the reduction of shortfall inequalities based on an indicator of length of life related to the central health capability of avoiding premature mortality. Moreover, using the maximum average life expectancy at birth in any given society as the potential average life expectancy at birth for all societies is favoured.[10] It would still be difficult to equate such a principle with the commitment to the higher order value of saving life described above. That said, if a choice must be made due to resource constraints, efforts to extend life up to the maximum average life expectancy for all societies should be prioritized over extending life beyond that threshold level, but many societies will have resources to devote to health beyond the threshold and should invest in extending the threshold further.

Notes

1. See Horton (2007) on NICE's fairness and rationality and the use of science in guideline development.
2. Other types of procedural models include citizen juries and citizen councils, which have been used with mixed success in the UK. Citizen advisory boards have also been used in environmental decision-making and offer many lessons. Ultimately, this is an area where research in empirical ethics can provide useful findings on the successes and drawbacks of different approaches.
3. For more on this, see Angell (1991); Atkinson et al. (1994); Brody and Halevy (1995); Callahan (1991); Council on Ethical and Judicial Affairs (1991); Curtis et al. (1995); Engelhardt (1996b); Engelhardt and Khushfk (1995); Esserman et al. (1995); Halevy and Brody (1996); Halevy et al. (1996); Howe (1994); Jecker and Schneiderman (1995); Lo (1991); Miles (1991); Society of Critical Care Medicine Ethics Committee (1994); Tomlinson and Brody (1990).
4. This is also a matter of gender equity. One US study found that women have, on average, 68 per cent more out-of-pocket health care expenditures than men, primarily because they have to pay for contraceptive drugs and devices. See Women's Research and Education Institute (1994).
5. See Brock (1995; 2002); Hadorn (1992); Menzel (1992, pp. 21–5); Orentlicher (1994, 1996) (arguing that the quality adjusted life year (QALY) discriminates against the disabled); Crossley (1993) (pointing out that disabilities should not be considered if they do not have a 'medical effect' on the proposed treatment). See also US Congress Office of Technology Assessment (1992), noting that the Bush administration rejected Oregon's waiver application, partly on the grounds that its use of quality of life measures violated the Americans with Disabilities Act (ADA). Also see generally Rai (1997).
6. Thanks go to Theodore W. Ruger for useful discussions on this topic.
7. Employing the 'reasonable accommodation' principle would involve using an incomplete eligibility criterion of medical appropriateness to avoid the 'bottomless pit' problem, and must be done on a case-by-case basis. See, for example, School Board of Nassau County v. Arline (1987) (stating that the court 'must conduct an individualized inquiry and make appropriate findings of fact, based on reasonable medical judgments'); see also Strathie v. Department of Transportation (1983) (noting that the determination of whether an individual with a disability poses a safety threat to others in the workplace must be made on a case-by-case basis).

8. There may be, in the short-run, reasons for modifying this interpretation if reaching this goal is a much longer-term prospect. In such cases, severe resource constraints and limited access to technology make this goal unattainable in the short term. That said, pressure to reach levels of health status is necessary (especially in developing countries) to spur greater prioritization of health and greater investments in health-related goods and services, and to motivate better performance of health systems.

9. Although discounting life years gained, for example, a 3 per cent discount rate as recommended by Weinstein et al. (1996), reduces the differences between the young and the elderly because additional years of life are counted less.

10. The maximum average life expectancy worldwide is 83 years, which is found in Japan.

Part IV

Domestic Health Reform

9

Political and Moral Legitimacy: A Normative Theory of Health Policy Decision-Making

In order to foster health capability for all and achieve just changes in health policy at the national level in any society, citizens and policy makers must be willing to pass federal legislation that ensures equity in health for all. This final chapter offers a normative theory for analysing federal health policy decisions, with specific application to the United States. This normative theory holds promise for analysing health reform efforts in many societies, especially pluralistic constitutional regimes in which deliberative democratic procedures are in place and offer political legitimacy. It recognizes that efforts to address health problems in developing and developed countries alike, will likely require norms and values to be restructured in a fundamental way—globally, but most importantly at the national level. The goal is to advance an understanding of health reform that takes both political and moral legitimacy as cornerstones and analyses the role of values and norms, particularly their level of generality, in health policy decision-making, and the extent to which different policy actors (political and non-political) *internalize norms themselves* and attempt to produce coalitions around them. Drawing attention to coalitions around, and internalization of, values and norms offers insights and prescriptions distinctive from those that prevailing analyses provide. It recognizes the need to introduce substantive normative principles (moral legitimacy) into a deliberative, democratic process (political legitimacy) for a comprehensive, integrative theory of health and social justice. From this perspective, pluralistic constitutional regimes are composed of individuals and their representatives, whose diverse beliefs create social tension and make social agreement difficult to achieve. Therefore, attempts to make collective decisions—for example, through the legislature—must emphasize shared values to achieve stability and social unity. It is necessary to determine shared values, even values shared for different reasons, to achieve social agreement for political and legal decision-making.

Under a health capability paradigm, such analysis is essential because the significant social change required to ensure individuals' health capability will require the political legitimacy that the support of citizens' values and beliefs ensures. Prior work on public values in health policy has overlooked the ways in which values of different levels of specificity connect to create a coherent rationale for health reform. This work aims to address these gaps by advancing an approach based on a more accurate framework of social agreement, which reflects the fact that values and norms operate at multiple levels of generality and degrees of internalization. This alternative framework, which is referred to here as social agreement theory, builds on political philosophy and democratic and legal theory. This normative framework is unique in that it integrates *public moral norm internalization* and the social agreement model of incomplete theorization. A *public moral norm* is a moral value that pertains to our individual and collective morality in the public sphere; an example of such a norm would be collective organization to achieve common goals. A public moral norm contrasts with an individual moral norm in that the moral value pertains not just to individual action but also to individual and collective action regarding the public sphere (e.g. norms about procedural justice, rules of accuracy, trust, ethicality, and neutrality). A particular type of public moral norm, a *distributive justice norm*, determines the distribution of societal resources. In this chapter, this theory of health and social justice brings together political legitimacy through the deliberative democratic process with moral legitimacy through the internalization of public moral norms and collective choice on public policy that is just (or at the very least is not unjust).

Studying health care reform efforts in the US reveals a key reason for their consistent failure. This failure can be understood by first analysing the extent of individual, societal, and political internalization of norms generally—and specifically the public moral norm that one has an ethical commitment to make financial sacrifices to support expansion of health insurance—then determining the extent to which social agreement about this ethical commitment has occurred. This agreement could occur even without consensus on abstract higher-level principles and on principles in other domains of social life (e.g. welfare). When this norm does become internalized, domestic legislation can follow, but it will be difficult for America to adopt universal health insurance coverage until this norm gains acceptance at the social and political level. Without this norm's acceptance, efforts to achieve public consensus on abstract principles (e.g. equality or egalitarianism) or on 'universal coverage' could continue to fail because they create more disagreement than agreement. Americans, especially liberal Americans, experience considerable ambivalence and conflict among the abstract higher-level principles invoked in debates about universal coverage. The theory developed here illustrates how these cleavages and uncertainties work and how they allow opponents of reform to launch value-based arguments that disrupt reformist coalitions. In so doing it provides a better understanding of how norms and values work together to form a coherent (or incoherent) basis for national reform. Efforts to involve national governments throughout the world in improving the health of their populations and to ensure access to quality health care for all require more than fragile agreement on mid-level principles. These efforts require invoking principles, values and norms, and honest discussion about the consequences of denying necessary and appropriate care for people's health and security. This final chapter of the book concludes with some preliminary prescriptions for future health reform efforts in the United States and elsewhere, with specific attention to social movements at the national level, such as the civil rights and feminist movements in the United States, which can provide guidance and principles for fundamentally restructuring norms and values. Collective reasoning about public policy requires a truthful deliberative process and a sincere and dedicated effort to achieve consensus on both the ends (values) and means (acceptable policy solutions) of public policy. These efforts are critical to citizens' self-determination in all constitutional democracies. The challenge is to create the conditions under which individuals can agree on a political conception governing health and health care and foster health capability for all.

9.1. Public moral norms and domestic health reforms

The distribution of public moral norms, their degree of internalization, and the social consensus, or lack thereof that applies to them, must be objects of study in the effort to better understand health policy reform.

An *internalized norm* is one that is so widely accepted as to have a 'taken-for-granted' quality (Finnemore and Sikkink 1998, p. 894). Individuals instinctively conform to internalized norms in the absence of external rewards or punishments (Bénabou and Tirole 2003). *Social internalization* occurs when the public legitimacy of a norm is such that there is widespread general adherence to it, whereas *political internalization* occurs when political elites accept the norm and promote its adoption as a matter of public policy (Koh 1998). A *public moral norm* pertains to our individual and collective morality in the public sphere; an example of such a norm would be collective organization to achieve common goals. A public moral norm contrasts with an individual moral norm in that the moral value pertains not just to individual action but also to individual and collective action regarding the public sphere. This work analyses a particular type of public moral norm, a *distributive justice norm*, which determines the distribution of societal resources for health care.

As discussed in Chapter 3, an *incompletely theorized agreement* (ITA) is one that is not uniformly theorized at all levels and across all dimensions of specificity and abstraction. Such agreements fail to produce *depth* (full accounts of foundations) or *width* (coherence with other dimensions). The theory offered here has roots in contemporary legal and political scholarship and builds on the ITA social decision-making framework. The ITA concept can be attributed to Cass Sunstein (1995, pp. 1733–72), but it also echoes John Rawls's notion of overlapping consensus (OC) (Rawls 1993). Both authors have tried to create frameworks for understanding how stability and social agreement might be established among elites (in law and the judiciary for ITA and in politics for OC) who disagree on fundamental matters. But neither has sufficiently applied these frameworks to public discourse about public policy and legislative reform or to how public values are effectively internalized by citizens. Moreover, neither framework has been applied to specific policy domains such as health policy.

An ethical commitment to make financial sacrifices to support the expansion of health insurance would be a public moral norm. Understanding health reform efforts requires analysing the extent of individual, societal, and political internalization of this norm. In the United States' case, for example, it will be difficult to adopt universal health insurance coverage until this more concrete ethical norm of willingness to pay for one's own and others' health care coverage is internalized and agreed upon at the social and political level. When this norm is internalized domestic legislation can follow.

This agreement might come at the expense of disagreement about abstract higher-level principles and principles in other domains of social life (e.g. welfare). Efforts to achieve public consensus on abstract principles (e.g. equality or egalitarianism) or on the vagaries of 'universal coverage' will continue to fail because they create more disagreement than agreement.

The following sections first review previous academic discussion of the role of values in motivating citizens' support for public policies. They then explore the differences between social agreement frameworks (such as ITA and OC) and the more traditional political science models of political decision-making that focus on political bargaining. They pay particular attention to how the more traditional models concentrate on what Rawls calls a *modus vivendi* as opposed to the formation of real and stable coalitions. This section also highlights theoretical differences between frameworks for decision-making among elites in the law and judiciary and in politics.

Building on the theory of the second section, the three types of ITA follow, briefly outlining how the ITA framework draws attention to the different levels of generality in value-based arguments and to the potential for building stable reform coalitions in public discourse among citizens. Studying how citizens and their representatives agree upon and internalize public values extends these frameworks to include public discourse about legislative and policy reform.

A literature survey follows, attempting to discover why the health reform efforts of the Clinton Administration failed. This chapter demonstrates that, while virtually all of the major scholarship in political science refers to the importance of underlying public values in understanding the fate of health care reform, it does not provide a theoretical framework for analysing these values.

An analysis follows about why American health care reform attempts in 1993 and 1994 generally fit into a norm- and value-based framework, one here characterized by ITA. The main argument here is that deliberations about health care in the United States represented agreement on the mid-level concept of universal coverage, but disagreement both on higher-level abstract principles and on low-level principles for particular outcomes. Further, while social internalization of and social agreement on some broadly defined health policy conceptions (such as universal coverage) might have occurred during the debate, both social and political internalization and agreement were lacking on the more concrete public moral norm of willingness to pay for universal health insurance. In short, the public and political elites faltered in their commitment to that norm.

Juxtaposing this second model with the other two models, the second model is found to be particularly susceptible to the destabilizing influence of competing values and is therefore less successful at producing social stability and social agreement. Social and political internalization of concrete norms works to *reduce* rather than to increase variation by stabilizing expectations and limiting options for policy choice. Without a shared and internalized norm of willingness to pay for universal coverage, the variation created by numerous floating policy ideas failed to stabilize expectations and ultimately limited rather than expanded policy options.

Applying social agreement theory to decision-making about reforms to universalize health insurance coverage in the United States, the last section explores the notion that agreement on a high-level principle (such as health equity) or on a low-level principle for a substantive outcome (such as willingness to pay for others' health insurance) might lead to more stable and broadly endorsed support for reform that universalizes insurance coverage in the United States.

9.2. Norms and values in the public's assessment of policy

Norms and values have always played a role in the study of public policy and political science, although they have typically been consigned to the categories of political culture or political ideology. Cultural and ideological explanations of political attitudes and behaviour typically focus on deeply ingrained social patterns, path dependency of historical events (e.g. the libertarian essence of the western frontier in American expansion, an aversion to state control in various social and economic activities, the legacy of slaves brought to the United States from Africa, or women's traditional societal roles), and key ideologies such as liberalism or conservativism. Although ideology and culture have at times been the focus in explaining policy outcomes, they have received less attention than the more widely studied economic and political factors (Feldman and Zaller 1992; Free and Cantril 1968; Lipset 1963; Hochschild 1986; Verba and Orren 1985).

For nearly half a century, scholars studying political culture and political ideology in the realm of social policy have focused on the degree to which the American public is either contradictory, oscillating between ideological convictions, or ideologically innocent, not coherently organizing policy preferences in accordance with liberal or conservative ideology (Converse 1976; Lane 1962). Some have focused on organized ideological conventions, which might serve to categorize Americans' values into distinct 'value sets' (e.g. conservative ideology favouring capitalism and liberal ideology stressing democratic values (McClosky and Zaller 1984)).

Even this conception reveals individuals' inconsistencies, which preclude their full participation in exclusively liberal or conservative ideologies, and unpredictability in their issue preferences (Feldman 1988). Others have focused on the value conflict that underlies Americans' political behaviour and the difficulty, inconsistency, or even lack of interest in resolving differences (Hochschild 1986; Reinarman 1987) between libertarian and socialist principles, for example. This work shows that individuals rarely resolve this conflict in a consistent or coherent manner. Some have argued that for many social welfare policy issues, liberal supporters are more conflicted in policy preferences and underlying values (that is, they are compassionate toward disadvantaged groups but opposed to higher taxes, expansion of budgets, and government) than are conservative opponents. Conservatives are generally more consistent in their ideological opposition to expanded services, arguing that individuals should get ahead on their own, without more taxes and bigger government (Feldman and Zaller 1992). In brief, American political culture is full of unresolved value conflicts, especially between freedom and equality, particularly when applied to social policy (Lipset 1963; McClosky and Zaller 1984). Indeed, those who generally support social welfare policies could be more conflicted about the abstract values they invoke to justify their support than social welfare opponents.

Another major finding from the literature on political ideology and political culture is that individual use of abstract principles and beliefs can vary by issue domain. This phenomenon is relevant for health policy because of the unique position of health and health care in political decision-making. Health differs from other social policy domains because the same feelings of individualism do not seem to apply to health as to welfare, job guarantees, guaranteed living standards, or spending on education. Health departs from welfare in a number of respects, mostly related to people's views of individualism, responsibility, dependency, and just desserts. Individuals do not always have full control over their health—people get cancer for unknown reasons, for instance—and health problems can arise even when individuals are doing everything they can to be healthy. In addition, welfare 'dependency' does not appear to have a health care equivalent (Cook and Barrett 1992, pp. 9–145). Although more recent work has shown some dependency stigma associated with means-tested health programmes like Medicaid, these biases are much less pronounced than cash assistance programmes (Stuber and Schlesinger 2006). Barring hypochondriacs or individuals with Munchausen's Syndrome and market failures, such as moral hazard or supplier-induced demand, individuals do not have the same dependency incentives in health as in welfare, because health care should be provided on an as-needed basis. Also, the principle of just desserts does not always apply to health. With some exceptions (e.g. lifestyle choices), people do not necessarily think that individuals should be denied health care because they are to blame for their health condition. This is different from attitudes about social welfare and poverty, where some individuals do believe that poor people deserve to be poor because America provides every opportunity to lift oneself out of poverty. Health disadvantage is not typically the result of lack of hard work or failure to take advantage of equal opportunity. Schlesinger and Lee (1993) found, for example, differences between people's views on health programmes and their views on general redistributive policies. By comparison, federal health initiatives were viewed by the public as: (1) 'less identified with racial minorities or economically disadvantaged groups'; (2) 'less constrained by notions of individual responsibility'; (3) 'more closely associated with concerns about equal opportunity in American society'; and (4) 'somewhat more constrained by choices between federal and local government' (Schlesinger and Lee 1993, p. 551).

When individuals experience ambivalence about abstract values and principles, they must draw on lower-level principles and concrete considerations that appeal to them (Kahan and Braman 2006) to justify policy choices. Otherwise conflict will prevent such choices. However, while past research has examined how individuals endorse particular values and policies on an ad hoc basis, these studies have overlooked the ways in which values of different levels of generality connect to form a coherent basis for policy reform. They have also overlooked the complex way in which individuals might incompletely theorize policy choice. Because of these missing pieces, the theoretical framework for analysing values and norms should do so at multiple levels of specificity and recognize the role of conflict and ambiguity underlying policy choice.

9.3. Alternative frameworks: political conceptions and political processes

Standard political science models of decision-making among policy makers generally focus on political and institutional factors. In the context of health reform in the United States, for example, many explanatory models focus on the American political process and the relationship between the

US legislative and executive branches of government. The roadblocks to health reform that scholars cite include:

(1) A fragmented and decentralized system of national policy making
(2) Weak political parties
(3) Personal politics
(4) Congressional policy-making strategies
(5) Strong interest group opposition
(6) Re-election incentives
(7) Financial contributions
(8) Presidential tactics and strategy
(9) Powerful congressional personalities
(10) Character and judgement flaws of key actors.

John Kingdon (2002, pp. 97–116) also notes other factors that make it difficult to reform policy, even during 'open' windows of opportunity. These factors include rules of procedure, the US Constitution, statutes, prescribed jurisdictions and other legal requirements, the budget, and political culture. Whether or not the political and institutional factors were adequate to explain the defeat of the Clinton health reform proposal, they could themselves have been the result of a public insufficiently mobilized by values and norms. Spotlighting coalitions around values and norms and their internalization at different levels offers unique new insights and prescriptions, distinctive from those prevailing analyses provide.

The alternative framework advanced here, social agreement theory, builds on political philosophy and legal theory. Pluralistic constitutional regimes, such as in the United States, are composed of individuals and their representatives, whose diverse comprehensive doctrines create social tension and make social agreement difficult to achieve. Therefore, attempts to make collective decisions—for example, through the legislature—must emphasize shared values to achieve stability and social unity. Both the overlapping consensus and incompletely theorized agreements frameworks emphasize the need to determine shared values, even values shared for different reasons, and to achieve social agreement for political and legal decision-making. Although these frameworks were originally intended to facilitate elite deliberation in law and politics, they have great potential for shaping, strengthening, and internalizing public norms.

Rawls draws a sharp distinction between political bargaining models and conceptual models rooted in political philosophy and legal doctrine. He suggests that political process models based on political bargaining are akin to a *modus vivendi*, or practical compromise—a 'social consensus founded on self-or group interests, or on the outcome of political bargaining: social unity is only apparent' (Rawls 1993, p. 147). A *modus vivendi* is thus a consensus on 'accepting certain authorities, or on complying with certain institutional arrangements, founded on a convergence of self-or group interests' (Rawls 1993, p. 147). For example, if both Orrin Hatch and Ted Kennedy accepted the principle of universal coverage by virtue of 'log rolling' (the process by which politicians trade political favours to support personal legislative interests), the agreement would be unstable because the bargain would be 'contingent on circumstances remaining such as not to upset the fortunate convergence of interests' (Rawls 1993, p. 147). Thus, if the senators' personal relationship dissolved or if the position of either person changed in Congress or within their respective parties, and they were no longer in a position to strike the bargain and hold their committee or party to it, universal coverage would lose its support. *Modus vivendi* agreements are also less stable than agreements based on a true overlapping consensus because the former depend more on 'happenstance and a balance of relative forces' (Rawls 1993, p. 148).

The ITA typology also contrasts with a political bargaining framework. It was originally designed for legal, particularly judicial, decision-making to achieve social agreement amid pluralism in law. This framework is usefully applied to legislation and to citizens' and their representatives' support for policies, and it augments the OC framework by describing the process of producing agreement on low-level principles when people are unable to agree on higher-level abstractions. Both the OC and the ITA models assume that actors are motivated by a good faith commitment to do the right thing. Thus, the decision or conception that is the object of a social agreement stands on its own merits. A social consensus based on an OC/ITA framework differs from a political bargaining approach because it will not change if the distribution of power among decision makers changes.

There are additional distinctions between social agreements based on an overlapping consensus or an incompletely theorized agreement and those that result from political bargaining. First, as Rawls notes, the object of an overlapping consensus is itself a *moral* conception, such that it is valued in itself. Second, the OC is 'affirmed on moral grounds' and 'includes conceptions of society and of citizens as persons, as well as principles of justice, and an account of the political virtues through which those principles are embodied in human character and expressed in public life' (Rawls 1993, p. 147). In other words, it represents a consensus among elites—and in this case citizens as well—on the public good, which can rise above the intersection of group or self-interest. Third, the OC is more stable because it is not simply a balance of power but is instead a *reasonable* consensus (Rawls 1993, p. 148). A *modus vivendi*, by contrast, reflects a temporary agreement among different and opposing peoples and parties. Thus, the OC/ITA framework increases stability because those who affirm a decision 'will not withdraw their support of it should the relative strength of their view in society increase and eventually become dominant' (Rawls 1993, p. 148). Fourth, a social agreement framework attempts to draw out 'certain fundamental ideas viewed as latent in the public political culture of a democratic society' (Rawls 1993, p. 175). As such, it attempts to tap into individuals' true values, even if individuals and their representatives have difficulty articulating those values in a completely theorized way. Fifth, this type of framework contrasts legitimate political authority with political power. For example, it differentiates 'an account of the legitimacy of political authority' from 'an account of how those who hold political power can satisfy themselves, and not citizens generally' (Rawls 1993, pp. 143–4). Legitimate political authority is not coercive: stability is not promoted by 'bringing others who reject a conception to share it, or to act in accordance with it, by workable sanctions' (Rawls 1993, p. 143). Instead, stability rises from a reasonable consensus on a politically legitimate conception or goal. Political legitimacy, in turn, involves a 'public basis of justification and appeals to public reason, and hence to free and equal citizens viewed as reasonable and rational' (Rawls 1993, p. 144).

From this social agreement perspective, legitimate political authority is not just a topic in political philosophy; it has pragmatic advantages in forging consensus and coalitions amid pluralism. A social agreement framework helps further traditional political process and bargaining arguments because it illuminates how political actors can undermine the conditions for reasoned agreement on common interests. It challenges the current scope of public opinion research in that it calls for research focused more on connecting values to public policy, not adequately addressed in most prior studies. Furthermore, it calls for research to examine whether the conditions of public communication help produce an informed, reasoning, and deliberative public that can come to agreement on norms and values to support policy formation. Jacobs and Shapiro's work, for example, sheds light on the barriers to social consensus posed by the efforts of political leaders and the mass media to distort and manipulate public opinion (Jacobs and Shapiro 2000). A social agreement model of policy decision-making thus shares an emphasis on public deliberation, responsible leadership, and mass communication with traditional political science models. Moreover, a social agreement model relies on popular sovereignty and political leadership to enhance deliberative public debate and public reasoning to agree on the common good. In the United States, common ground for reaching agreement on the ethical principles that govern health and health care has yet to be achieved, beyond the libertarian principle that promotes the market and *ad hoc* public programmes like Medicare as the default way to allocate health care resources.

9.4. Case study: the Clinton Administration and failed health reform

The year 2008 marked the fifteenth anniversary of the rapid rise and demise of the Clinton Administration's health reform efforts. Analysts still disagree over why large-scale health reform efforts continue to fail in the American political landscape. A *normative theory* for analysing federal health policy decision-making in the United States is offered here. This theory states that values and norms, particularly their level of generality, and the social agreement or lack thereof around them have a central role in shaping health policy reform. This theory does not attempt to arrive at a single unified framework for explaining health policy reform, and it recognizes the complementary roles of political science and economic explanations. Nonetheless, it argues that unarticulated values and norms have a critical role to play in health policy making and reform; this role has been inadequately studied and has lacked a theoretical framework.

There are many explanations of why accord on policy never developed during the Clinton Administration and why the Health Security Act (HSA) was defeated. Skocpol (1996) argues, for example, that despite its popularity during the 1992 campaign, by 1994 health reform and the HSA in particular became 'ideal targets' for their political enemies (conservatives) to distort, while its promoters failed to gain the support necessary to pass it in Congress. Even though the HSA was actually a compromise between market-oriented and government-centred reform, she argues, it was portrayed as a liberal, big-government proposal. She rejects explanations that point to the failures of key participants and divided public opinion. Tuohy (1999) argues that, while factors such as institutional barriers, interest-group mobilization, public opinion, and strategic miscalculations all played a role, the failure of the Clinton proposal was primarily due to the inability of political actors to mobilize authority on an 'extraordinary scale' in order to enact a programme of universal health insurance. Hacker (1997) asserts that there was an inadequate constituency for Clinton's proposed compromise, and he failed to obtain sufficient support from either liberals or conservatives.

Johnson and Broder (1996) believe that private interests triumphed over public interests and that a small but powerful minority manipulated public opinion to dismantle the proposal. They reject explanations that point to the decentralized structure of the American political process, although they do not discount this as one factor that makes comprehensive reform more difficult than incremental reform. They highlight three major political mistakes made by the Clinton Administration. The Administration's first mistake was to 'mismatch' Clinton's political capital (having been elected by only 43 per cent of the popular vote) with the scale of the reform (comprehensive instead of incremental). The Administration erred twice more by choosing to make a secretive task force the centre of policy making and by failing to distinguish between strategies suited to the House (where the Democratic left was predominant) and the Senate (where Democrats forwarded legislation through consensus and strong support by moderates in both parties). A fourth problem, which was beyond the Clinton Administration's control, included institutional barriers and 'historical forces' that 'have weakened the presidency as a vehicle for change' and have led to a 'perpetual campaign' whereby 'the politics of governing have been all but overwhelmed by the demands of seeking and retaining office' (Johnson and Broder 1996, p. 613). All this is exacerbated by a 'credibility gap' that makes it increasingly difficult for presidents to communicate with the American public on complex issues and a set of public and private institutions (including the media) that attempts to manufacture and control public opinion rather than inform, clarify alternatives, and help search for consensus. Johnson and Broder's work has been criticized by some, however, for being primarily descriptive and not analytical.

Jacobs and Shapiro (2000) use this point about political manipulation and the loss of democratic responsiveness as their main thesis about contemporary politics in America. They argue that during the Clinton Administration health reform efforts, policy makers were driven by ideology and personal preferences and focused on political calculations of allies and opponents. Rather than follow public opinion as their guide, they instead used 'crafted talk' to shape their policy options in efforts to gain public support. Opponents of the Clinton plan achieved their goal of reducing public support for the plan (a 20 percentage point decline in a year) by polarizing public debates and the press's coverage of them so as to create uncertainty and fears among the public about their personal interest in the policies being proposed. Jacobs and Shapiro have also argued that increases in partisan conflict and public opinion manipulation have actually reduced the effectiveness of the governing process and public confidence in American politics.

Finally, Mashaw and Marmor (1996) critique policy development explanations, stating that they tend to focus on solutions that respond to circumstantial failures and attempt to 'fix' the process of American policy development. Instead, they argue that the 'same structural conditions that defeated universal health insurance in the 1930s, the 1950s, the 1960s, and the 1970s' were responsible for the stalemate in 1994 (Mashaw and Marmor 1996, p. 63). Their main argument is that the United States faces structural, institutional, and fiscal problems that limit its ability to function as the 'guarantor of the population's health security' (Mashaw and Marmor 1996, p. 64). The structural impediments relate to the mismatch between political legitimacy—and thus governmental authority—and the level of government. For example, state governments might have the political legitimacy to ensure universal health insurance, but they lack the fiscal and legal authority to do so. Conversely, the federal government has the fiscal and legal abilities but lacks the political legitimacy needed to enact comprehensive health reforms.

Each of the major explanations of the Clinton debacle provides insight into what went wrong in 1993–1994, and together they offer a partial explanation for the failure to achieve comprehensive reform. However, although political scientists emphasize different factors as their particular favourites in explaining health reform failure, virtually all of them agree that public values are an important but neglected aspect of these policy episodes. Some of the major scholarship in political science alludes to the importance of underlying values, but no major scholarship provides a framework for analysing these values. Skocpol, for example, discusses the need for 'a renewed social vision . . . with frank statements about social justice and moral values' in an effort to promote comprehensive health reform (Skocpol 1996, p. 187). Johnson and Broder state that health reform is centrally about 'American values, raising the question of whether our handling of public programs reflects those values of charity and compassion or suggests a sharp change in attitudes. . . . It sets the stage for the most fundamental debate about national values America has had in decades' (Johnson and Broder 1996, p. 638). In addition, they argue the need for a 'great public debate about what kind of health care Americans want' (Johnson and Broder 1996, p. 629). Jacobs and Shapiro contend that individuals' values and fundamental preferences differ from the public's perceptions, evaluations, and choices regarding specific policy proposals and that during the 1993–1994 health reform debate policy makers were focused on personal preferences and ideology and political calculations about their opponents and allies rather than responding to public opinion. As a result, polarized policy debates and the press's coverage of them reduced support for the Clinton plan by creating uncertainty and fear about people's self-interest. Public opinion is much more than the addition of discrete individual preferences, they argue; instead, it requires a community-oriented process that deals with 'complex motivations . . . and multiple and competing tendencies,' and more thought and public reasoning than the contemporary concept of public opinion suggests (Jacobs and Shapiro 2000, p. xix). They also highlight the destabilizing and delegitimizing force of deceptive and manipulative crafted talk. Thus, more work must be done to better understand the values and norms necessary to create agreement on the political conception underlying policy reform.

9.5. A model of American health care reform and incomplete theorization

The Clinton Administration's plan for health care reform was an example of the second type of ITA, an *incompletely specified and generalized agreement*. The nation had formed a consensus on the mid-level principle of universal health care coverage, but no single high-level principle was invoked to explain why such coverage was justified. Moreover, the connection between this agreed upon mid-level principle and the particulars of how society should achieve and pay for universal coverage were equally unclear.

9.5.1. Agreement on universal health care coverage

In the early 1990s, most Americans and their representatives supported the view that universal health insurance should be a priority for policy makers. Jacobs and Shapiro found, for example, 'that through September 1993 clear majorities (close to two-thirds in some cases)' favoured universal coverage (Jacobs and Shapiro 2000, p. 96). In 1992, support for national health insurance was at 66 per cent—the highest it had been in 40 years (CBS News/New York Times Poll 1992). Moreover, public opinion surveys in September and November 1993 and January 1994 found that Americans were willing to increase government spending for health insurance coverage (Jacobs and Shapiro 2000, p. 228). Several public opinion studies

(Blendon and Donelan 1989; 1990; Blendon et al. 1994; Shapiro and Young 1989) revealed that:

(1) Relative to other social policies, consensus about health policy had grown among groups that previously had been separated by traditional social cleavages such as race, socio-economic status, gender, age, and education level.

(2) There was long-standing and near-universal support for equal access to health care regardless of ability to pay.

(3) Though an overwhelming majority of Americans thought that health care was too costly, they ranked universal access high on opinion polls.

Thus, agreement on universal coverage characterized the debate about comprehensive health reform during the 1990s. President Clinton made it the centrepiece of his presidential campaign, his presidency, and his health care reform package.

9.5.2. Multiple high-level theories for universal coverage

Many high-level principles could justify the mid-level principle of universal coverage (Kymlicka 1990). Among them are:

(1) communitarian theories of justice that require the expression of accepted community values and collective responsibility;

(2) utilitarian or welfare economic theories of justice that require maximization of utility or social welfare;

(3) liberal egalitarian theories of justice that require equality of opportunity (Daniels 1985; Rawls 1971);

(4) a Rawlsian theory of justice that requires fair distribution of resources (primary goods (Rawls 1971));

(5) a Kantian theory of justice that requires others to be respected as moral agents;

(6) ethical theories (virtue ethics) that emphasize compassion, charity, and altruism, such as moral concern for others;

(7) a right to health care; and

(8) the principle that society should provide social conditions to maintain and improve individuals' capability for health (Ruger 1998; 2003b; 2004a; 2004b).

Additional higher-level justifications for universal coverage include human capital concerns about workforce productivity and global competitiveness; financial risks associated with lack of insurance or underinsurance; and the notion that citizens have political, legal, and social rights (Marshall 1950).

The problem with having multiple high-level justifications for one mid-level principle is that it restricts policy options to those that fit with certain high-level schemes. It also reveals significant conceptual vagueness about the underlying values that could guide health policy. For instance, a communitarian theory would allow the justification for health care to vary by community (Walzer 1990), arguing that each society constructs its own principles as it evolves politically and that morality is therefore determined by each culture (cultural or moral relativism). Taken to the extreme, this viewpoint could undermine political and social cooperation in societies that respect individual liberties and diversity (Buchanan et al. 2000). Similarly, a strict liberal egalitarian approach that offers a more literal interpretation of equal health care access might restrict free-market principles by not allowing wealthy citizens to buy health care unavailable to the poor (Gutmann 1981). A single-payer system such as the Canadian health system is an approximate example, because participating physicians, hospitals, and clinics have not been allowed to offer services outside the provincial system until recently. In contrast, a focus on human capital would favour health reform that improved worker productivity and therefore global competitiveness, whereas a focus on charity or compassion would emphasize the importance of voluntary charitable acts toward others by non-governmental organizations and individuals.

The 1993–1994 debate surrounding universal health care coverage never settled on one general theory or ethical conception. For example, Americans' support for collective responsibility for medical care was deeply divided. When surveyed about a collective or individual commitment for medical care in 1993 and 1994, a slight majority of the American public in 1993 (52 per cent) favoured collective responsibility, whereas 16 per cent favoured individual responsibility, and 33 per cent favoured divided responsibility between the collective and the individual (Schlesinger 2004, p. 977). In 1994, the American public remained divided (48 per cent favoured collective, 34 per cent favoured split responsibility, 21 per cent favoured individual responsibility). When asked, Americans were also divided on whether or not they supported a 'right to health care': in 1993, while 59 per cent favoured a right to health care, 36 per cent thought of health care as merely a privilege (Schlesinger 2004, p. 978). In another survey of American values at the time,

Robert Blendon and colleagues found that Americans held conflicting core values, which included (1) 'a moral commitment to the uninsured', (2) 'a desire to achieve personal peace of mind', (3) 'a lack of self-blame', (4) 'a limited willingness to sacrifice', (5) 'reasoned self-interest in what changes are enacted', (6) 'a distrust of government', and (7) 'a healthy cynicism about the behavior of our major institutions' (Blendon et al. 1994, p. 274). While moral concern for the uninsured was a strong core value among the American public, this value alone was not enough to generate strong support for national health insurance. In these and other surveys, researchers found Americans to have competing core values, to express ambivalence about health and health care, and to exhibit a conflict among core beliefs (Blendon et al. 1995).

These results are consistent with findings from Schlesinger and Lau (2000), who speculate that health reform failure resulted from efforts to combine two diverse policy conceptions—societal rights and marketable commodity—that individuals perceived as incompatible. They are consistent also with research from Frohlich and Oppenheimer (1993) and Mitchell et al. (1993, pp. 629–39), who find that individuals contemplate multiple principles (e.g. equality, merit, efficiency, need) and make trade-offs among them, but that conflict among such principles leads to contradictory results. Nearly all political science research on higher-level norms of distributive justice has shown that individuals have conflicting views on justice (Hochschild 1986; Kluegel et al. 1995; Verba and Orren 1985). More recent work on values and democratic decision-making adds more evidence of a lack of coherence among the public (and political elites) regarding deep values for health reform. At the same time that Americans strongly supported health reform that would help them personally, they also supported the notion that health care should be provided based on medical need, not ability to pay, and that the medical care system should treat everyone equally (Schlesinger 2002, pp. 889–925). Conflict among principles resulted in a failure to develop a widespread principle or set of principles supporting health reform. Thus, although these studies rely primarily on public opinion surveys and more extensive studies of value-based reasoning in political science are needed, this evidence suggests significant higher-level value differences underlying Americans' views about health care reform.

9.5.3. Strategies for attaining universal coverage

Two types of strategies for attaining universal coverage dominated the debate of the early 1990s, an employer mandate (plus an individual mandate) and a single-payer option. The employer mandate would have required all employers to make health insurance available to all employees—part-time, seasonal, and temporary in the strictest model—and to pay a defined proportion of the cost. The advantages of this mandate were its ability to supplement the existing American employer-based system and its potential to increase the financial risk pool. A disadvantage was the perceived harm to businesses such as restaurants and stores that are small or employ mostly low-wage or part-time workers (even though small businesses would have been likely to receive government subsidies). There was also speculation that employers would lay off workers and that small-group insurance reform would be required. The insurance industry was concerned about and forcefully opposed to the employer mandate. Additionally, to achieve universal coverage, the employer mandate would need supplementation with an individual mandate or other mechanism for covering those not in the workforce.

The single-payer option involves one public payer for health care services and health-related products. Thus, the government would provide health insurance, using funds collected from individuals and employers. Because the single-payer system largely eliminates private health insurance, the insurance and related industries oppose it. In some single-payer systems, health care services are organized and delivered by a central body, simplifying administration and reducing costs. The Canadian universal health insurance programme is an example of a single-payer system, as is the US Medicare programme (though the latter was not presented as such during the debate). Canada and many other countries have single-payer programmes, but opponents (especially the Health Insurance Association of America) argue that introducing such a system into the United States would require social transformation of American health care and public health.

Numerous other health care proposals emerged in 1993–1994, including, but not limited to, managed competition, price controls and copayments, health purchasing cooperatives, quality controls, standardized benefits, payroll taxes, medical savings accounts, electronic billing, freedom of choice, and global budgets. Some of the competing proposals fused elements of different 'categories' of reform (Marmor and Goldberg 1994). One such proposal was the 'pay or play' plan, which gave companies the option of covering health insurance for their employees or opting out by paying a payroll tax (Hacker 1997).

Despite all these options, Americans disagreed on how best to achieve universal coverage and on specific strategies for reform. The public was deeply divided in its support for alternative approaches, in particular the single-payer and employer mandate option. In a survey of Americans' views on health policy, researchers found that most Americans do not favour a single-payer type of national health plan (Blendon and Benson 2001). These researchers found that, generally speaking, the majority of Americans in January 1993 (63 per cent) and March 1993 (59 per cent) favoured some type of national health insurance; however, they were unsure about what type of health plan they wanted. As Blendon and Benson note:

> Among the confounding factors is the lack of an underlying consensus among the American public over the preferred type of national health plan. Polls that offer only one plan as a possible solution often show majority support for that proposal. But when other major alternative proposals are offered, . . . public support splinters (Blendon and Benson 2001, p. 36)

Among the employer mandate, single-payer, and tax credit strategies, Americans were nearly equally divided with 28 per cent, 32 per cent, and 33 per cent public support, respectively, in 1992 (Blendon et al. 1992, p. 3373). As Jacobs and Shapiro note, for example, the public 'tortured' itself but ultimately failed 'to reach a verdict that would give a "full endorsement" to one of the leading proposals' (Jacobs and Shapiro 2000, p. 220).

The Clinton plan, the Health Security Act, was an employer mandate model, based on a managed competition framework. It relied on government regulation rather than market forces alone to control costs. It created a system of regional purchasing monopolies and placed price controls on health plan premiums. It also set up a National Health Board to oversee health care quality. Opponents quickly pointed to inefficiencies and bureaucratic problems they surmised the plan would create. Divergence on policy particulars was one factor in the plan's failure. And although most lawmakers supported universal coverage, they did not want to take political risks by raising taxes or upsetting small businesses. They perceived that the voting public, while generally supportive of universal coverage, was unwilling to pay higher taxes or to have its health care rationed.

Americans not only disagreed on how to achieve universal coverage, but they gave weak responses on their opinions about universal coverage when higher taxes were envisioned. The conflict and limited willingness to pay is illustrated by responses to public opinion surveys. While one survey, for example, found that only 22 per cent of Americans were willing to pay an additional $200 a year in new taxes to support national health care (Blendon and Donelan 1990), another survey, which did not quantify willingness to pay in dollars, found that 61–64 per cent of Americans indicated *some* willingness to pay higher taxes to cover the cost of universal health insurance (Jacobs and Shapiro 2000, p. 228). However, the majority of Americans at the time (55 per cent in 1993 and 66 per cent in 1994) indicated that the amount of federal taxes they had to pay in general was already too high (Blendon and Benson 2001, p. 42).

This pattern of differentiated responses at different levels of generality emphasizes the need for further clarity about the balance between underlying values and consensus on political conceptions of the health system. Clearly, the American public as a whole has not agreed to and internalized the public moral norm of willingness to pay extra taxes to support universal health care. Furthermore, Americans shifted toward self-interest over the course of the health reform debate: fierce opposition to the specific objective of expanding health insurance coverage undercut the public's support, which dropped from 64 per cent in 1993 to roughly 55 per cent in 1994 (Jacobs and Shapiro 2000, p. 228). It appears that Americans were interested in reform based on whether or not they personally would be better off as a result. As political analysts note, 'Americans' strong support for reform could be quickly tempered by messages implying that personal sacrifices might be required to deal with the broader problems', especially if reform would 'require more than a modest tax increase' (Blendon et al. 1995, p. 12). Americans' focus on limiting the harm to themselves personally 'created a serious constraint to maintaining public support for comprehensive reform' (Blendon et al. 1995, p. 12). Americans' unwillingness to pay sufficient taxes to support universal health insurance coverage reflects an ITA; indeed, supporting values were never effectively marshalled to provide a rationale for internalizing a collective commitment to pay for universal coverage. Table 9.1 shows the levels involved in the incomplete theorization of health care reform in America and suggested explanations of stability.

9.6. A wedge theory of health care reform

This analysis offers an additional way of evaluating the failure of the Clinton plan: the consensus on the need for universal coverage at that time was an *incompletely specified and generalized agreement* and therefore lacked both high-level and low-level agreements. This second type of ITA can be particularly problematic in achieving stability and permanence because, without a consensus on higher-level principles *and* without agreement on lower-level principles for particulars, the idea of universal coverage was vulnerable to value-based attacks from opponents. A failure

Table 9.1. Models of Incompletely Theorized Agreements

Model	High-level	Mid-level	Low-level	Stability
Incompletely Specified Agreement	Agreement	Disagreement	Disagreement	Stable
Incompletely Specified and Generalized Agreements	Disagreement	Agreement	Disagreement	Unstable
Incompletely Theorized Agreements on Particular Outcomes	Disagreement	Disagreement	Agreement	Stable

to more clearly articulate and agree on values left the Clinton proposal vulnerable to Republican attacks. Opponents used value- and norm-based assaults to insert a wedge between competing models of health care reform, preventing agreement on particular outcomes. These attacks generally took the form of libertarian and individualistic arguments and emphasized the value conflict between freedom and equality.

Jacobs and Shapiro's (2000) work on crafted talk and the loss of democratic responsiveness reinforces the wedge theory, as do Marmor and Oberlander (1994), whose analysis demonstrates how opponents of reform exploited the fragility of the universal coverage agreement and enhanced the appeal of competing values. These adversaries prevented major health care system changes by convincing the public that reform threatened core values in America's liberal tradition. These values included individualism, distrust of government, and the capitalist conviction that the private sector is more efficient than government. Republican strategists created further confusion about reform because their party did not want to concede too much political ground to the Democrats.

Entrenched Republican interests blocked reform by manipulating people's fears and misunderstandings (Marmor and Oberlander 1994). Several themes contributed to this confusion. First, opponents questioned whether a health care crisis actually existed and thus whether a moral concern for others or even reasoned self-interest justified legislative efforts. Second, they created false dichotomies between regulation and competition and thus confusion about the role of the private sector and government in American liberal society. Third, they also created false dichotomies between radical and conservative plans and mounted efforts to polarize citizens into ideological camps with which they might not entirely identify.

226

Efforts to categorize Americans' values into 'value sets' reveal that supporters of health reform (liberals) are more conflicted in policy preferences and underlying values than are opponents (conservatives). These efforts, which tend to push values toward the poles and away from the centre—for example, contrasting freedom and equality—thus leave liberals more fragmented and divided than conservatives on underlying values. Furthermore, the style of opponents' attacks, adversarial and based on ideological cant, name calling, exaggeration, and distortion, is in itself value based, taking the focus off collective efforts to achieve the common good and toward a 'us-versus-them' way of thinking. Jacobs and Shapiro (2000) similarly argue that the media's focus on political conflict and strategy heightened public cynicism and fears about altering the status quo, causing concern about government effectiveness and the personal risk of health reform to individuals. For example, opponents of reform distorted the choice issue in health care, marshalling a threat to individualism, all the while failing to note that the private sector's quest for cost containment was restricting choice more than any reform might do. They also exaggerated the role of government in the Clinton plan and other reform packages, causing the public to question whether loss of freedom through regulation was worth the potential benefits of comprehensive reform. Senator Bob Dole, with his organizational charts, was particularly skilled at this type of dialogue. He and others used competing values to drive a wedge between the parties, destabilizing the mid-level agreement on universal coverage. By 1994, 'as the media conveyed the genuinely fractious nature of policy debates, the public became increasingly fearful ... of the personal costs of higher taxes and lower quality care, and many people switched from supporters ... to opponents of the Clinton plan or any reform' (Jacobs and Shapiro 2000, p. 237).

Value articulation does not inoculate the public against disruptive arguments. But the failure to achieve an ethical consensus on wealth redistribution to support health care coverage left the reform effort vulnerable to the depredations of opposing forces. For large-scale reform, individuals must be willing to pay for health insurance for themselves and fellow citizens; otherwise universal coverage is unachievable. Any policy enacted to achieve universal coverage will require individuals to make a financial commitment to fulfil claims by others. Because universal coverage requires social organization in the form of redistribution of resources and related legislation and regulation, it requires an ethical commitment on the part of a majority of individuals. Without this ethical commitment, it will not be possible to redistribute resources from the wealthy to those less fortunate. The effort to do so is—and must be—essentially voluntary, not coercive (Ruger 2006a).

ITA analysis tells us that health care reform would not have been as susceptible to the wedge strategy if social agreement on either a high-level conception (such as health equity) or low-level principle (willingness to help pay for others' health insurance) had occurred. A shared high-level political conception or shared lower-level principles provide a focal point around which agreements can coalesce and shape policy, enabling deep social compromise upon which to build new policy proposals. Such compromise takes as given the numerous disagreements that divide citizens and policy makers. By accepting disagreement (and its plurality), promoting social compromise, and putting forward conceptual tools for coming to agreement on policy proposals (legislation), social agreement theory has prescriptive advantages in facilitating consensus on health reform through deliberation in a pluralistic constitutional democracy like the United States. Such a consensus might have promoted further agreement at lower levels of policy by putting the focus on discrete trade-offs in willingness to pay (e.g. paying $200 more in taxes for universal coverage). It also might have forced Americans to define their priorities, obliging them to decide collectively how much they valued health as compared, for example, to national security (at a higher level) *or* how to trade off public and private sector or federal and state initiatives as was done in the State Children's Health Insurance Program (S-CHIP) (at a lower level). Such decision-making would ultimately require more objective and explicit information on how society spends its money and whether such expenditures match up with Americans' own values. The result would be greater clarity—not uncertainty—about Americans' core values and social consensus on the principles that should guide health care decisions. Americans should be given the opportunity to weigh the costs and trade-offs between health policy and policies that achieve other social ends.

Although many high-level principles could justify universal coverage, certain principles—equality of opportunity, health equity, human rights (right to health), altruism, health need, equal treatment—might have improved the health policy debates of the early 1990s, especially if policy elites or grassroots organizations had focused on mobilizing and seeking a consensus among the American public—and representing that consensus—on norms of health care equity and fairness. The American public has expressed strong support for equal health care treatment (65–93 per cent) and for meeting health care needs (38–84 per cent) (Schlesinger 2002, p. 910). Policy leaders could have argued, for instance, that health insurance is important for ensuring all American's ability to be healthy and financially secure. These sentiments have deep roots in American political thought and philosophy about the human condition, yet reformers failed to tap into them. From this perspective, reformers might need to address value conflict among potential *supporters* as much, if not more than, among potential *opponents*. A lower level agreement on a single or set of principles could be useful, especially for drawing out fundamental ideas latent in the public political culture.

One important idea incorporated into the debates was that America was experiencing a multidimensional health care crisis: costs were too high, people were uninsured or underinsured, and quality was too variable. Americans were willing to address these problems, but they shifted toward self-interest over the course of the reform debate. Because of this shift, consensus on individuals' willingness to sacrifice or pay for others' health insurance never solidified. As Jacobs and Shapiro note, during the period 1990–1993, 'Americans consistently looked beyond their own personal situation to focus on national and collective benefits such as easing the burden of health expenditures... and making altruistic efforts to provide others with quality care' (Jacobs and Shapiro 2000, p. 236). During 'this period of public-spiritedness, the influence of personal costs on the public's preferences for reform were relatively weak, while expectations toward the potentially positive consequences of national reform were comparatively strong' (Jacobs and Shapiro 2000, p. 236). This climate led to the beginnings of health care reform. But as the debate progressed, Americans changed, increasingly judging reform based on its effect on them personally (Blendon et al. 1995, p. 12). Indeed, when the American public was asked about willingness to pay higher taxes so that the uninsured could have the same benefits available to the average person (or pay somewhat lower taxes and provide the uninsured with a scaled-down plan), only 40 per cent of middle-class Americans said they would support higher taxes (Blendon et al. 1995, p. 20).

In the absence of sufficient public support for paying taxes, the Clinton Administration had to focus on delivering a plan that promised not to increase costs. As a result, the HSA was held to a tough financial standard and was expected to generate economic efficiencies from the health care system to pay for expanded health insurance coverage. This need to fiddle with the health care system left the proposal vulnerable to attacks, which evoked public fears that government was tinkering with health care and that individuals were going to lose more than they gained as a result of reform. This is the point where the absence of internalized values of sacrifice is especially relevant for the fate of the Clinton reforms. If reformers had engaged the public's values enough to create a willingness to pay

229

more taxes, then the Clinton plan would have never needed to tinker with the health care system and would therefore not have been vulnerable to Republican attacks about 'big government' and 'government control'. The Clinton plan could potentially have been a reform primarily, even solely, about financing health care, where the public is comfortable with a government role. Or reformers might have been able to engage the public with a values-based argument about the need to sacrifice a bit financially and perhaps even a bit in terms of health care convenience, in order to help others deprived of health care. Such efforts could have helped to inoculate the Clinton plan against opponents' attacks.

9.7. Internalization and agreement on moral values

Despite these daunting features of American public policy discourse, some reform efforts have succeeded. They include large-scale social movements such as the New Deal, the civil rights movement, and the women's movement, and smaller scale efforts like the S-CHIP. A number of factors underlie the success of reforms, including changes in collective policy preferences resulting from gradual social and economic trends, social movements, organized interests, and mass media reports. Page and Shapiro, for example, argue that civil rights support was energized by a series of events that were 'manifestations of a powerful social movement that ultimately raised white as well as black Americans' consciousness of the mistreatment suffered by black people' (Page and Shapiro 1992, p. 77). There is little doubt, they add, that the civil rights movement had a 'major impact on public opinion' (Page and Shapiro 1992 p. 72). Indeed, the impact was so great that it connected to fundamental American values— through the use of norms-based arguments—to forge a consensus on legislative and judicial action to ensure equal treatment for all persons, regardless of race. In this case, both the public (through grassroots organizers) and elites worked to address gaps in public values by making value-based arguments (Lee 2002). Ultimately, Americans changed and broadened their commitment to equality. Through a struggle over moral principles, norms became internalized and equal protection and anti-discrimination were enshrined in legislation and judicial doctrine.

With respect to equal rights for women, Page and Shapiro argue that the 'shift in favor of equal employment opportunities for women seems, like the similar movement with respect to blacks, to have followed naturally from basic American values of individualism and equal opportunity' (Page and Shapiro 1992, p. 101). Public opinion on domestic aspects of the economy has been fairly stable over time. It demonstrates a 'coherent view of public policy' and a 'substantial, though bounded, welfare state' that 'reflects a sense of societal obligation, a strong commitment to government action...to protect the helpless, and to provide a substantial degree of equal opportunity for all' (Page and Shapiro 1992, p. 118). Rawls might say that this 'coherent' view reflects a political conception of justice that centres on the principle of equal opportunity. Indeed, successfully implemented social welfare programmes typically have reflected Americans' "enduring commitments to social insurance and equal opportunity" while also appealing to commitments to the market, individualism, and limited government (Marmor et al. 1990, p. 241). Writing about the Social Security programme, Page and Shapiro note that the system of aiding broad categories of the 'truly needy' under the logic of self-insurance seems to fit the American conception of fairness. This agreement on policy particulars through lower-level reasoning on person categories and type of insurance comports with the ITA framework of social agreement as well. It also fits with the notion of norm internalization—that these norms have a 'taken for granted' quality (Finnemore and Sikkink 1998).

To truly address the nation's health problems is likely to require revising norms and values, as with the civil rights movement. That movement generated strong opposition from interest groups, but the high moral vision and rhetoric of leaders such as Martin Luther King Jr. informed and energized its focus on racial justice and equality. At the same time, grassroots organizations and local protests by individual citizens pressed for social change in the moral consciousness of the American public (Lee 2002). Indeed, the strong support of clergy and grassroots organizations around the nation and the corresponding moral rhetoric that these leaders and citizens deployed in support of the Civil Rights Act of 1964 were influential factors leading to the bill's enactment. No such coalition of moral thinkers or grassroots organizers took centre stage in the health reform debates of the early 1990s. Although agreement on particulars, such as affirmative action, is still incomplete, this high-level moral vision has established racial equality as a defining principle—an internalized norm—of American political thought. In contrast, though Americans have expressed concern for others and have indicated general support for a right to health care, they have yet to clarify and internalize the underlying values that relate to health reform and the health system. Because high-level theory was important to major American reforms in other policy areas, it seems that abstract arguments about higher-level principles can be important to democratic politics generally and to health reform specifically. Agreements on low-level principles have also been important and can be the product of reforms that succeed despite the threat of political impasse between opposing parties.

Thus, one way to achieve comprehensive health care reform might be to put a higher-level theory of the right or the good at the centre of public deliberation about comprehensive health reform. This proposal is consistent with Bruce Ackerman's discussion of 'constitutional moments' in which citizens become excited and mobilize around a 'big idea' (Ackerman 1991). The United States needs *a constitutional moment for health* to infuse Americans with a vision of universal health care as the right thing to do. This social and then political internalization will lead political elites to accept the norm and promote its adoption for health policy. As Elster and Slagstad argue, deontological claims can help produce large-scale social change (Elster and Slagstad 1988). Such a consensus might better withstand attack by opposing theoretical camps. High-level principles can play a defining role in American social reform.

Public opinion polls suggest that high-level principles about health care exist or are latent in American political culture. Page and Shapiro found that 'large majorities of the public have seen medical care as a "right" to which all citizens are entitled: NORC [National Opinion Research Center] found 87% so responding in 1968, and Roper, asking a slightly different question, found 78% in 1975 and 81% in 1979' (Page and Shapiro 1992, p. 129). But support for health care rights has since dissipated to the point that it is not, in itself, sufficient as a high-level principle to support reform. Clinton did not take this tack in his health reform efforts and explicitly did not evoke rights in his speeches introducing the Health Security Act.

Indeed, as a Rawlsian OC framework might suggest, the common high-level values for reform need to represent an overlapping consensus among higher-level principles, perhaps including rights with other justifications. From a Rawlsian perspective, developing an OC might be necessary, given the gaps in values supporting health reform, to draw out certain fundamental ideas latent in the public political culture.

Jacobs and Shapiro's work during the 1993–1994 health reform debate suggests that public opinion was motivated partly by concern for others, although self-interest still played a role. For example, 'the public receptiveness to rebuilding the country's health system was...a persuasive indicator of the public's concern for others who are most vulnerable' (Jacobs and Shapiro 2000, p. 241). A social agreement model demonstrates that, while complete theorization might not be necessary or possible, some degree of agreement—even if incompletely theorized—is important for stable governance and policy selection. According to Rawls, as long as a strong social consensus is achieved around a political conception that is agreed upon for its own sake, such agreements can provide guidance for specific policy proposals. Agreement at lower levels can then follow as a separate step, after public debate about principles and priorities for specific policy alternatives. A report from the Institute of Medicine (IOM 2004), for example, identified several principles (universality, continuity, affordability, and enhanced health and well-being) around which social agreement could be achieved. Collectively, such principles might form a framework for designing and evaluating new approaches to universal health insurance coverage. Some innovative methods of democratic deliberation, such as national issues forums, citizen juries, and deliberative polling, could be instructive here in efforts to define a model of respectful public exchange in creating consensus (Fishkin 1991; Kahan and Braman 2006).

Social consensus for health reform might occur at different levels, but it will require conditions that permit truth telling and rational debate. Collective reasoning about public policy requires a truthful deliberative process as an essential component of democracy and a sincere and dedicated effort to achieve consensus on both the ends (values) and means (acceptable policy solutions) of public policy. These efforts are critical to citizens' ability to 'rule themselves' (Richardson 2002). Public opinion can be manipulated and distorted, so the challenge in a constitutional democracy is to create conditions of honest debate under which Americans can agree on a political conception that governs health and health care. Such a conception is likely to be latent in the political culture and could well emerge through public deliberation and social consensus: public opinion research suggests that the American public is capable of rational collective policy preferences that reflect underlying social values (Page and Shapiro 1992). It is therefore important to invoke principles such as equal opportunity, health equity, altruism or moral concern for others, or public spiritedness in order to clarify what Americans value to guide policy makers. Efforts to involve the government in improving the health of the nation and to ensure access to quality health care for all require more than fragile agreement on mid-level principles.

These efforts require invoking principles, values and norms, and honest discussion about the impact of denying necessary and appropriate care on the health and security of Americans. There are numerous ethical values that can be invoked to mobilize support for health reform—protecting

233

opportunities or financial security, fostering human flourishing, human rights, health equity—but whatever the value, the objective in invoking higher-level theory is to gain greater clarity of thought, centre on norm internalization, and to achieve social consensus. This agreement must then translate into implementable public policies (such as Medicare and Medicaid) that give priority to public investments in health and health care over less important social goals. In a world of scarce resources, such trade-offs must and should be made through informed choice by the people who are ultimately affected by those decisions: the citizenry. Agreement across the political spectrum by Democrats and Republicans (Menzel and Light 2006) alike is required. The Medicare programme, though not universal, represents a successful partial reform that has achieved agreement about both ends (values) and means (Marmor and Barer 1997).

Even if society achieves clarity of thought at a higher level, reform must take place at the level of policy. It is thus more likely that agreement on lower-level principles will occur on the path to achieving health care reform. The passage of the S-CHIP is an example of lower-order consensus to achieve health reform. In this case, legislators agreed to expand coverage for children (through S-CHIP) without agreeing on universal coverage and without justifying this outcome on the basis of any one overarching political philosophy (e.g. utilitarianism or communitarianism). In fact, they might have offered very different reasons for reaching the same conclusion: some legislators might have wanted to enact S-CHIP on the basis of equality among children, regardless of income, while some agreed on S-CHIP because they prioritized children's health over that of adults, and still others might have viewed children as the most vulnerable members of society. Furthermore, the S-CHIP was designed to allow states to implement it using different models (e.g. public insurance, Medicaid extension, or private insurance), in such a way that Congress could get agreement on reform without forcing agreement on lower-order strategies. Congress was able to find common ground and coalesced to approve S-CHIP legislation despite the rationale's incomplete theorization.

In conclusion, the remarkably quick collapse and fragmentation of the seemingly potent movement for universal health coverage in the United States during 1993–1994 can be viewed as evidence for the inherent fragility of values that the public has not embraced at either a higher or lower level of generality.

Conclusion

Are the current approaches to fostering good health for all bearing fruit in the United States and in many other countries? Clearly, they are not. Utilitarian, communitarian, libertarian, egalitarian, and democratic procedural approaches have fallen short of providing either adequate theoretical grounding or sufficient practical impetus for health system reform.

Can the world become a far healthier place? Unquestionably. Can its nation states use their institutional structures, public, private, and non-profit, to reform health systems and foster better health for their peoples? The health capability paradigm answers that question with an emphatic yes, and provides the theoretical foundation on which to construct that effort.

Starting with the fundamental imperative of justice to support human flourishing, the health capability paradigm assembles this foundation brick by brick. It frames health capabilities in terms of health functioning, health agency, and health needs. It draws on social choice theory and introduces incompletely theorized agreements as a means to find a way forward through conflicting views. It proposes shortfall equality as an objective, realistic measure of health performance. It demands efficiency and provides pragmatic principles to promote it, in criteria for medical necessity and appropriateness, and in a robust grasp of the opportunity costs issue. It illuminates the central role of norms, both positive ones that advance justice and negative ones that undermine health, and the need for inspired leadership and grassroots efforts to foster new commitments to justice in health. It examines the theory underlying health insurance and argues for universal coverage. It respects medical and public health expertise and insists on scientific as well as ethical rationality. It focuses centrally on the health capability and health agency of patients and thus honours their voice in the deliberative process.

The building blocks of this theory come from philosophy, law, economics, political science, medicine, and the biological sciences. This integrated construct is a radical alternative, and it forms the inner architecture necessary if we are to build health systems in which all can strive to realize their health capabilities.

It is time for this new model. It is time for this vision of human flourishing. It is time to move forward.

Bibliography

Aaron, H. and Schwartz, W. (1984) *The Painful Prescription: Rationing Hospital Care*. Washington, DC: Brookings Institution.

Abigail Alliance for Better Access to Developmental Drugs v. Von Eschenbach (2007) 495 F.3d 695 (DC Cir.).

Ackerman, B. (1991) *We the People*. Cambridge, MA: Belknap Press of Harvard University Press.

Aetna Health Inc. v. Davila (2004) 542 US 200.

Agency for Healthcare Research and Quality (2000a) 'Research on caring for children with asthma.' *AHRQ Publication No. 00–P025*.

——(2000b) 'Research on Diabetes Care.' *AHRQ Publication No. 00-P018*.

Albrecht, G. and Fitzpatrick, R. (eds) (1994) *Quality of Life in Health Care* Greenwich, CT: JAI Press.

Alkire, S. and Black, R. (1997) 'A Practical Reasoning Theory of Development Ethics: Furthering the Capabilities Approach.' *Journal of International Development* 9(2): 263–79.

Altman, S. and Ostby, E. (1991) 'Paying for Hospital Care: The Impact on Federal Policy', in E. Ginzberg (ed.), *Health Services Research: Key to Health Policy*: 46–68.

American Association of Community Psychiatrists (2007) 'Keystones for Collaboration and Leadership: Issues and Recommendations for the Transformation of Community Psychiatry.' Available at http://www.comm.psych.pitt.edu/finds/TransformationofPsychiatryReport.pdf accessed on 8 January 2009.

American Thoracic Society (1991) 'Withholding and Withdrawing Life-Sustaining Therapy.' *American Review of Respiratory Diseases* 144(3 Pt 1): 726–31.

Americans with Disabilities Act (1994) 42 U.S.C. §§ 12101–12213.

Amick, B., Levine, S., Tarlov, A. and Walsh, D. (eds) (1995) *Society and Health*. New York: Oxford University Press.

Anand, P. (2005) 'Capabilities and health.' *Journal of Medical Ethics* 31(5): 299–303.

Anand, S. and Hanson, K. (1997) 'Disability-adjusted life years: a critical review.' *Journal of Health Economics* 16(6): 685–702.

Anand, S. and Peter, F. (2000) 'Equal Opportunity', in N. Daniels et al., *Is Inequality Bad for Our Health?*: 48–52.

Anand, S., Peter, F. and Sen A. (eds) (2004) *Public Health, Ethics and Equity*. New York: Oxford University Press.

Bibliography

Anand, S. and Sen, A. (1994) 'Sustainable human development: concepts and priorities.' *U.N. Human Development Report Office Occasional Paper No. 9.*

——(1995) 'Gender inequality in human development: theories and measurement.' *U.N. Human Development Report Office Occasional Paper No. 19.*

Anderson, C., Mhurchu C., Rubenach S., Clark M., Spencer C. and Winsor, A. (2000) 'Home or Hospital for Stroke Rehabilitation? Results of a Randomized Controlled Trial II Cost Minimization Analysis at 6 months.' *Stroke* 31 (5): 1032–7.

Anderson, E. (1993) *Value in Ethics and Economics.* Cambridge, MA: Harvard University Press.

——(1999) 'What is the point of equality?' *Ethics* 109(2): 287–337.

Anderson, G., Hurst, J., Hussey, P. and Jee-Hughes, M. (2000) 'Health Spending and Outcomes: Trends in OECD Countries, 1960–1998.' *Health Affairs* 19(3): 150–7.

Angell, M. (1991) 'The case of Helga Wanglie: a new kind of "right to die" case' [editorial]. *New England Journal of Medicine* 325(7): 511–12.

——(2000) 'Pockets of Poverty', in N. Daniels et al., *Is Inequality Bad for Our Health* 42–7.

Annas, G. (2003) 'The Right to Health and the Nevirapine Case in South Africa.' *New England Journal of Medicine* 348(8): 750–4.

Arneson, R. (1989) 'Equality and equal opportunity for welfare.' *Philosophical Studies* 56(1): 77–93.

——(1990) 'Liberalism, Distributive Subjectivism, and Equal Opportunity for Welfare.' *Philosophy & Public Affairs* 19(2): 158–94.

——(2000) 'Perfectionism and Politics.' *Ethics* 111(1): 37–63.

——(2006) 'Distributive Justice and Basic Capability Equality: "Good Enough" is Not Good Enough.' In A. Kaufman (ed.) *Capabilities Equality: Basic Issues and Problems*: 17–43.

Arrow, K. (1951) *Social Choice and Individual Values* [book review]. New York: John Wiley & Sons, Inc.

——(1963) 'Uncertainty and the Welfare Economics of Medical Care.' *American Economic Review* 53(5): 941–73.

——(1973) 'Some Ordinalist-Utilitarian Notes on Rawls's Theory of Justice.' *Journal of Philosophy* 70(9): 245–63.

Asch, S., Kerr, E., Keesey, J., Adams, J., Setodji, C., Malik S. and McGlynn, E. (2006) 'Who Is at Greatest Risk for Receiving Poor-Quality Health Care?' *New England Journal of Medicine* 354(11): 1147–56.

Atkinson, S., Bihari, D., Smithies, M., Daly, K., Mason, R. and McColl, I. (1994) 'Identification of futility in intensive care.' *Lancet* 344(8931): 1203–6.

Auster, R., Leveson, I. and Sarachek, D. (1969) 'The Production of Health, An Exploratory Study.' *Journal of Human Resources* 4(4): 411–36.

Autism Program Quality Indicators (2001) *A Self-Review and Quality Improvement Guide for Schools and Programs Serving Students with Autism Spectrum Disorders*. New York State Education Department. Available at: http://www.vesid.nysed.gov/specialed/autism/apqi.htm accessed on 8 January 2009.

Baily, M. (1994) 'The democracy problem.' *Hastings Center Report* 24(4): 39–42.

Baumrin, B. (2002) 'Why There Is No Right to Health Care', in R. Rhodes et al. (eds) *Medicine and Social Justice: Essays on the Distribution of Health Care*: 78–83.

Beauchamp, T. and Childress, J. (1994) *Principles of Biomedical Ethics, 4th Edition*. New York: Oxford University Press.

——(2001) *Principles of Biomedical Ethics, 5th Edition*. New York: Oxford University Press.

Beauchamp, T. and Walters, L. (1994) *Contemporary Issues in Bioethics, 4th Edition*. Belmont: Wadsworth Publishing Company.

Beitz, C. (1986) 'Amartya Sen's Resources, Values, and Development.' *Economics and Philosophy* 2: 282–90.

Bénabou, R. and Tirole J. (2003) 'Intrinsic and Extrinsic Motivation.' *Review of Economic Studies* 70(3): 489–520.

Benatar, S., Daar, A. and Singer, P. (2005) 'Global Health Challenges: The Need for an Expanded Discourse on Bioethics.' *Public Library Of Science Medicine* 2(7 e143): 587–9.

Bennett, S., Creese, A. and Monasch, R. (1998) 'Health insurance schemes for people outside formal sector employment.' ARA Paper No. 16, *Division of Analysis Research and Assessment*. Geneva: WHO.

Berger, M. and Leigh, J. (1989) 'Schooling, Self-selection, and Health.' *Journal of Human Resources* 24(3): 433–55.

Bergner, M., Bobbitt, R., Kressel, S., Pollard, W., Gilson, B. and Morris, J. (1976) 'The sickness impact profile: conceptual formulation and methodology for the development of a health status measure.' *International Journal of Health Services* 6(3): 393–415.

Bergthold, L. (1995) 'Medical necessity: do we need it?' *Health Affairs* 14(4): 180–90.

Berkman, L. and Kawachi, I. (eds) (2000) *Social Epidemiology*. New York: Oxford University Press.

Berkowitz, A. (2005) 'An Overview of the Social Norms Approach', in L. Lederman and L. Stewart (eds), *Changing the Culture of College Drinking: A Socially Situated Health Communication Campaign*: 193–214.

Bernstein, S., McGlynn, E., Siu, A., Roth, C., Sherwood, M., Keesey, J., Kosecoff, J., Hicks, N. and Brook, R. (1993) 'The appropriateness of hysterectomy. A comparison of care in seven health plans.' *Journal of the American Medical Association* 269(18): 2398–402.

Bhargava, A. (1994) 'Modelling the health of Filipino children.' *Journal of the Royal Statistical Society, Series A* 157(3): 417–32.

Birch, S. and Gafni, A. (2003) 'Economics and the evaluation of health care programmes: generalisability of methods and implications for generalisability of results.' *Health Policy* 64(2): 207–19.

Black, C., Peterson, S., Mansfield, J. and Thliveris, M. (1999) 'Using population-based data to enhance clinical practice guideline development.' *Medical Care* 37 (6 Suppl): JS254–63.

Blank, R. (1992) 'Regulatory Rationing: A Solution to Health Care Resource Allocation.' *University of Pennsylvania Law Review* 140(5): 1573–96.

Blendon, R. (1988) 'What should be done about the uninsured poor?' *Journal of the American Medical Association* 260(21): 3176–7.

Blendon, R., Altman, D., Benson, J., Taylor, H., James, M. and Smith, M. (1992) 'The implications of the 1992 Presidential election for health care reform.' *Journal of the American Medical Association* 268(23): 3371–5.

Blendon, R. and Benson, J. (2001) 'Americans' Views On Health Policy: A Fifty-Year Historical Perspective.' *Health Affairs* 20(2): 33–46.

Blendon, R., Brodie, M. and Benson, J. (1995) 'What happened to Americans' support for the Clinton health plan?' *Health Affairs* 14(2): 7–23.

Blendon, R. and Donelan, K. (1989) 'The 1988 election: how important was health?' *Health Affairs* 8(3): 6–15.

——(1990) 'The public and the emerging debate over national health insurance.' *New England Journal of Medicine* 323(3): 208–12.

Blendon, R., Leitman, R., Morrison, I. and Donelan, K. (1990) 'Satisfaction with health systems in ten nations.' *Health Affairs* 9(2): 185–92.

Blendon, R., Marttila, J., Benson, J., Shelter, M., Connolly, F. and Kiley, T. (1994) 'The beliefs and values shaping today's health reform debate.' *Health Affairs* 13(1): 274–84.

Bloche, M. (2002) 'Trust and Betrayal in the Medical Marketplace.' *Stanford Law Review* 55(3): 919–54.

Boorse, C. (1975) 'On the Distinction between Disease and Illness.' *Philosophy and Public Affairs* 5(1): 49–68.

Borsari, B. and Carey, K. (2003) 'Descriptive and Injunctive Norms in College Drinking: A Meta-Analytic Integration.' *Journal of Studies on Alcohol* 64(3): 331–41.

Boyd, C., Darer, J., Boult, C., Fried, L., Boult, L. and Wu, A. (2005) 'Clinical Practice Guidelines and Quality of Care for Older Patients with Multiple Comorbid Diseases: Implications for Pay for Performance.' *Journal of the American Medical Association* 294(b): 716–24.

Bradley, E., Roumanis, S., Radford, M., Webster, T., McNamara, R., Mattera, J., Barton, B., Berg, D., Portnay, E., Moscovitz, H., Parkosewich, J., Holmboe, E., Blaney, M. and Krumholz, H. (2005) 'Achieving door-to-balloon times that meet quality guidelines: how do successful hospitals do it?' *Journal of American College of Cardiology* 46(7): 1236–41.

Breyer, S. (1993) *Breaking the vicious circle: toward effective risk regulation.* Cambridge, MA: Harvard University Press.

Brock, D. (1993) 'Quality of Life Measures in Health Care and Medical Ethics', in M. Nussbaum and A. Sen (eds), *The Quality of Life*: 95–132.

——(1995) 'Justice and the ADA: does prioritizing and rationing health care discriminate against the disabled?' *Social Philosophy and Policy* 12(2): 159–85.

——(2000) 'Broadening the Bioethics Agenda.' *Kennedy Institute of Ethics Journal* 10(1): 21–38.

——(2002) 'Priority to the Worse Off in Health-Care Resource Prioritization', in R. Rhodes et al. (eds) *Medicine and Social Justice: essays on the distribution of health care*: 362–72.

Brody, B. and Halevy, A. (1995) 'Is Futility a Futile Concept?' *Journal of Medicine and Philosophy* 20(2): 123–44.

Brook, R. (1994) 'The RAND/ UCLA Appropriateness Method', in K. McCormick et al, (eds) *Methodology Perspectives*: 59–70.

Brook, R., Kamberg, C., Lohr, K., Goldberg, G., Keeler, E. and Newhouse, J. (1990) 'Quality of ambulatory care: Epidemiology and comparison by insurance status and income.' *Medical Care* 28(5): 392–433.

Brook, R. and Lohr, K. (1986) 'Will We Need to Ration Effective Health Care?' *Issues in Science and Technology* 3: 68–77.

Brook, R., Ware, J., Rogers, W., Keeler, E., Davies, A., Sherbourne, C., Goldberg, G., Lohr, K., Camp, P. and Newhouse, J. (1984) *The Effect of Coinsurance on the Health of Adults: Results from the RAND Health Insurance Experiment*. Santa Monica, CA: Rand.

Brooks, W., Jordan, J., Divine, G., Smith, K. and Neelon, F. (1990) 'The impact of psychologic factors on measurement of functional status: Assessment of the sickness impact profile.' *Medical Care* 28(9): 793–804.

Broome, J. (1994) 'Fairness versus doing the most good.' *Hastings Center Report* 24(4): 36–9.

Brown, L. (1993) *The New Shorter Oxford Dictionary, 4th Edition*. Oxford: Oxford University Press.

Buchanan, A. (1984) 'The right to a decent minimum of health care.' *Philosophy & Public Affairs* 13(1): 55–78.

Buchanan, A., Brock, D., Daniels, N. and Wikler, D. (2000) *From Chance to Choice: Genetics and Justice*. Cambridge: Cambridge University Press.

Bunker, J., Gomby, D. and Kehrer, B. (eds) (1989) *Pathways to Health: The Role of Social Factors*. Menlo Park: Kaiser Family Foundation.

Bush, J. (1984) 'General Health Policy Model/ Quality of Well-Being (QWB) Scale', in N. Wenger et al., *Assessment of Quality of Life in Clinical Trials of Cardiovascular Therapies*: 189–99.

Butler, S. and Haislmaier, E. (eds) (1989) *A National Health System for America*. Washington, DC: Heritage Foundation.

Callahan, D. (1976) 'Biomedical progress and the limits of human health', in R. Veatch and R. Branson (eds) *Ethics and Health Policy*: 157–65.

——(1990) *What kind of life: the limits of medical progress*. Washington, DC: Georgetown University Press.

Callahan, D. (1991) 'Medical futility, medical necessity. The-problem-without-a-name.' *Hastings Center Report* 21(4): 30–5.

Cameron, J. (2000) 'Amartya Sen on Economic Inequality: The Need for an Explicit Critique of Opulence.' *Journal of International Development*, 12(7): 1031–45.

Campbell, E. (1964) 'The internalization of moral norms.' *Sociometry* 27(4): 391–412.

Caplan, A. (2006) 'Ethical issues surrounding forced, mandated, or coerced treatment.' *Journal of Substance Abuse Treatment* 31(2): 117–20.

Carmen, R. (2000) 'Prima Mangiare, Poi Filosofare.' *Journal of International Development*, 12(7): 1019–30.

CBS News/New York Times Poll (1992).

Center for Health Economics Research for the Robert Wood Johnson Foundation (1993) *Access to Health Care: Key Indicators for Policy.* Princeton, NJ Robert Wood Johnson Foundation.

Chaoulli v. Quebec (Attorney General) (2005) 1 S.C.R. 791, 2005 SCC 35.

Chayes, A. and Chayes, A. (1993) 'On compliance.' *International Organization* 47(2): 175–205.

Chayes, A., Ehrlich, T. and Lowenfeld, A. (1968) *International Legal Process: Materials for an Introductory Course.* Boston: Little, Brown and Company.

Chen, L., Evans, T., Anand, S., Boufford, J., Brown, H., Chowdhury, M., Cueto, M., Dare, L., Dussault, G. and Elzinga, G et al., (2004) 'Human Resources for Health: Overcoming the Crisis.' *The Lancet* 364(9449): 1984–90.

Chen, L., Evans, T. and Cash, R. (1999) 'Health as a Global Public Good', in I. Kaul, I. Grunberg and M. Stern (eds) *Global Public Goods.* New York: Oxford University Press: 284–306.

Children's Hospital & Regional Medical Center: Heart Center 2006. Available at: http://heartcenter.seattlechildrens.org/conditions_treated/patent_ductus_arteriosus.asp accessed on 8 January 2009.

Clarke, A., Phillips, D., Brown, R. and Harper, P. (1987) 'Clinical aspects of X-linked hypohidrotic ectodermal dysplasia.' *Archives of Disease in Childhood* 62(10): 989–96.

Cluff, L. (1981) 'Chronic disease, function and the quality of care.' *Journal of Chronic Disease* 34(7): 299–304.

Coast, J. (2001) 'Citizens, their agents and health care rationing: an exploratory study using qualitative methods.' *Health Economics* 10(2): 159–74.

Code of Federal Regulations (2004) 29 C.F.R. § 1630.2.

Cohen, G. (1989) 'On the Currency of Egalitarian Justice.' *Ethics* 99(4): 906–44.

——(1993) 'Equality of What? On Welfare, Goods, and Capabilities', in M. Nussbaum and A. Sen (eds) *The Quality of Life:* 9–29.

Cohen, J. and Rogers, J. (2000) 'Editors' Preface', in N. Daniels et al., *Is Inequality Bad for Our Health?*: xix.

Cohn, S., Berk, M., Berry, S., Bozzette, S., Duan, N., Frankel, M., Klein, J., McKinney, M., Rastegar, A., Smith, S., and Shapiro, M. (2001) 'The Care of HIV-Infected Adults in Rural Areas of the United States.' *Journal of Acquired Immune Deficiency Syndromes* 28(4): 385–92.

Constitution of the World Health Organization (1946) 62 Stat. 2679. 14 U.N.T.S. 185.

Converse, P. (1976) *The Dynamics of Party Support: Cohort-analyzing Party Identification*. Beverly Hills: Sage.

Conway, C. (2003) 'The Pros and Cons of Pharmaceutical Patents.' *Regional Review*, Quarter 1: 10–18.

Cook, F. and Barrett, E. (1992) *Support for the American welfare state: the views of Congress and the public*. New York: Columbia University Press.

Cook, R. and Dickens, B. (2002a) 'Human rights to safe motherhood.' *International Journal of Gynecology and Obstetrics* 76(2): 225–31.

——(2002b) 'Human rights and HIV-positive women.' *International Journal of Gynecology and Obstetrics* 77(1): 55–63.

Cook, R., Dickens, B. and Fathalla, M. (2003) *Reproductive Health and Human Rights: Integrating Medicine, Ethics and Law*. New York: Oxford University Press.

Cookson, R. (2005) 'QALYs and the capability approach.' *Health Economics* 14(8): 817–29.

Coppola, K., Ditto, P., Danks, J. and Smucker, W. (2001) 'Accuracy of Primary Care and Hospital-Based Physicians' Predictions of Elderly Outpatients' Treatment Preferences With and Without Advance Directives.' *Archives of Internal Medicine* 161(3): 431–40.

Council on Ethical and Judicial Affairs, American Medical Association (1991) 'Guidelines for the Appropriate Use of Do-Not-Resuscitate Orders.' *Journal of the American Medical Association* 265(14): 1868–71.

——(1995) 'Ethical Issues in Managed Care.' *Journal of the American Medical Association* 273(4): 330–5.

Courtwright, A. (2008) 'Health Disparities and Autonomy.' *Bioethics* 22(8): 431–9.

Cranston, M. (1983) 'Are There Any Human Rights?' *Daedalus* 112(4): 1–17.

Crocker, D. (1995) 'Functioning and Capability: The Foundations of Sen's and Nussbaum's Development Ethic, Part 2', in M. Nussbaum and J. Glover (eds) *Women, Culture and Development: A Study of Human Capabilities*: 153–98.

Crocker, D. and Linden, T. (eds) (1998) *Ethics of Consumption: The Good Life, Justice and Global Stewardship*. Lanham: Rowman and Littlefield Publishers.

Cross, F. (2001) 'The Error of Positive Rights.' *UCLA Law Review* 48: 857–924.

Crossley, M. (1993) 'Of Diagnoses and Discrimination: Discriminatory Non-treatment of Infants with HIV Infection.' *Columbia Law Review* 93(7): 1581–667.

CSDH (2008) *Closing the gap in a generation: health equity through action on the social determinants of health*. Final report of the Commission on Social Determinants of Health. Geneva: World Health Organization.

Culyer, A. and Newhouse, J. (eds) (2000). *Handbook of Health Economics*. Amsterdam: Elsevier.

Curtis, J., Park, D., Krone, M. and Pearlman, R. (1995) 'Use of the medical futility rationale in do-not-attempt-resuscitation orders.' *Journal of the American Medical Association* 273(2): 124–8.

Cutler, D. and McClellan, M. (2001) 'Is Technological Change In Medicine Worth It?' *Health Affairs* 20(5): 11–29.

Cutler, D., McClellan, M. and Newhouse, J. (2000) 'How Does Managed Care Do It?' *Rand Journal of Economics Vol. 1* 31(3): 526–48.

Cutler, D. and Reber, S. (1998) 'Paying for Health Insurance: The Trade-Off between Competition and Adverse Selection.' *Quarterly Journal of Economics* 113(2): 433–66.

Cutler, D. and Zeckhauser, R. (2000) 'The Anatomy of Health Insurance', in A. Culyer and J. Newhouse (eds), *Handbook of Health Economics*: 563–643.

——(2004) 'Extending the Theory to Meet the Practice of Insurance.' *Brookings-Wharton Papers on Financial Services* 2004(1): 1–53.

Daniels, N. (1981) 'Health-care needs and distributive justice.' *Philosophy and Public Affairs* 10(2): 146–79.

——(1985) *Just Health Care*. New York: Cambridge University Press.

——(1988) *Am I my Parents' Keeper?: An Essay on Justice Between the Young and the Old*. New York: Oxford University Press.

——(1992) 'Liberalism and medical ethics.' *Hastings Center Report* 22(6): 41–3.

——(1993) 'Rationing fairly: programmatic considerations.' *Bioethics* 7(2–3): 224–33.

——(1994) 'Four unsolved rationing problems: A challenge.' *Hastings Center Report* 24(4): 27–9.

——(1996) 'Justice, fair procedures, and the goals of medicine.' *Hastings Center Report* 26(6): 10–12.

——(1998) 'Rationing Medical Care: A Philosopher's Perspective on Outcomes and Process.' *Economics and Philosophy* 14: 27–50.

——(2001) 'Justice, Health, and Healthcare.' *American Journal of Bioethics* 1(2): 2–16.

——(2008) *Just health: meeting health needs fairly*. New York: Cambridge University Press.

Daniels, N., Kennedy, B., Kawachi, I., Cohen, J. and Rogers, J. (2000) *Is Inequality Bad for Our Health?* Boston: Beacon Press.

Daniels, N. and Sabin, J. (2002) *Setting Limits Fairly: Can We Learn to Share Medical Resources?* New York: Oxford University Press.

Danis, M., Clancy, C. and Churchill, L. (eds) (2002) *Ethical Dimensions of Health Policy*. New York: Oxford University Press.

Danzon, P. and Kim, J. (2002) *The Life Cycle of Pharmaceuticals: a cross-national perspective*. London: Office of Health Economics.

Davies, A. and Ware, J. Jr. (1981) *Measuring Health Perceptions in the Health Insurance Experiment*. Santa Monica: Rand.

Davies, E. and Cleary, P. (2005) 'Hearing the patient's voice? Factors affecting the use of patient survey data in quality improvement.' *Quality and Safety in Health Care* 14(6): 428–32.

Davis, K. and Rowland D. (1991) 'Financing Health Care for the Poor', in E. Ginzberg (ed.) *Health Services Research: Key to Health Policy:* 93–125.

Day, P., Fox, D., Maxwell, R. and Scrivens, E. (eds) (1996) *The State, Politics and Health: Essays for Rudolf Klein.* Cambridge, MA: Blackwell Publishing.

Deaton, A. and Paxson, C. (1998) 'Aging and Inequality in Income and Health.' *American Economic Review* 88(2): 248–53.

Deyo, R., Cherkin, D., Weinstein, J., Howe, J., Ciol, M. and Mulley, A. Jr. (2000) 'Involving Patients in Clinical Decisions: Impact of an Interactive Video Program on Use of Back Surgery.' *Medical Care* 38(9): 959–69.

Ditto, P., Danks, J., Smucker, W., Bookwala, J., Coppola, K., Dresser, R., Fagerlin, A., Gready, R., Houts, R., Lockhart, L. and Zyzanstri, S. (2001) 'Advance Directives as Acts of Communication: A Randomized Controlled Trial.' *Archives of Internal Medicine* 161(3): 421–30.

Dorsey, J., Holtz, P., Griffiths, R., McGrath, M. and Steinberg, E. (1996) 'Costs and Charges Associated with Three Alternative Techniques of Hysterectomy.' *New England Journal of Medicine* 335(7): 476–82.

Dreze, J. and Sen, A. (1989) *Hunger and Public Action.* Oxford: Clarendon Press.

Durkheim, E. (1951) *Suicide: a study in sociology.* New York: The Free Press.

Dworkin, G. (1981) 'Taking risks, assessing responsibility.' *Hastings Center Report* 11(5): 26–31.

Dworkin, R. (1981a) 'What is equality? Part I: Equality of Welfare.' *Philosophy and Public Affairs* 10(3): 185–246.

——(1981b) 'What is equality? Part II: Equality of resources.' *Philosophy and Public Affairs* 10(4): 283–345.

——(1993) 'Justice in the Distribution of Health Care.' *McGill Law Journal* 38(4): 883–98.

——(2000) *Sovereign Virtue: the theory and practice of equality.* Cambridge, MA: Harvard University Press.

Dybul, M., Chun, T., Yoder, C., Hidalgo, B., Belson, M., Hertogs, K., Larder, B., Dewar, R., Fox, C., Hallahan, C., Justement, J., Migueles, S., Metcalf, J., Davey, R., Daucher, M., Pandya, P., Baseler, M., Ward, D. and Fauci, A. (2001) 'Short-cycle structured intermittent treatment of chronic HIV infection with highly active antiretroviral therapy: Effects on virologic, immunologic, and toxicity parameters.' *Proceedings of the National Academy of Sciences* 98(26): 15161–6.

Eddy, D. (1991a) 'Clinical decision-making: from theory to practice. The individual vs society. Is there a conflict?' *Journal of the American Medical Association* 265(11): 1446–50.

——(1991b) 'Oregon's methods. Did cost-effectiveness analysis fail?' *Journal of the American Medical Association* 266(15): 2135–41.

Eddy, D. (1992) 'Cost-effectiveness analysis. A conversation with my father.' *Journal of the American Medical Association* 267(12): 1669–75.

Elhauge, E. (1994) 'Allocating Health Care Morally.' *California Law Review* 82(6): 1449–544.

Elster, J. and Hylland, A. (eds) (1986) *Foundations of Social Choice Theory*. New York: Cambridge University Press.

Elster, J. and Slagstad, R. (eds) (1988) *Constitutionalism and Democracy*. Cambridge: Cambridge University Press.

Emanuel, E. (1991) *The Ends of Human Life: Medical Ethics in a Liberal Polity*. Cambridge, MA: Harvard University Press.

——(1996) 'Cost savings at the end of life. What do the data show?' *Journal of the American Medical Association* 275(24): 1907–14.

——(2000) 'Political Problems', in N. Daniels et al., *Is Inequality Bad for Our Health?*: 59–66.

——(2002) 'Setting Limits Fairly: Can We Learn to Share Medical Resources? [book review].' *New England Journal of Medicine* 347(12): 953–4.

Emanuel, E., Young-Xu, Y., Levinsky, N., Gazelle, G., Saynina, O. and Ash, A. (2003) 'Chemotherapy Use among Medicare Beneficiaries at the End of Life.' *Annals of Internal Medicine* 138(8): 639–43.

Emergency Medical Treatment and Active Labor Act (2005) 42 U.S.C. § 1395dd.

Emmons, K. (2000) 'Health Behaviors in a Social Context', in L. Berkman and I. Kawachi (eds) *Social Epidemiology*: 242–66.

Emmons, K., Sorensen, G., Klar, N., Digianni, L., Barclay, G., Schmidt, K. and Hammond, S. (2000) 'Healthy Baby Second-Hand Smoke Study: Project Brief.' *Tobacco Control*, 9 (Suppl 3): iii58–60.

Engelhardt Jr., H. (1974) 'The disease of masturbation: values and the concept of disease.' *Bulletin of the History of Medicine* 48(2): 234–48.

——(1986) *The Foundations of Bioethics, 1st Edition*. New York: Oxford University Press.

——(1996a) *The Foundations of Bioethics, 2nd Edition*. New York: Oxford University Press.

——(1996b) 'Rethinking Concepts of Futility in Critical Care.' Center for Medical Ethics and Health Policy, Baylor College of Medicine.

——(2000) *The Foundations of Christian Bioethics*. Lisse: Swets and Zeitlinger.

Engelhardt Jr., H. and Khushtfk, G. (1995) 'Futile care for the critically ill patient.' *Current Opinion in Critical Care* 1(4): 329–33.

Enthoven, A. (1980) *Health Plan: The Practical Solution to the Soaring Cost of Medical Care*. Reading: Addison-Wesley Publishing Company.

——(1988) 'Managed competition: an agenda for action.' *Health Affairs* 7(3): 25–47.

Enthoven, A. and Kronick, R. (1989) 'A consumer-choice health plan for the 1990s: Universal health insurance in a system designed to promote quality and economy (2).' *New England Journal of Medicine* 320(2): 94–101.

Equal Employment Opportunity Commission (2002) *Enforcement Guidance: Reasonable Accommodation and Undue Hardship Under the Americans with Disabilities Act.* Available at: http://www.eeoc.gov/policy/docs/accommodation.html accessed on 8 January 2009.

Escarce, J., Van Horn, R., Pauly, M., Williams, S., Shea, J. and Chen, W. (1999) 'Health Maintenance Organizations and Hospital Quality for Coronary Artery Bypass Surgery.' *Medical Care Research and Review* 56(3): 340–62.

Esserman, L., Belkora, J. and Lenert, L. (1995) 'Potentially ineffective care: A new outcome to assess the limits of critical care.' *Journal of the American Medical Association* 274(19): 1544–51.

Evans, N., Gilpin, E., Farkas, A., Shenassa, E. and Pierce, J. (1995) 'Adolescents' perceptions of their peers' health norms.' *American Journal of Public Health* 85(8): 1064–9.

Evans, T. (2002) 'A Human Right to Health?' *Third World Quarterly* 23(2): 197–215.

Evans, T., Whitehead, M., Diderichsen, F., Bhuiya, A. and Wirth, M. (eds) (2001) *Challenging Inequities in Health: From Ethics to Action.* New York: Oxford University Press.

Falit, B. and Gross, C. (2008) 'Access to Experimental Drugs for Terminally Ill Patients'. *Journal of the American Medical Association* 300(23): 2793–5.

Fallik, D. (2002a) 'Disorder Demands Love, Strength: Mennonite Family Says Early Detection Made the Difference For Their Son.' *St. Louis-Post Dispatch*, 6 January: A9.

——(2002b) 'A Swab Saves Lives: Doctor Develops Genetic Test to Solve Decades-Old Mystery Surrounding Deaths of Mennonite Babies: Maple Syrup Urine Disease.' *St. Louis Post-Dispatch*, A1.

Farmer, P. (2003) *Pathologies of Power: Health, human rights and the new war on the poor.* Berkeley: University of California Press.

Farmer, P. and Kim, J. (2008) 'Surgery and Global Health: A view from beyond the OR.' *World Journal of Surgery* 32(4): 533–6.

Farrell, P. and Fuchs, V. (1982) 'Schooling and health: The cigarette connection.' *Journal of Health Economics* 1(3): 217–30.

Feldman, S. (1988) 'Structure and Consistency in Public Opinion: The Role of Core Beliefs and Values.' *American Journal of Political Science* 32(2): 416–40.

Feldman, S. and Zaller, J. (1992) 'The Political Culture of Ambivalence: Ideological Responses to the Welfare State.' *American Journal of Political Science* 36(1): 268–307.

Fidler, D. (2004) 'Fighting the Axis of Illness: HIV/AIDS, Human Rights, and US Foreign Policy.' *Harvard Human Rights Journal* 17: 99–136.

Finnemore, M. and Sikkink, K. (1998) 'International Norm Dynamics and Political Change.' *International Organization* 52(4): 887–917.

Fishkin, J. (1991) *Democracy and Deliberation: New Directions for Democratic Reform.* New Haven: Yale University Press.

Fleck, L. (1992) 'Just Health Care Rationing: A Democratic Decisionmaking Approach.' *University of Pennsylvania Law Review* 140(5): 1597–636.

——(2001) 'Healthcare Justice and Rational Democratic Deliberation.' *American Journal of Bioethics* 1(2): 20–1.

Floyd, R., Rimer, B., Giovino, G., Mullen, P. and Sullivan, S. (1993) 'A Review of Smoking in Pregnancy: Effects on Pregnancy Outcomes and Cessation Efforts.' *Annual Review of Public Health*, 14: 379–411.

Folland, S. (1990) 'A Critique of Pure Need: An Analysis of Norman Daniels' Concept of Health Care Need.' *International Journal of Social Economics* 17(3): 36–45.

Francis, L. and Silvers, A. (eds) (2000) *Americans with Disabilities: Exploring Implications of the Law for Individuals and Institutions.* New York: Routledge.

Free, L. and Cantril, H. (1968) *The Political Beliefs of Americans: A study of public opinion.* New York: Simon and Shuster.

Freedberg, K., Losina, E., Weinstein, M., Paltiel, A., Cohen, C., Seage, G., Craven, D., Zhang, H., Kimmel, A. and Goldie, S. (2001) 'The Cost Effectiveness of Combination Antiretroviral Therapy for HIV Disease.' *New England Journal of Medicine* 344(11): 824–31.

Freedberg, K., Scharfstein, J., Seage, G. III, Losina, E., Weinstein, M., Craven, D. and Paltiel, A. (1998) 'The Cost-effectiveness of Preventing AIDS-Related Opportunistic Infections.' *Journal of the American Medical Association* 279(2): 130–6.

Fried, C. (1976) 'Equality and rights in medical care.' *Hastings Center Report* 6(1): 29–34.

Friedman, W., Hirschklau, M., Printz, M., Pitlick, P. and Kirkpatrick, S. (1976) 'Pharmacologic closure of patent ductus arteriosus in the premature infant.' *New England Journal of Medicine* 295(10): 526–9.

Frohlich, N. and Oppenheimer, J. (1993) *Choosing Justice: An Experimental Approach to Ethical Theory.* Berkeley: University of California Press.

Fuchs, V. (1982) *Economic Aspects of Health.* Chicago: University of Chicago Press.

——(1993) *The Future of Health Policy.* Cambridge, MA: Harvard University Press.

Gakidou, E., Frenk, J. and Murray, C. (2000) 'A Health Agenda', in N. Daniels et al., *Is Inequality Bad for Our Health?*: 71–8.

Gallup Organization (2005) 'National Survey of Organ and Tissue Donation Attitudes and Behaviors.' Available at: http://www.organdonor.gov/survey2005/introduction.shtm accessed on 8 January 2009.

Garber, A. and Phelps, C. (1997) 'Economic foundations of cost-effectiveness analysis.' *Journal of Health Economics* 16(1): 1–31.

Gardner, M. (1998) 'Cost Analysis in Obstetrics and Gynecology.' *Clinical Obstetrics and Gynecology* 41(2): 296–306.

Gardner, M., Rouse, D., Goldenberg, R., Lanning, J., Thom, E. and Zachary, J. (1996) 'Cost Comparison of Induction of Labor Versus Expectant Management in Pregnancies Lasting Longer Than 41 Weeks.' *American Journal of Managed Care* 2 (7): 814–18.

Gasper, D. (1997a) 'Sen's Capability Approach and Nussbaum's Capabilities Ethic.' *Journal of International Development* 9(2): 281–302.

——(1997b) 'Development Ethics, Capabilities and the Work of W.I.D.E.R.' *Journal of International Development* 9(2): 231–3.

——(2000) 'Development as Freedom: Taking Economics Beyond Commodities - The Cautious Boldness of Amartya Sen.' *Journal of International Development* 12(7): 989–1001.

Gasper, D. and Cameron, J. (2000) 'Introduction: Assessing and Extending the work of Amartya Sen.' *Journal of International Development* 12(7): 985–8.

Gibbard, A. (1982) 'The prospective Pareto Principle and equity of access to health care.' *Milbank Memorial Fund Quarterly* 60(3): 399–428.

——(1986) 'Interpersonal Comparisons: Preference, Good, and the Intrinsic Reward of a Life', in J. Elster and A. Hylland (eds) *Foundations of Social Choice Theory*: 165–94.

Gilbert, D., Pinel, E., Wilson, T., Blumberg, S. and Wheatley, T. (2002) 'Durability Bias in Affective Forecasting', in T. Gilovich et al. (eds) *Heuristics and Biases: The Psychology of Intuitive Judgement*: 292–312.

Gilovich, T., Griffin, D. and Kahneman, D. (eds) (2002) *Heuristics and Biases: The Psychology of Intuitive Judgement*. New York: Cambridge University Press.

Ginsburg, P. and Lee, P. (1991) 'Physician Payment', in E. Ginzberg (ed.) *Health Services Research: Key to Health Policy*: 69–92.

Ginzberg, E. (ed.) (1991) *Health Services Research: Key to Health Policy*. Cambridge, MA: Harvard University Press.

Giri, A. (2000) 'Rethinking Human Well Being: A Dialogue with Amartya Sen.' *Journal of International Development*, 12(7): 1003–18.

Glied, S. and Little, S. (2003) 'The uninsured and the benefits of medical progress.' *Health Affairs* 22(4): 210–19.

Gold, M., Siegel, J., Russell, L. and Weinstein, M. (eds) (1996) *Cost-Effectiveness in Health and Medicine*. New York: Oxford University Press.

Goldie, S., Kaplan, J., Losina, E., Weinstein, M., Paltiel, A., Seage G., III, Craven, D., Kimmel, A., Zhang, H., Cohen, C. and Freedberg, K. (2002) 'Prophylaxis for Human Immunodeficiency Virus-Related Pneumocystis carinii Pneumonia: Using Simulation Modeling to Inform Clinical Guidelines.' *Archives of Internal Medicine* 162(8): 921–8.

Gorovitz, S. (2001) 'Justice in Healthcare and Dimpled Chads.' *American Journal of Bioethics* 1(2): 29–30.

Gostin, L. (2001) 'The human right to health: a right to the "highest attainable standard of health."' *Hastings Center Report* 31(2): 29–30.

——(ed.) (2002) *Public Health Law and Ethics: A Reader*. Berkeley: University of California Press.

Green, R. (2001) 'Access to Healthcare: Going Beyond Fair Equality of Opportunity.' *American Journal of Bioethics* 1(2): 22–3.

Grossman, M. (1972) 'The Demand for Health: A Theoretical and Empirical Investigation.' *National Bureau of Economic Research Occasional Paper No. 119.*

Gruskin, S. and Dickens, B. (2006) 'Human Rights and Ethics in Public Health.' *American Journal of Public Health* 96(11): 1903–5.

Gruskin, S., Grodin, M., Annas, G. and Marks, S. (eds) (2005) *Perspectives on health and human rights.* New York: Routledge.

Gruskin, S. and Tarantola, D. (2001) 'Health and Human Rights' in R. Detels and R. Beaglehole'. (eds) *Oxford Textbook on Public Health.* Oxford: Oxford University Press: 311–35.

Gutmann, A. (1981) 'For and against equal access to health care.' *Milbank Memorial Fund Quarterly Health and Society* 59(4): 542–60.

Gutmann, A. and Thompson, D. (1996) *Democracy and Disagreement 2nd Edition.* Cambridge, MA: Harvard University Press.

Hacker, J. (1997) *The Road to Nowhere: The Genesis of President Clinton's Plan for Health Security.* Princeton: Princeton University Press.

Hadley, J., Steinberg, E. and Feder, J. (1991) 'Comparison of uninsured and privately insured hospital patients. Condition on admission, resource use, and outcome.' *Journal of the American Medical Association* 265(3): 374–9.

Hadorn, D. (1991) 'Setting health care priorities in Oregon Cost-effectiveness meets the rule of rescue.' *Journal of the American Medical Association* 265(17): 2218–25.

——(1992) 'The problem of discrimination in health care priority setting.' *Journal of the American Medical Association* 268(11): 1454–9.

Haines, M., Barker, G. and Rice, R. (2003) 'Using social norms to reduce alcohol and tobacco use in two Midwestern high schools', in H. Perkins (ed.) *The Social Norms Approach to Preventing School and College Age Substance Abuse: A Handbook for Educators, Counselors, and Clinicians.* San Franciso: Jossey–Bass.

Halevy, A. and Brody, B. (1996) 'A Multi-Institution Collaborative Policy on Medical Futility.' *Journal of the American Medical Association* 276(7): 571–4.

Halevy, A., Neal, R. and Brody, B. (1996) 'The low frequency of futility in an adult intensive care unit setting.' *Archives of Internal Medicine* 156(1): 100–104.

Hall, M. (1997) *Making Medical Spending Decisions: the Law, Ethics, and Economics of Rationing Mechanisms.* New York: Oxford University Press.

Hall, M. and Anderson, G. (1992) 'Health Insurers' Assessment of Medical Necessity.' *University of Pennsylvania Law Review* 140(5): 1637–712.

Hall, M., Bobinski, M. and Orentlicher, D. (2003) *Health Care Law and Ethics, 6th Edition.* New York: Aspen Law & Business.

Hardin, G. (1968) 'The Tragedy of the Commons.' *Science* 162: 1243–8.

Harris, J. (1985) *The Value of Life.* London: Routledge and Kegan Paul.

——(1987) 'QALYfying the value of life.' *Journal of Medical Ethics* 13(3): 117–23.

Hartmann, O., Le Corroller, A., Blaise, D., Michon, J., Philip, I., Norol, F., Janvier, M., Pico, J., Baranzelli, M., Rubie, H., Coze, C., Pinna, A., Meresse, V., and Benhamou, E. (1997) 'Peripheral Blood Stem Cell and Bone Marrow Transplantation for Solid Tumors and Lymphomas: Hematologic Recovery and Costs. A Randomized, Controlled Trial.' *Annals of Internal Medicine* 126(8): 600–7.

Havighurst, C. (1995) *Health Care Choices: Private Contracts as Instruments of Health Reform.* Washington, DC: American Enterprise Institute for Public Policy Research.

Hawthorn, G. (ed.) (1988) *The Standard of Living.* Cambridge: Cambridge University Press.

Hays, R. and Stewart, A. (1990) 'The structure of self-reported health in chronic disease patients.' *Psychological Assessment* 2(1): 22–30.

HealthAtoZ: Your Family Health Site. Patent ductus arteriosus. Available at: http://www.Lifesteps.com/gm/Atoz/default.jsp?status=L accessed on 8 January 2009.

Health Security Act (1993) 'H. R. 3600.' 103d Congress.

Heaney, D., Shorvon, S. and Sander, J. (1998) 'An Economic Appraisal of Carbamazepine, Lamotrigine, Phenytoin and Valproate as Initial Treatment in Adults with Newly Diagnosed Epilepsy.' *Epilepsia* 39 (Suppl 3): S19–25.

—— et al.(2000) 'Cost minimization analysis of antiepileptic drugs in newly diagnosed epilepsy in 12 European countries.' *Epilepsia* 41 (Suppl 5): S37–44.

Henkin, L. (1979) *How Nations Behave: Law and Foreign Policy, 2nd Edition.* New York: Columbia University Press.

Hessler, K. and Buchanan, A. (2002) 'Specifying the Content of the Human Right to Health Care', in R. Rhodes et al. (eds) *Medicine and Social Justice: essays on the distribution of health care*: 84–96.

Hiatt, H. (1987) *America's Health in the Balance: Choice or Chance?* New York: Harper and Row Publishers.

Hochschild, J. (1986) *What's Fair? American Beliefs about Distributive Justice.* Cambridge, MA: Harvard University Press.

Hoffman, J., Mower, W., Wolfson, A., Todd, K. and Zucker, M. (2000) 'Validity of a Set of Clinical Criteria to Rule Out Injury to the Cervical Spine in Patients with Blunt Trauma.' *New England Journal of Medicine* 343(2): 94–9.

Holmes, S. and Sunstein, C. (1999) *The Cost of Rights: Why Liberty Depends on Taxes.* New York: W. W. Norton and Company.

Horton, R. (2007) 'NICE vindicated in UK's High Court.' *Lancet* 370(9587): 547–8.

Horton, S. (1996) 'Persistent vegetative state: what decides the cut-off point?' *Intensive & Critical Care Nursing* 12(1): 40–4.

House, J. (2002) 'Understanding social factors and inequalities in health: 20th Century Progress and 21st Century Prospects.' *Journal of Health and Social Behavior* 43(2): 125–42.

Howe, E. (1994) 'Discussing futility.' *Journal of Clinical Ethics* 5(2): 91–9.

Humber, J. and Almeder, R. (eds) (1995) *Allocating Health Care Resources*. Totowa, NJ: Humana Press.

Ignatieff, M. (2001) *Human Rights as Politics and Idolatry*. Princeton: Princeton University Press.

IOM (1999) *To Err is Human: Building a Safer Health System*. Washington D.C.: The National Academies Press.

——(2001) *Crossing the Quality Chasm: A New Health System for the 21st Century*. Washington D.C.: The National Academies Press.

——(2004) *Insuring America's Health: Principles and Recommendations*. Washington DC: The National Academies Press.

ICESCR (International Covenant on Economic, Social and Cultural Rights) (1966) 993 U.N.T.S. 3.

Irwin, T. (1999) *Aristotle, Nicomachean Ethics 2nd Edition*. Indianapolis: Hackett Publishing Company.

Jacobs, L. and Shapiro, R. (2000) *Politicians Don't Pander: Political Manipulation and the Loss of Democratic Responsiveness*. Chicago: University of Chicago Press.

Jacobson, P. and Parmet W. (2007) 'A New Era of Unapproved Drugs: The Case of Abigail Alliance v. Von Eschenbach.' *Journal of the American Medical Association* 297(2): 205–8.

Jamar, S. (1994) 'The International Human Right to Health.' *Southern University Law Review* 22: 1–68.

Jecker, N. and Schneiderman, L. (1995) 'When families request that everything possible be done.' *Journal of Medicine and Philosophy* 20(2): 145–63.

Johnson, H. and Broder, D. (1996) *The System: The American Way of Politics at the Breaking Point*. Boston: Little Brown and Company.

Kahan, D. and Braman, D. (2006) 'Cultural Cognition and Public Policy.' *Yale Law & Policy Review* 24: 149–72.

Kahneman, D. and Tversky, A. (1979) 'Prospect theory: An Analysis of Decision under Risk.' *Econometrica* 47(2): 263–91.

Kaiser Commission on Medicaid and the Uninsured. (2006) *The Uninsured: A Primer*. Washington D.C.

Kaiser Family Foundation (2000) *National Survey on Americans as Health Care Consumers: An Update on the Role of Quality Information*. Menlo Park, CA.

——(2001) State Health Facts Online. Available at: http://statehealthfacts.kff.org

Kamm, F. (1993). *Morality, Mortality Vol. 1: Death and Whom to Save From it*. Oxford: Oxford University Press.

——(1994) 'To Whom?' *Hastings Center Report* 24(4): 29–32.

——(2001) 'Health and Equality of Opportunity.' *American Journal of Bioethics* 1(2): 17–19.

Kant (1898) *Critique of Practical Reason and Other Works on the Theory of Ethics*. English translation by T. Abbott. London: Longmans, Green and Co.

Kaplan, E. and Merson, M. (2002) 'Allocating HIV-Prevention Resources: Balancing Efficiency and Equity.' *American Journal of Public Health* 92(12): 1905–7.

Kaplan, R. and Anderson, J. (1988) 'A general health policy model: update and applications.' *Health Services Research* 23(2): 203–35.

Karasek, R. and Theorell, T. (1990) *Healthy Work: Stress, Productivity, and the Reconstruction of Working Life*. New York: Basic Books.

Kass, N. (2001) 'An Ethics Framework for Public Health.' *American Journal of Public Health* 91(11): 1776–82.

Keck, M. and Sikkink, K. (1998) *Activists Beyond Borders: Advocacy Networks in International Politics*. Ithaca: Cornell University Press.

Kenkel, D. (1991) 'Health Behavior, Health Knowledge, and Schooling.' *Journal of Political Economy* 99(2): 287–305.

Kesselheim, A. and Mello, M. (2007) 'Confidentiality laws and secrecy in medical research: improving public access to data on drug safety.' *Health Affairs* 26 (2): 483–91.

Kickbusch, I. (2003) 'Global health governance: Some theoretical considerations on the new political space', in K. Lee (ed.) *Health impacts of globalization: Towards global governance*: 192–203.

Kilner, J. (1990) *Who Lives? Who Dies? Ethical Criteria in Patient Selection*. New Haven Yale University Press.

Kingdon, J. (2002) 'The Reality of Public Policy Making', in M. Danis et al. (eds) *Ethical Dimensions of Health Policy*: 97–116.

Kleinman, L., Kosecoff, J., Dubois, R. and Brook, R. (1994) 'The medical appropriateness of tympanostomy tubes proposed for children younger than 16 years in the United States.' *Journal of the American Medical Association* 271 (16): 1250–5.

Kluegel, J., Mason, D. and Wegener, B. (eds) (1995) *Social Justice and Political Change: Public Opinion in Capitalist and Post-Communist States*. New York: Aldine de Gruyter.

Koh, H. (1996) 'Transnational Legal Process.' *Nebraska Law Review* 75(1): 181–207.

——(1998) 'The 1998 Frankel Lecture: Bringing International Law Home.' *Houston Law Review* 35(3): 623–82.

——(1999) 'How Is International Human Rights Law Enforced?' *Indiana Law Journal* 74(4): 1397–417.

Kohn, L., Corrigan, J. and Donaldson, M. (2000) *To Err is Human: Building a Safer Health System*. Washington, DC: National Academies Press.

Korsgaard, C. (1993) 'The Reasons We Can Share: An Attack on the Distinction Between Agent-Relative and Agent-Neutral Values.' *Social Philosophy and Policy* 10(1): 24–51.

——(1993b) 'Commentary on Cohen and Sen' in M. Nussbaum and A. Sen. (eds) *The Quality of Life*: 54–61.

Kramer, P. (1993) *Listening to Prozac*. New York: Viking Press.

Krieger, N. (2007) 'Why epidemiologists cannot afford to ignore poverty.' *Epidemiology* 18(6): 658–6.

Bibliography

Kuntz, K., Tsevat, J., Weinstein, M. and Goldman, L. (1999) 'Expert Panel vs Decision-Analysis Recommendations for Postdischarge Coronary Angiography After Myocardial Infarction.' *Journal of the American Medical Association* 282(23): 2246–51.

Kymlicka, W. (1990) *Contemporary Political Philosophy: An Introduction*. Oxford: Clarendon Press.

Lane, R. (1962) *Political Ideology: Why the American Common Man Believes What He Does*. New York: Free Press of Glencoe.

Leape, L., Hilborne, L., Park, R., Bernstein, S., Kamberg, C., Sherwood, M. and Brook, R. (1993) 'The appropriateness of use of coronary artery bypass graft surgery in New York State.' *Journal of the American Medical Association* 269(6): 753–60.

Leary, V. (1994) 'The right to health in international human rights law.' *Health and Human Rights* 1(1): 24–56.

Lederman, L. and Stewart, L. (eds) (2005) *Changing the Culture of College Drinking: A Socially Situated Health Communication Campaign*. Cresskill: Hampton Press.

Lee, T. (2002) *Mobilizing Public Opinion: Black Insurgency and Racial Attitudes in the Civil Rights Era*. Chicago: University of Chicago Press.

Leichter, H. (1992) 'Political Accountability in Health Care Rationing: In Search of a New Jerusalem.' *University of Pennsylvania Law Review* 140(5): 1939–63.

Lerner, D. and Levine, S. (1994) 'Health Related Quality of Life: Origins, Gaps and Directions', in G. Albrecht and R. Fitzpatrick, *Quality of Life in Health Care*: 43–65.

Leslie, J. and Jamison D. (1990) 'Health and nutrition considerations in education planning. 1. Educational consequences of health problems among school-age children.' *Food and Nutrition Bulletin* 12(3): 191–203.

Letiche, J. (1987) 'Foreword', in A. Sen, *On Ethics and Economics*: ix–xiii.

Lipset, S. (1963) *The First New Nation: The United States in Historical Perspective*. New York: Basic Books.

Litman T. and L. Robins. (eds) (1997) *Health Politics and Policy, 3rd Edition*. Albany: Delmar.

Lo, B. (1991) 'Unanswered questions about DNR orders.' *Journal of the American Medical Association* 265(14): 1874–5.

Loewenstein G., Brennan, T. and Volpp, K. (2007) 'Asymmetric paternalism to improve health behaviors.' *Journal of the American Medical Association* 298(20): 2415–17.

Lohr, J. (1999) Gale Encyclopedia of Medicine, Gale Research. Search item: Patent Ductus Arteriosus. Available at: http://findarticles.com/p/articles/mi_g2601/is_0010/ai_2601001031?tag=content;col1 accessed on 8 January 2009.

Lohr, K., Brook, R., Kamberg, C., Goldberg, G., Leibowitz, A., Keesey, J., Reboussin, D. and Newhouse, J. (1986) 'Use of medical care in the Rand Health Insurance Experiment. Diagnosis-and service-specific analyses in a randomized controlled trial.' *Medical Care* 24(9 Suppl): S1–87.

Lohr, K. and Mock, G. (1989) *Advances in the Assessment of Health Status: Overview and Report of a Conference.* Washington, DC: National Academy Press.

Lomasky, L. (1981) 'Medical Progress and National Health Care.' *Philosophy and Public Affairs* 10(1): 65–88.

Lord, C. (1984) *Aristotle, The Politics.* Chicago: Chicago University Press.

Luft, H. (1978) 'How do health-maintenance organizations achieve their 'savings'?' *New England Journal of Medicine* 298(24): 1336–43.

MacIntyre, A. (1981) *After Virtue: A Study in Moral Theory.* London: Gerald Duckworth & Co. Ltd.

——(1988) *Whose Justice? Which Rationality?* Notre Dame: University of Notre Dame Press.

Mann, J. (1996) 'Health and Human Rights.' *British Medical Journal* 312 (7036): 924–5.

——(1999) 'Human Rights and AIDS: The Future of the Pandemic', in J. Mann et al., *Health and Human Rights*: 216–228.

Mann, J., Gostin, L., Brennan, T., Lazzarini, Z. and Fineberg, H. (1999) 'Health and Human Rights', in J. Mann et al. (eds) *Health and Human Rights*: 7–20.

Mann, J., Gruskin, S., Grodin, M., and Annas, G. (eds) (1999) *Health and Human Rights: A Reader* New York: Routledge.

Manning, W., Keeler, E., Newhouse, J., Sloss, E. and Wasserman, J. (1989) 'The taxes of sin. Do smokers and drinkers pay their way?' *Journal of the American Medical Association* 261(11): 1604–609.

Manning, W., Newhouse, J. and Ware, J. (1982) 'The Status of Health in Demand Estimation; or, Beyond Excellent, Good, Fair, and Poor', in V. Fuchs (ed.) *Economic Aspects of Health*: 143–84.

Maple Syrup Urine Disease Family Support Group. Available at: http://www.msud-support.org/ accessed on May 29, 2009.

Marchand, S., Wikler, D. and Landesman, B. (1998) 'Class, health and justice' *Milbank Quarterly Journal.* 76(3): 449–67.

Marmor, T. (ed.) (1994) *Understanding Health Care Reform.* New Haven: Yale University Press.

——(2000) 'Policy Options', in N. Daniels et al., *Is Inequality Bad for Our Health?*: 53–8.

Marmor, T. and Barer, M. (1997) 'The Politics of Universal Health Insurance: Lessons for and from the 1990s', in T. Litman and L. Robins (eds) *Health Politics and Policy, 3rd Edition.*

Marmor, T. and Goldberg, M. (1994) 'American Health Care Reform: Separating Sense from Nonsense', in T. Marmor (ed.), *Understanding Health Care Reform*: 1–18.

Marmor, T., Mashaw, J. and Harvey, P. (1990) *America's Misunderstood Welfare State: Persistent Myths, Enduring Realities*. New York: Basic Books.

Marmor, T. and Oberlander, J. (1994) 'A Citizen's Guide to the Healthcare Reform Debate.' *Yale Journal on Regulation* 11(2): 495–506.

Marmot, M. (2000) 'Do Inequalities Matter?' in N. Daniels et al. *Is Inequality Bad for Our Health?*: 37–41.

——(2005) *The Status Syndrome: How social standing affects our health and longevity.* New York: MacMillan.

Marshall, T. (1950) *Citizenship and Social Class*. Cambridge: Cambridge University Press.

Mashaw, J. and T. Marmor. (1996) 'Can the American State Guarantee Access to Health Care?' in P. Day et al. (eds) *The State, Politics, and Health: Essays for Rudolf Klein*: 61–75.

Mathews, S. and Pronovost, P. (2008) 'Physician autonomy and informed decision making: Finding the balance for patient safety and quality.' *Journal of the American Medical Association* 300(24): 2913–15.

Maynard, A. and Bloor, K. (1998) 'Universal coverage and cost control: the United Kingdom National Health Service.' *Journal of Health and Human Services Administration* 20(4): 423–41.

McClosky, H. and Zaller, J. (1984) *The American Ethos: Public Attitudes Toward Capitalism and Democracy*. Cambridge, MA: Harvard University Press.

McCormick, K., Moore, S. and Siegel, R. (eds) (1994) *Clinical Practice Guideline Development Methodology Perspectives AHCPR Pub No. 95–0009*. Rockville: Public Health Service, U.S. Department of Health and Human Services.

McGlynn, E., Asch, S., Adams, J., Keesey, J., Hicks, J., DeCristofaro, A. and Kerr, E. (2003) 'The Quality of Health Care Delivered to Adults in the United States.' *New England Journal of Medicine* 348(26): 2635–45.

McIver, S. (1995) 'Information for public choice.' *British Medical Bulletin* 51(4): 900–13.

Mechanic, D. (1989) 'Socioeconomic status and health: an examination of Underlying Processes', in J. Bunker et al. (eds) *Pathways to Health: the Role of Social Factors*: 9–26.

Meel, B. (2003) 'The myth of child rape as a cure for HIV/AIDS in Transkei: A case report.' *Medicine, Science and the Law* 43(1): 85–8.

Menzel, P. (1987) 'Economic competition in health care: a moral assessment.' *Journal of Medicine and Philosophy* 12(1): 63–84.

——(1990) *Strong Medicine: The Ethical Rationing of Health Care*. New York: Oxford University Press.

——(1992) 'Oregon's denial: Disabilities and quality of life.' *Hastings Center Report* 22(6): 21–5.

——(1995) 'QALYs: Maximization, Distribution and Consent. A Response to Alan Williams. *Health Care Analysis* 3(3): 226–9.

—— (1999) 'How Should What Economists Call "Social Values" Be Measured?' *Journal of Ethics* 3(3): 249–73.

Menzel, P. and Light, D. (2006) 'A conservative case for universal access to health care.' *Hastings Center Report* 36(4): 36–45.

Merson, M., Black, R. and Mills, A. (eds) (2001) *International Public Health: Diseases, Programs, Systems, and Policies*. Gaithersburg: Aspen Publishers.

Michelman, F. (1999) 'What (If Anything) Is Progressive-Liberal Democratic Constitutionalism?' *Widener Law Symposium Journal* 4: 181–99.

Miles, S. (1991) 'Informed demand for "non-beneficial" medical treatment.' *New England Journal of Medicine* 325(7): 512–15.

Mills, A. and Ranson, M. (2001) 'The Design of Health Systems', in M. Merson et al., *International Public Health: Diseases, Programs, Systems, and Policies*: 515–57.

Mishan, E. (1976) *Cost-Benefit Analysis*. New York: Praeger.

Mitchell, G., Tetlock, P., Mellers, B. and Ordonez, L. (1993) 'Judgments of Social Justice: Compromises between Equality and Efficiency.' *Journal of Personality and Social Psychology* 65(4): 629–39.

Morone, J. (1992) 'The Bias of American Politics: Rationing Health Care in a Weak State.' *University of Pennsylvania Law Review* 140(5): 1923–38.

Morton, D., Strauss, K., Robinson, D., Puffenberger, E. and Kelley, R. (2002) 'Diagnosis and treatment of maple syrup disease: A study of 36 patients.' *Pediatrics* 109(6): 999–1008.

Murray, C. and Acharya, A. (1997) 'Understanding DALYs.' *Journal of Health Economics* 16(6): 703–30.

Nagel, J. (1992) 'Combining Deliberation and Fair Representation in Community Health Decisions.' *University of Pennsylvania Law Review* 140(5): 1965–85.

Nagel, T. (1979) 'Equality', in T. Nagel, *Mortal Questions*. Cambridge University Press: 106–27.

——(1991). *Equality and Partiality*. New York: Oxford University Press.

National Committee of Quality Assurance (1997) 'The State of Managed Care Quality.' Available by sending an e-mail through the customer service link at www.ncqa.org or to marketing@ncqa.org

National Institute of Allergy and Infectious Diseases (2001) '7-Day-On, 7-Day-Off Regimen Could Reduce Cost, Toxicities of HIV therapy.' Available at: http://www3.niaid.nih.gov/news/newsreleases/2001/dayon.htm accessed on May 29 2009.

National Institute of Mental Health (1999) *Mental Health: A Report of the Surgeon General*. Report from the Department of Health and Human Services, Substance Abuse and Mental Health Services Administration, Center of Mental Health Services. Available at: http://www.surgeongeneral.gov/library/mentalhealth/home.html accessed on May 29 2009.

Newhouse, J. (1984) 'Cream skimming, asymmetric information, and a competitive insurance market.' *Journal of Health Economics* 3(1): 97–100.

—— et al., (1993) *Free for All? Lessons from the RAND Health Insurance Experiment*. Cambridge, MA: Harvard University Press.

Nord, E. (1993a) 'The trade-off between severity of illness and treatment effect in cost-value analysis of health care.' *Health Policy* 24(3): 227–38.

——(1993b) 'The Relevance of Health State after Treatment in Prioritising Between Different Patients.' *Journal of Medical Ethics* 19(1): 37–42.

Newhouse, J. (1994) 'The QALY-a measure of social value rather than individual utility?' *Health Economics* 3(2): 89–93.

——(1995) 'The Person-trade-off Approach to Valuing Health Care Programs.' *Medical Decisionmaking* 15(3): 201–8.

——(1999) *Cost-Value Analysis in Health Care: Making Sense Out of QALYs*. Cambridge: Cambridge University Press.

Nord, E., Pinto, J., Richardson, J., Menzel, P. and Ubel, P. (1999) 'Incorporating Societal Concerns for Fairness in Numerical Valuations of Health Programmes.' *Health Economics* 8(1): 25–39.

Nord, E., Richardson, J., Street, A., Kuhse, H. and Singer, P. (1995) 'Maximizing health benefits vs egalitarianism: An Australian survey of health issues.' *Social Science & Medicine* 41(10): 1429–37.

Nozick, R. (1974) *Anarchy, State and Utopia*. New York: Basic Books.

Nussbaum, M. (1986) *The Fragility of Goodness: Luck and Ethics in Greek Tragedy and Philosophy*. New York: Cambridge University Press.

——(1988) 'Nature, Function and Capability: Aristotle on Political Distribution.' *Oxford Studies in Ancient Philosophy* Suppl: 145–84.

——(ed.) (1990) *Love's Knowledge: Essays on Philosophy and Literature*. Oxford: Oxford University Press.

——(1990a) 'Plato on Commensurability and Desire', in M. Nussbaum (ed.), *Love's Knowledge: Essays on Philosophy and Literature*.

——(1990b) 'Nature, Function, and Capability: Aristotle on Political Distribution', in G. Patzig, *Aristoteles' 'Politik Gottingen: Vandenhoeck and Ruprecht'*: 152–86.

——(1992) 'Human Functioning and Social Justice: In Defense of Aristotelian Essentialism.' *Political Theory* 20(2): 202–46.

——(1993) 'Non-Relative Virtues: An Aristotelian Approach', in M. Nussbaum and A. Sen (eds) *The Quality of Life*: 242–70.

——(1997) 'Capabilities and Human Rights.' *Fordham Law Review* 66(2): 273–300.

——(1998) 'The Good as Discipline, the Good as Freedom', in D. Crocker and T. Linden, (eds) *Ethics of Consumption: The Good Life, Justice, and Global Stewardship*: 312–41.

——(2000a) 'Brave Good World.' Review of Buchanan et al., *From Chance to Choice*: Genetics and Justice. New Republic 12/04/2000: 38–48.

——(2000b) *Women and Human Development: The Capabilities Approach*. New York: Cambridge University Press.

Nussbaum, M. and Glover, J. (eds) (1995) *Women, Culture and Development—A Study of Human Capabilities*. New York: Oxford University Press.

Nussbaum, M. and Sen, A. (eds) (1993) *The Quality of Life*. Oxford: Clarendon Press.

Oliver, A. and Mossialos, E. (2004) 'Equity of access to health care: outlining the foundations for action.' *Journal of Epidemiology and Community Health* 58(8): 655–8.

Olmstead, T., Sindelar, J., Easton, C. and Carroll, K. (2007) 'The cost-effectiveness of four treatments for marijuana dependence.' *Addiction* 102(9): 1443–53.

O'Neill, O. (1996) *Towards Justice and Virtue: A Constructive Account of Practical Reasoning*. Cambridge: Cambridge University Press.

Orentlicher, D. (1994) 'Rationing and the Americans with Disabilities Act.' *Journal of the American Medical Association* 271(4): 308–14.

——(1996) 'Destructuring Disability: Rationing of Health Care and Unfair Discrimination against the Sick.' *Harvard Civil Rights—Civil Liberties Law Review* 31(1): 49–87.

——(2000) 'Utility, Equality, and Health Care Needs of Persons with Disabilities: interpreting the ADA's requirement of reasonable accommodations', in L. Francis and A. Silvers, (eds) *Americans with Disabilities: Exploring Implications of the Law for Individuals and Institutions*: 236–43.

Osaba, D. (ed.) (1991) *Effect of Cancer on Quality of Life*. Boca Ralton: CRC Press.

Page, B. and Shapiro, R. (1992) *The Rational Public: Fifty Years of Trends in Americans' Policy Preferences*. Chicago: University of Chicago Press.

Parfit, D. (2001) 'Equality or Priority', in J. Harris, (ed.) *Bioethics*, Oxford: Oxford University Press: 347–86.

Patrick, D. and Erickson, P. (1993) *Health Status and Health Policy: Quality of Life in Health Care Evaluation and Resource Allocation*. New York: Oxford University Press.

Patzig, G. (ed.) (1990) *Aristoteles' 'Politik.'* Gottingen: Vandenhoeck & Ruprecht.

Pauly, M. (1979) 'What is unnecessary surgery?' *Milbank Memorial Fund Quarterly* 57(1): 95–117.

Pauly, M., Zweifel, P., Scheffler, R., Preker, A. and Bassett, M. (2006) 'Private Health Insurance in Developing Countries.' *Health Affairs* 25(2): 369–79.

Perkins, H. (ed.) (2003) *The Social Norms Approach to Preventing School and College Age Substance Abuse: A Handbook for Educators, Counselors, and Clinicians*. San Francisco: Jossey-Bass.

Perkins, H. (2003a) 'The Emergence and Evolution of the Social Norms Approach to Substance Abuse Prevention', in H. Perkins (ed.) *The Social Norms Approach to Preventing School and College Age Substance Abuse: A Handbook for Educators, Counselors, and Clinicians*: 3–17.

Perkins, H., Haines, M. and Rice, R. (2005) 'Misperceiving the college drinking norm and related problems: a nationwide study of exposure to prevention information, perceived norms and student alcohol misuse.' *Journal of Studies on Alcohol* 66(4): 470–8.

Pettit, P. (1995) 'A Review of "The Quality of Life."' *Contemporary Sociology*, 24(3): 427–9.

Pildes, R. and Anderson, E. (1990) 'Slinging Arrows at Democracy: Social Choice Theory, Value Pluralism, and Democratic Politics.' *Columbia Law Review* 90(8): 2121–214.

Po, A. (2001) 'Too much, too little, or none at all: dealing with substandard and fake drugs.' *Lancet* 357(9272): 1904.

Pogge, T. (2002a) *World Poverty and Human Rights: Cosmopolitan Responsibilities and Reforms*. Cambridge: Polity.

——(2002b) 'Can the Capability Approach be Justified?' *Philosophical Topics* 30(2): 167–228.

Pogge, T. (2004) 'Relational Conceptions of Justice: Responsibilities for Health Outcomes', in S. Anand, F. Peter, and A. Sen (eds) *Public Health, Ethics, and Equity*: 135–62.

Powers, M. (1995) 'Hypothetical Choice Approaches to Health Care Allocation', in J. Humber and R. Almeder, *Allocating Health Care Resources*: 147–76.

Powers, M. and Faden, R. (2000) 'Inequalities in Health, Inequalities in Health Care: Four Generations of Discussion about Justice and Cost-Effectiveness Analysis.' *Kennedy Institute of Ethics Journal* 10(2): 109–27.

——(2006) *Social justice: the moral foundations of public health and health policy*. New York: Oxford University Press.

President's Commission for the Study of Ethical Problems in Medicine and Biomedical and Behavioral Research (1983) *Securing Access to Health Care: Volume 1*. Washington, D.C.: US Government Printing Office.

Qizilbash, M. (1996a) 'Ethical Development.' *World Development* 24(7): 1209–21.

——(1996b) 'Capabilities, Well-being, and Human Development: A Survey.' *Journal of Development Studies* 33(2): 143–62.

——(1997) 'Needs, Incommensurability and Well-Being.' *Review of Political Economy*, 9(3): 261–76.

——(1998) 'The Concept of Well-Being.' *Economics and Philosophy* 14(1): 51–73.

Rai, A. (1997) 'Rationing through choice: a new approach to cost-effectiveness analysis in health care.' *Indiana Law Journal* 72(4): 1015–97.

Rakowski, E. (1991) *Equal Justice*. Oxford: Clarendon Press.

——(1993) 'Taking and Saving Lives.' *Columbia Law Review* 93(5): 1063–156.

——(1994) 'The aggregation problem.' *Hastings Center Report* 24(4): 33–6.

Rawls, J. (1971) *A Theory of Justice*. Cambridge, MA: Belknap Press.

——(1993) *Political Liberalism*. New York: Columbia University Press.

——(1999) *The Law of Peoples*. Cambridge, MA: Harvard University Press.

Raz, J. (1986) *The Morality of Freedom*. Oxford: Clarendon Press.

Rehabilitation Act (1994) 29 U.S.C. §§ 701–797 (b).

Reinarman, C. (1987) *American States of Mind: Political Beliefs and Behavior Among Private and Public Workers*. New Haven: Yale University Press.

Reinhardt, U. (1991) 'Health Manpower Forecasting: The Case of Physician Supply', in E. Ginzberg (ed.) *Health Services Research: Key to Health Policy*: 234–83.

Rhodes, R., Battin, M. and Silvers, A. (eds) (2002) *Medicine and Social Justice: essays on the distribution of health care*. New York: Oxford University Press.

Rice, D., MacKenzie, E., and Associates (1989) *Cost of injury in the United States: a report to Congress*. San Francisco, CA: Institute for Health & Aging, University of California, and Injury Prevention Center, the Johns Hopkins University.

Richardson, H. (2002) *Democratic Autonomy: Public Reasoning about the Ends of Policy*. New York: Oxford University Press.

Richardson, J. and Nord, E. (1997) 'The Importance of Perspective in the Measurement of Quality-adjusted Life Years.' *Medical Decision Making* 17(1): 33–41.

Rid, A. (2009) 'Justice and Procedure: how does "accountability for reasonableness" result in fair limit-setting decisions?' *Journal of Medical Ethics* 35(1): 12–16.

Rid, A. and Biller-Andorno, N. (2009) 'Justice in action? Introduction to the mini-symposium on Norman Daniels' Just health: meeting health needs fairly.' *Journal of Medical Ethics* 35(1): 1–2.

Ritter, G., Thomas, C. and Wallack, S. (2001) 'Greater Use of Generics: A Prescription for Drug Cost Savings.' Unpublished manuscript, Brandeis University.

Robert Wood Johnson Foundation. (2001) New Survey snows language barriers causing many Spanish-Speaking Latinos to skip care [press release]. Available from:http://www.rwjf.org.

Roberts, M. and Reich M. (2002) 'Ethical Analysis in Public Health.' *Lancet* 359(9311): 1055–9.

Robinson, R. (1993) 'Costs and cost-minimisation analysis.' *British Medical Journal* 307(6906): 726–8.

Roemer, J. (1994) 'Inequality Reexamined' [book review]. *The Philosophical Review* 103(3): 554–7.

——(1995) 'Equality and Responsibility.' *Boston Review* 20(2): 3–7.

——(1996) *Theories of Distributive Justice*. Cambridge, MA: Harvard University Press.

Romano, P., Bloom, J. and Syme, L. (1991) 'Smoking, Social Support, and Hassles in an Urban African-American Community.' *American Journal of Public Health*, 81(11): 1415–22.

Rosenbaum, S. (1992) 'Mothers and Children Last: The Oregon Medicaid Experiment.' *American Journal of Law & Medicine* 18(1–2): 97–126.

Rosser, R. and Kind, P. (1978) 'A Scale of Valuations of States of Illness: Is There a Social Consensus?' *International Journal of Epidemiology* 7(4): 347–58.

Ruger, J. (1995a) 'Health, Health Care and Incompletely Theorized Agreements.' Mimeographed, Harvard University.

——(1995b) 'Value Formation, Democratic Choice Process, and Health Care Rationing.', Mimeographed, Harvard University.

——(1997) 'Social Justice and Health Policy' [lecture]. Health Policy Doctoral Seminar Series, Harvard University.

——(1998) 'Aristotelian Justice and Health Policy: Capability and Incompletely Theorized Agreements', unpublished Ph.D. dissertation on file with the Harvard University Library.

——(2003a) 'Catastrophic health expenditure.' *Lancet* 362(9388): 996–7.

——(2003b) 'Health and development.' *Lancet* 362(9385): 678.

——(2004a) 'Health and social justice.' *Lancet* 364(9439): 1075–80.

——(2004b) 'Ethics of the social determinants of health.' *Lancet* 364(9439): 1092–7.

——(2004c) 'Combating HIV/AIDS in developing countries.' *British Medical Journal* 329(7458): 121–2.

——(2005a) 'Global Tobacco Control: An Integrated Approach to Global Health Policy.' *Development* 48(2): 65–9.

——(2005b) 'Democracy and health.' *Quarterly Journal of Medicine* 98(4): 299–304.

Ruger, J. (2005c) 'Fatal Indifference: The G8, Africa and Global Health' [book review], *Journal of Public Health Policy* 26(3): 377–82.

——(2005d) 'Disease and Democracy: the Industrialized World Faces AIDS' [book review], *British Medical Journal* 331(7522): 970.

——(2006a) 'Toward a Theory of a Right to Health: Capability and Incompletely Theorized Agreements.' *Yale Journal of Law & the Humanities* 18: 273–326.

——(2006b) 'Ethics and Governance of Global Health Inequalities.' *Journal of Epidemiology and Community Health* 60(11): 998–1003.

——(2006c) 'Measuring Disparities in Health Care.' *British Medical Journal* 333: 274.

——(2006d) 'Health, Capability, and Justice: Toward a New Paradigm of Health Ethics, Policy and Law.' *Cornell Journal of Law and Public Policy* 15(2): 403–82.

——(2007a) 'Rethinking Equal Access: Agency, Quality, and Norms.' *Global Public Health* 2(1): 78–96.

——(2007b) 'Health, Health Care, and Incompletely Theorized Agreements: A Normative Theory of Health Policy Decision Making.' *Journal of Health Politics, Policy and Law* 32(1): 51–87.

——(2007c) 'The Moral Foundations of Health Insurance.' *Quarterly Journal of Medicine* 100(1): 53–7.

——(2008a) 'Governing Health.', *Harvard Law Review Forum* 121: 43–56.

——(2008b) 'Social Risk Management - Reducing Disparities in Risk, Vulnerability and Poverty Equitably.' *Medicine and Law* 27: 109–18.

——(2008c) 'Ethics in American Health 1: Ethical Approaches to Health Policy.' *American Journal of Public Health* 98(10): 1751–6.

——(2008d) 'Ethics in American Health 2: An Ethical Framework for Health System Reform.' *American Journal of Public Health* 98(10): 1756–63.

——(in press) 'Health Capability: Conceptulization and Operationalization.' *American Journal of Public Health*.

Ruger, J. and Emmons, K. (2008) 'Economic Evaluations of Smoking Cessation and Relapse Prevention Programs for Pregnant Women: A Systematic Review.' *Value in Health* 11(2): 180–90.

Ruger, J., Jamison, D., and Bloom, D. (2001) 'Health and the Economy', in M. Merson et al., (eds), *International Public Health: Diseases, Programs, Systems, and Policies*: 617–66.

Ruger, J. and Kim, H. (2006) 'Global health inequalities: an international comparison.' *Journal of Epidemiology & Community Health* 60(11): 928–36.

——(2007) 'Out-of-Pocket Healthcare Spending by the Poor and Chronically Ill in the Republic of Korea.' *American Journal of Public Health* 97(5): 804–11.

Ruger, J., Richter, C. and Lewis, L. (2003) 'Association Between Insurance Status and Admission Rate for Patients Evaluated in the Emergency Department.' *Academic Emergency Medicine* 10(11): 1285–8.

Ruger, J., Richter, C. and Lewis, L. (2006) 'Clinical and Economic Factors Associated with Ambulance Use to the Emergency Department.' *Academic Emergency Medicine* 13(8): 879–85.

——(2007) 'Identifying High-Risk Patients for Triage and Resource Allocation in the ED.' *The American Journal of Emergency Medicine* 25(7): 794–8.

Ruger, J., Richter, C., Spitznagel, E. and Lewis, L. (2004) 'Analysis of Costs, Length of Stay, and Utilization of Emergency Department Services by Frequent Users: Implications for Health Policy.' *Academic Emergency Medicine* 11(12): 1311–17.

Ruger, J., Weinstein, M., Kearney, M., Hammond, K. and Emmons, K. (2008) 'Cost-effectiveness of Motivational Interviewing for Smoking Cessation and Relapse Prevention among Low-income Pregnant Women: A Randomized Controlled Trial.' *Value in Health* 11(2):191–8.

Ruger, T. (2004) 'The United States Supreme Court and Health Law: The Year in Review: The Supreme Court Federalizes Managed Care Liability.' *The Journal of Law, Medicine & Ethics* 32(3): 528–31.

Russell, L., Gold M., Siegel J., Daniels, N. and Weinstein, M. (1996) 'The role of cost-effectiveness analysis in health and medicine. Panel on Cost-Effectiveness in Health and Medicine.' *Journal of the American Medical Association* 276(14): 1172–7.

Sabin, J. and Daniels, N. (1994) 'Determining "medical necessity" in mental health practice.' *Hastings Center Report* 24(6): 5–13.

Safran, D. and Ruger, J. (1994) 'The Massachusetts Health Care Industry: Pathway to the Future (Governor's Task Force on Health Care Industry).' Boston, Massachusetts.

Samuelson, P. (1954). 'The Pure Theory of Public Expenditure.' *Review of Economics and Statistics* 36(4): 387–9.

Sandel, M. (1982) *Liberalism and the Limits of Justice*. Cambridge: Cambridge University Press.

——(1984) *Liberalism and Its Critics*. New York: New York University Press.

Scanlon, T. (1975) 'Preference and Urgency.' *Journal of Philosophy* 72(19): 655–69.

——(1993) 'Value, Desire, and Quality of Life', in M. Nussbaum and A. Sen (eds), *The Quality of Life*: 185–201.

Schiavo ex rel. Schindler v. Schiavo (2005). 403 F.3d 1289 (11th Cir.).

Schieber, G. (ed.) (1997) *Innovations in Health Care Financing*. World Bank Discussion Paper No. 365.

Schieber, G. and Maeda, A. (1997). 'A Curmudgeon's Guide to Financing Health Care in Developing Countries', in G. Schieber (ed.) *Innovations in Health Care Financing: 1–38.*

Schlesinger, M. (2002) 'On Values and Democratic Policy Making: The Deceptively Fragile Consensus around Market-Oriented Medical Care.' *Journal of Health Politics, Policy and Law* 27(6): 889–926.

——(2004) 'Reprivatizing the Public Household? Medical Care in the Context of American Public Values.' *Journal of Health Politics, Policy and Law* 29(4–5): 969–1004.

Schlesinger, M. and Lau, R. (2000) 'The Meaning and Measure of Policy Metaphors.' *American Political Science Review* 94(3): 611–26.

Schlesinger, M. and Lee, T. (1993) 'Is Health Care Different? Popular Support of Federal Health and Social Policies.' *Journal of Health Politics, Policy and Law* 18(3): 551–628.

Schmitz, N., Linch, D., Dreger, P., Goldstone, A., Boogaerts, M., Ferrant, A., Demuynck, H., Link, H., Zander, A. and Barge, A. (1996) 'Randomised trial of filgrastim-mobilised peripheral blood progenitor cell transplantation versus autologous bone-marrow transplantation in lymphoma patients.' *Lancet* 347 (8998): 353–7.

School Board of Nassau County v. Arline. (1987) 480 U.S. 273, 274.

Schuster, M., McGlynn, E. and Brook, R. (2005) 'How Good Is the Quality of Health Care in the United States?' *Milbank Quarterly* 76(4): 517–63.

Scitovsky, A. and Capron, A. (1986) 'Medical Care at the End of Life: The Interaction of Economics and Ethics.' *Annual Review of Public Health* 7(1): 59–75.

Sen, A. (1980) 'Plural Utility.' *Proceedings of the Aristotelian Society* 81: 193–215.

——(1982) *Choice, Welfare, and Measurement*. Cambridge, MA: MIT Press.

——(1984) *Resources, Values and Development*. Cambridge, MA: Harvard University Press.

——(1985) *Commodities and Capabilities*. Amsterdam: North-Holland.

——(1987a) *On Ethics and Economics*. New York: Wiley Blackwell.

——(1987b) *The Standard of Living*. Cambridge: Cambridge University Press.

——(1992) *Inequality Reexamined*. Cambridge, MA: Harvard University Press.

——(1993a) 'Positional objectivity.' *Philosophy & Public Affairs* 22(2): 126–45.

——(1993b) 'Capability and Well-Being', in M. Nussbaum and A. Sen (eds) *The Quality of Life*: 30–53.

——(1993c) 'The Economics of Life and Death.' *Scientific American* 268(5): 40–47.

——(1995a) 'Rationality and Social Choice.' *American Economic Review*, 85(1): 1–24.

——(1995b) 'Rational Choice Theory.' Lecture given at Harvard University Graduate School of Art and Science, Cambridge MA. Economics Course 2057. 20 November.

——(1997) 'Human rights and Asian Values: What Lee Kuan Yew and Le Peng don't understand about Asia.' *The New Republic*, 217: 33–40.

——(1999) *Development as Freedom*. New York: Knopf.

——(2000) 'Foreword', in N. Daniels et al., *Is Inequality Bad for Our health?: vii–xviii*.

——(2002) *Rationality and Freedom*. Cambridge, MA: Belknap Press.

——(2004) 'Elements of a theory of human rights.' *Philosophy & Public Affairs* 32(4): 315–56.

Sexton, M. and Hebel, J. (1984) 'A Clinical Trial of Change in Maternal Smoking and its Effect on Birth Weight.' *Journal of the American Medical Association*, 251(7): 911–15.

Shapiro, R. and Young, J. (1989) 'Public Opinion and the Welfare State: The United States in Comparative Perspective.' *Political Science Quarterly* 104(1): 59–89.

Shojania, K., Yokoe, D., Platt, R., Fiskio, J., Ma'luf, N. and Bates, D. (1998) 'Reducing vancomycin use utilizing a computer guideline: Results of a Randomized Controlled Trial.' *Journal of American Medical Informatics Association* 5(6): 554–62.

Skocpol, T. (1996) *Boomerang: Clinton's Health Security Effort and the Turn against Government in U.S. Politics.* New York: W. W. Norton.

Smith, T., Hillner, B., Schmitz, N., Linch, D., Dreger, P., Goldstone, A., Boogaerts, M., Ferrant, A., Link, H., Zander, A., Yanovich, S., Kitchin, R. and Erder, M. (1997) 'Economic analysis of a randomized clinical trial to compare filgrastim-mobilized peripheral-blood progenitor-cell transplantation and autologous bone marrow transplantation in patients with Hodgkin's and non-Hodgkin's lymphoma.' *Journal of Clinical Oncology* 15(1): 5–10.

Snead, O. (2007) 'Unenumerated Rights and the Limits of Analogy: A Critique of the Right to Medical Self-Defense.' *Harvard Law Review Forum* 121: 1–12.

Snyder, R., Cunningham, W., Nakazono, T. and Hays, R. (2000) 'Access to Medical Care Reported by Asians and Pacific Islanders in a West Coast Physician Group Association.' *Medical Care Research and Review* 57(2): 196–215.

Sober, E. (2000). 'Appendix One: The Meaning of Genetic Causation', in A. Buchanan et al., *From Chance to Choice: Genetics and Justice*: 347–70.

Socialist Health Association (2005) 'National Policy Forum Document on Health July 2005.' Available at: http://www.sochealth.co.uk/news/npf2005.htm accessed on 8 January 2009.

Society of Critical Care Medicine Ethics Committee (1994) 'Consensus Statement on the Triage of Critically Ill Patients.', *Journal of the American Medical Association* 271(15): 1200–3.

Soobramoney v. Minister of Health (1998) (1) SA 765 (CC).

Stanford University Center for Health Policy (2002) *Model Contractual Language for Medical Necessity.* Palo Alto: Integrated Health Care Association.

Starfield, B. (2000) 'Primary Care', in N. Daniels et al., *Is Inequality Bad for Our Health?*: 67–70.

Starr, P. (1982) *The Social Transformation of American Medicine.* New York: Basic Books.

Stedman (2000) *Stedman's Medical Dictionary, 27th Edition.* New York: Lippincott, Williams and Wilkins.

Sterba, J. (1994) 'Book review of "The Quality of Life."' *Ethics* 105(1): 198–201.

Stern, L. (1983) 'Opportunity and health care: criticisms and suggestions.' *Journal of Medicine and Philosophy* 8(4): 339–61.

Stewart, A., Hays, R. and Ware, J. Jr (1988) 'The MOS short-form general health survey. Reliability and validity in a patient population.' *Medical Care* 26(7): 724–35.

Stewart, A. and Ware, J. (eds) (1992) *Measuring Functioning and well-being: The Medical Outcomes Study Approach*. Durham, NC: Duke University Press.

Strathie v. Department of Transportation. 716 F.2d 227 (3rd Cir. 1983).

Streeten, P. et al., (1981) *First Things First: Meeting Basic Human Needs in Developing Countries*. New York: Oxford University Press.

Stuber, J. and Schlesinger, M. (2006) 'Sources of stigma for means-tested government programs.' *Social Science and Medicine* 63(4): 933–45.

Sugden, R. (1993) 'Welfare, Resources and Capabilities: A Review of *Inequality Reexamined* by Amartya Sen.' *Journal of Economic Literature* 31(4): 1947–62.

Sun, R., Watcha, M., White, P., Skrivanek, G., Griffin, J., Stool, L. and Murphy, M. (1999) 'A Cost Comparison of Methohexital and Propofol for Ambulatory Anesthesia.' *Anesthesia and Analgesia* 89(2): 311–16.

Sunstein, C. (1994) 'Incommensurability and Valuation in Law.' *Michigan Law Review* 92(4): 779–861.

——(1995) 'Incompletely Theorized Agreements.' *Harvard Law Review* 108(7): 1733–72.

Swartz, K. (1989) *The Medically Uninsured: Special Focus on Workers*. Washington, DC: Urban Institute Press.

——(1994) 'Dynamics of people without health insurance: don't let the numbers fool you.' *Journal of the American Medical Association* 271(1): 64–6.

Sweetenham, J., Hieke, K., Kerrigan, M., Howard, P., Smartt, P., McIntyre, A. and Townshend, S. (1999) 'Cost-minimization analysis of CHOP, fludarabine and rituximab for the treatment of relapsed indolent B-cell non-Hodgkin's lymphoma in the UK.' *British Journal of Haematology* 106(1): 47–54.

Tarlov, A., Ware, J., Greenfield, S., Nelson, E., Perrin, E. and Zubkoff, M. (1989) 'The Medical Outcomes Study. An application of methods for monitoring the results of medical care.' *Journal of the American Medical Association* 262(7): 925–30.

Taurek, J. (1977) 'Should the numbers count?' *Philosophy and Public Affairs* 6(4): 293–316.

Taylor, A., Beauregard, K. and Vistnes, J. (1995) 'Who Belongs to HMOs: A Comparison of Fee-for-Service versus HMO Enrollees.' *Medical Care Research and Review* 52 (3): 389–408.

Tengs, T., Adams, M., Pliskin, J., Safran, D., Siegel, J., Weinstein, M. and Graham, J. (1995) 'Five-Hundred Life-Saving Interventions and Their Cost-Effectiveness.' *Risk Analysis* 15(3): 369–90.

Tengs, T., Meyer, G., Siegel, J., Pliskin, J., Graham, J. and Weinstein, M (1996) 'Oregon's Medicaid Ranking and Cost-Effectiveness: Is There Any Relationship?' *Medical Decision Making* 16(2): 99–107.

Thaler, R. (1980) 'Toward a Positive Theory of Consumer Choice.' *Journal of Economic Behavior and Organization* 1(1): 39–60.

Thaler, R. and Sunstein, C. (2003) 'Libertarian Paternalism.' *American Economic Review* 93(2): 175–9.

Duchon, L., Schoen, C., Doty, M., Davis, K., Strumpf, E., and Bruegman (2001) *Security Matters: How Instability in Health Insurance Puts U.S. Workers at Risk*. The Commonwealth Fund.

Thomas, C., Ritter, G. and Wallack, S. (2001) 'Growth in prescription drug spending among insured elders.' *Health Affairs* 20(5): 265–77.

Tolley, G., Kenkel, D. and Fabian, R. (eds) (1994) *Valuing Health for Policy: An Economic Approach*. Chicago: University of Chicago Press.

Tomlinson, T. and Brody, H. (1990) 'Futility and the ethics of resuscitation.' *Journal of the American Medical Association* 264(10): 1276–80.

Tuohy, C. (1999) *Accidental Logics: The Dynamics of Change in the Health Care Arena in the United States, Britain, and Canada*. New York: Oxford University Press.

Ubel, P. (2000) *Pricing Life: why it's time for health care rationing*. Cambridge, MA: MIT Press.

UN CESCR (2000) 'The Right to the Highest Attainable Standard of Health' General Comment 14, 22nd Session, U.N. Doc. E/C.12/2000/4.

——(2003) *Human Development Report 2003*. New York: Oxford University Press.

UN Development Program (2001) *Human Development Report 2001*. New York: Oxford University Press.

US Congress Office of Technology Assessment (1992) *Evaluation of the Oregon Medicaid Proposal, OTA-H-531*. Washington, DC: US Government Printing Office.

US Department of Health and Human Services (2000) 'Clinical Practice Guideline: Treating Tobacco Use and Dependence.' Available at: http://www.surgeongeneral.gov/tobacco/treating_tobacco_use.pdf accessed on 8 January 2009.

United States General Purchasing Office (1973) *Health Maintenance Organization Act*. Washington, DC: US General Purchasing Office.

Van Doorslaer, E., Wagstaff, A. and Rutten, F. (eds) (1993) *Equity in the finance and delivery of health care: an international perspective*. New York: Oxford University Press.

Van Parijs, P. (1991) 'Why Surfers Should Be Fed: The Liberal Case for an Unconditional Basic Income.' *Philosophy and Public Affairs* 20(2): 101–31.

Vande Zande v. Wisconsin Department of Administration (1995) 44 F.3d538 (7th Cir.)

Veatch, R. (1976) 'What is a "just" health care delivery', in R. Veatch and R. Branson (eds) *Ethics and Health Policy*: 127–53.

——(1996) 'Which grounds for overriding autonomy are legitimate?' *Hastings Center Report* 26(6): 42–3.

Veatch, R. and Branson, R. (eds) (1976) *Ethics and Health Policy*. Cambridge, MA: Ballinger Publishing Company.

Verba, S. and Orren, G. (1985) *Equality in America: The View from the Top*. Cambridge, MA: Harvard University Press.

Viscusi, W. (1992) *Fatal Tradeoffs: Public and Private Responsibilities for Risk*. New York: Oxford University Press.

Volokh, E. (2007) 'Medical Self-Defense, Prohibited Experimental Therapies, and Payment for Organs.' *Harvard Law Review* 120(7): 1813–46.

Walt, G. and Buse, K. (2006) 'Global Cooperation in International Public Health', in M. Merson et al. (eds) *International Public Health*, 2nd Edition: 649–80.

Walzer, M. (1983) *Spheres of Justice: A Defense of Pluralism and Equality*. New York: Basic Books.

——(1990) 'The Communitarian Critique of Liberalism.' *Political Theory* 18(1): 6–23.

—— (1993) 'Objectivity and Social Meaning', in M. Nussbaum and A. Sen (eds) *The Quality of Life*: 165–77.

Ward, P. (1997) 'Health care rationing: can we afford to ignore euthanasia?' *Health Services Management Research* 10(1): 32–41.

Ware, J. (1991) 'Measuring Functioning, Well-being, and other Generic Health Concepts', in D. Osoba (ed.) *Effect of Cancer on Quality of Life*: 7–24.

Waymack, M. (2001) 'Daniels on Justice and Healthcare: Laudable Goals—Questionable Method.' *American Journal of Bioethics* 1(2): 28.

Webster's Third New International Dictionary of the English Language (1981) [unabridged] Editor-in-chief P. Gove and Merriam-Webster editorial staff. Springfield: G. & C. Merriam Co.

Weiner, J., Parente, S., Garnick, D., Fowles, J., Lawthers, A. and Palmer, R. (1995) 'Variation in office-based quality. A claims-based profile of care provided to Medicare patients with diabetes.' *Journal of the American Medical Association* 273 (19): 1503–8.

Weinick, R. and Krauss, N. (2000) 'Racial/ethnic differences in children's access to care.' *American Journal of Public Health* 90(11): 1771–4.

Weinstein, M. (1990) 'Principles of cost-effective resource allocation in health care organizations.' *International Journal of Technology Assessment in Health Care* 6(1): 93–103.

Weinstein, M., Siegel, J., Gold, M., Kamlet, M. and Russell, L. (1996) 'Recommendations of the Panel on Cost-effectiveness in Health and Medicine.' *Journal of the American Medical Association* 276(15): 1253–8.

Weinstein, M. and Stason, W. (1977) 'Foundations of cost-effectiveness analysis for health and medical practices.' *New England Journal of Medicine* 296(13): 716–21.

Wenger, N., Mattson, M., Furberg, C. and Elinson, J. (eds) (1984) *Assessment of Quality of Life in Clinical Trials of Cardiovascular Therapies*. New York: Le Jacq.

Whitelaw, N. and Liang, J. (1991) 'The structure of the OARS physical health measures.' *Medical Care* 29(4): 332–47.

Wikler, D. (2004) 'Personal and Social Responsibility for Health', in S. Anand, F. Peter, A. Sen (eds) *Public Health Ethics and Equity*: 109–34.

Williams, A. (1996) 'QALYs and ethics: A health economist's perspective.' *Social Science & Medicine* 43(12): 1795–804.

Williams, B. (1987) 'The Standard of Living: Interests and Capabilities', in A. Sen, *The Standard of Living*: 94–102.

Wilson, J. (2009) 'Not so special after all? Daniels and the social determinants of health.' *Journal of Medical Ethics* 35(1): 3–6.

Windsor, R., Cutter, G., Morris, J., Reese, Y., Manzella, B., Bartlett, E., Samuelson, C. and Spanos, D. (1985) 'The Effectiveness of Smoking Cessation Methods for Smokers in Public Health Maternity Clinics: A Randomized Trial.' *American Journal of Public Health*, 75(12): 1389–92.

Winslow, C., Kosecoff, J., Chassin, M., Kanouse, D. and Brook, R. (1988a) 'The appropriateness of performing coronary artery bypass surgery.' *Journal of the American Medical Association* 260(4): 505–9.

Winslow, C., Solomon, D., Chassin, M., Kosecoff, J., Merrick, N. and Brook, R. (1988b) 'The appropriateness of carotid endarterectomy.' *New England Journal of Medicine* 318(12): 721–7.

Wolfson, S. (2000) 'Students' estimates of the prevalence of drug use: evidence for a false consensus effect.' *Psychology of Addictive Behaviors* 14(3): 295–8.

Women's Research and Education Institute (1994) *Women's Health Insurance Costs and Experiences*. Available at: http://www.wrei.org/Publications_HealthInsurancecCosts.htm accessed on May 27 2009.

Woodard, G. and Edouard, L. (1992) 'Reaching Out: A Community Initiative for Disadvantaged Pregnant Women.' *Canadian Journal of Public Health*, 83(3): 188–90.

Woolf, S., Johnson, R., Fryer, G., Rust, G. and Satcher, D. (2004) 'The health impact of resolving racial disparities: an analysis of US mortality data.' *American Journal of Public Health* 94(12): 2078–81.

World Bank (1990) *World Development Report: Poverty*. New York: Oxford University Press.

——(1993) *World Development Report: Investing in Health*. New York: Oxford University Press.

——(1997) *World Development Report: The State in a Changing World*. New York: Oxford University Press.

——(2000) *World Development Indicators*. New York: Oxford University Press.

World Bank Key Development Data and Statistics. Available at: http://web.worldbank.org/WBSITE/EXTERNAL/DATASTATISTICS/0, contentMDK.20535285~menuPK:1390200~pagePK:64133150~piPK:64133175~theSitePK:239419,00.html accessed on 1 February 2009.

WHO (2001) *Macroeconomics and Health: Investing in Health for Economic Development*. Report on the Commission on Macroeconomics and Health. Geneva: WHO.

——(2003) *Investing in Health: A Summary of the Findings of the Commission on Macroeconomics and Health*. Geneva: WHO.

WHO Statistical Information System (2006). *Tough Choices: Investing in Health for Development. Experiences from national follow-up*. Available at: http://www.who.int/whosis/data/Search.jsp?indicators=[Indicator]. Members accessed on 11 January 2009.

Younis, R., Hesse, S. and Anand, V. (2001) 'Evaluation of the Utility and Cost-Effectiveness of Obtaining Histopathologic Diagnosis on All Routine Tonsillectomy Specimens.' *Laryngoscope* 111(12): 2166–9.

Ysander, B. (1993) 'Robert Erikson: Descriptions of Inequality', in M. Nussbaum and A. Sen (eds) *The Quality of Life:* 84–7.

Index